BUSINESS POWER
IN GLOBAL GOVERNANCE

BUSINESS POWER
IN GLOBAL
GOVERNANCE

DORIS FUCHS

LYNNE
RIENNER
PUBLISHERS

BOULDER
LONDON

Published in the United States of America in 2007 by
Lynne Rienner Publishers, Inc.
1800 30th Street, Boulder, Colorado 80301
www.rienner.com

and in the United Kingdom by
Lynne Rienner Publishers, Inc.
3 Henrietta Street, Covent Garden, London WC2E 8LU

Library of Congress Cataloging-in-Publication Data
Fuchs, Doris A.
    Business power in global governance / Doris Fuchs.
        p. cm.
    Includes bibliographical references and index.
    ISBN 978-1-58826-492-3 (hardcover : alk. paper) — ISBN 978-1-58826-468-8
(pbk. : alk. paper)
    1. International business enterprises—Political aspects.
2. Globalization. 3. Corporate power. 4. Business and politics. I. Title.
    HD2755.5.F827 2007
    338.8'81—dc22

                                                              2007004528

British Cataloguing in Publication Data
A Cataloguing in Publication record for this book
is available from the British Library.

Printed and bound in the United States of America

The paper used in this publication meets the requirements
of the American National Standard for Permanence of
Paper for Printed Library Materials Z39.48-1992.

5 4 3 2 1

Contents

Tables and Figures

Tables

Figures

Preface

Electoral representation and the existence of checks and balances on political power are core principles of democracy. In the era of globalization and global governance, however, the nature of the political game is changing. Important political decisions increasingly are being made at levels other than the national one, and by actors other than governments. Do checks and balances still function in this new game? Or have new powerful actors arisen and processes developed whose influence circumvents them?

The critical globalization literature frequently has claimed that transnational corporations (TNCs) are such actors. However, these claims have tended to remain rather broad and unspecific. Are TNCs really these all-powerful political actors in today's world? And if so, how do they exercise their power? These are the questions I had in mind when setting out to write this book.

Only on the basis of answers to these questions can we seriously discuss the need for and desirable design of new checks and balances in support of democratic legitimacy and social justice. As I hope the analysis presented in this book shows, such a discussion is urgently needed. While not omnipotent and, in fact, vulnerable in some respects, TNCs have gained political power in a range of dimensions and are exercising influence via a wide variety of political activities that traditional checks and balances fail to control. The balance of interests in the political arena clearly does not exist anymore and requires targeted intervention to be restored, if government of the people, by the people, and for the people is to be assured.

* * *

The argument presented in this book owes a great deal to many people, in terms of both inspiration and guidance. My thinking on corporate power in global governance has been particularly influenced by discussions and research collaborations with Jennifer Clapp, Claire Cutler, Matthias Finger, Virginia Haufler, Agni Kalfagianni, Markus Lederer, David Levy, Sylvia Lorek, Daniel Mazmanian, Andreas Nölke, Louis Pauly, Tom Princen, and Klaus Dieter Wolf. Moreover, Maarten Arentsen, Ulrich Beck, Andreas Busch, Edgar Grande, Friedrich Kratochwil, Renate Mayntz, Frank Schimmelfennig, and Stefan Schirm commented on earlier versions of the manuscript and gave valuable advice. Special thanks are due to Philipp Forstner for excellent editorial assistance. Finally, I am grateful to Marilyn Grobschmidt at Lynne Rienner Publishers for her enthusiasm and unrelenting support in the completion of the manuscript, as well as to two anonymous reviewers for their insightful comments. All remaining errors are, of course, my responsibility.

—*Doris Fuchs*

1

Exploring the Role of Business in Global Governance

Global Governance, Business, and the Question of Power

It has been a little more than ten years now since *global governance* assumed a prominent spot on the international agenda, spurred by the euphoria at the end of the Cold War and hopes of more cooperation and harmony in global problem solving. In the early 1990s the "Commission on Global Governance" met to deliberate the future of world politics. Simultaneously, the academic community started to explore the topic. In 1992 James Rosenau and Ernst-Otto Czempiel published *Governance Without Government*, a scholarly treatment of a new type of global politics in a globalizing world no longer separated by an iron curtain and with new political actors on the scene. Since then, global governance has become a paradigm in analyses of the organization of the international system and global problem-solving. Under this paradigm, scholars and practitioners discuss changes in political actors, issues, practices, and perspectives. Most important, they highlight the rise in political decisionmaking by nonstate, suprastate, and substate actors, in particular civil society, international governmental organizations (IGOs), and transnational corporations[1] (TNCs), and explore the contribution these actors can make to global problem-solving.

In spite of a flurry of research and debate, however, global governance today remains a vague and controversial concept. Scholars and practitioners agree about little except that new actors are participating in political decisionmaking. Even the extent of the actual and potential contribution of these actors and the remaining actual and potential contribution of traditional political actors, specifically the state, are subject to serious disagreement. More problematic, however, is that a substantial share of contributions to the global governance debate, especially early on, failed to pay sufficient attention to the role of power, the "key concept" in political science (Lasswell and Kaplan 1950). Focusing on participatory global rule-making, they forgot to ask questions about who rules, how, and in whose interest. Clearly, these questions have to be of pivotal importance for anybody interested in the implications of global governance for democracy, social justice, and global sustainable development.

The need to ask questions about power and the implications of the pursuit of private interests for global governance are particularly apparent in the case of TNCs. An increasing number of publications in the popular and academic literature perceive a shift in power toward TNCs due to globalization. Scholars, activists, and politicians charge that corporations have become extremely powerful actors and are increasingly able to shape governance at national and supranational levels. At the same time, the desirability of the contribution of business actors in general and TNCs in particular to governance cannot always be taken for granted. On the one hand, the notion of corporate citizenship and the environmental and social responsibility of business actors is gaining ground. On the other hand, however, scandals and catastrophes caused by business actors from Seveso and Bhopal to the Exxon *Valdez,* Enron, and WorldCom suggest that the economic and political activities of business actors still need to be embedded in an appropriate regulatory framework. TNCs, in particular, may be simultaneously the "principal agent and architect" and the major "villain" and "beneficiary" of globalization and global governance (Drache 2001, 6).

Meanwhile, TNCs have grown in number and, more dramatically, in size. UNCTAD (2000) reports the existence of approximately 63,000 TNCs with 700,000 foreign affiliates. Moreover, TNCs command financial and human resources of a magnitude previously unknown. The last wave of mergers that started in the late twentieth century has led to the development of new economic units with gigantic budgets and staff sizes.

Despite these developments and concerns about their political implications, however, there has been surprisingly little systematic research on the role of business in general and TNCs in particular in global governance. Only recently, more power-oriented and broader inquiries into the role of TNCs in global politics have started to appear (Levy and Newell 2005; May 2006a). In addition, the literature has highlighted a variety of "new" forms of political activities by business, including self-regulation, the role of rating agencies, public-private and private-private partnerships (PPPs), and the privatization of areas traditionally considered the task of public actors, such as security. In this context, scholars have drawn attention to the development of "private authority" in the international system.

Yet a comprehensive and systematic understanding of the political activities employed by businesses with respect to global governance and their meaning and development in terms of business's political power is missing. This fact is also surprising, since assumptions about the power of business frequently inform arguments about the role of other actors in global governance, in particular the state and civil society. This lack of information on the "big picture" with respect to business's political power is partly a function of methodological problems, of course. Numerous case studies on the topic exist. While these provide a wealth of case-specific detail, however, they tend to offer little reliable information on overarching trends. In contrast, quantitative assessments in this field frequently rely on macro-level data that do not allow the identification of the complex dynamics of the underlying political processes. In consequence, we still lack important insights on broader developments with respect to the role of business in global governance.

The present analysis responds to this lack of information. Its primary objective is to provide an encompassing yet lucid picture of the role of business in global governance and to thereby better understand its role as a political actor. In the pursuit of this objective, the study explores the broad range of political activities by businesses, including lobbying and campaign finance activities, rule-setting activities as well as influence deriving from structural dependencies, and efforts to influence governance-relevant norms and ideas. The analysis is thereby able to consider actor-specific, structural, and systemic dimensions of business's power and its material and ideational sources. Adopting a comprehensive conceptualization of global governance, the analysis takes into account activities at the national, transnational, and supranational levels (Messner and Nuscheler 1996a, 2003).

In pursuit of its research objectives, the analysis takes the following two steps. First, it develops a systematic and comprehensive framework locating the various political activities of business in global governance in a typology of power. Second, it applies this framework to evidence on trends in the respective political activities of business since the 1970s, that is, since the arrival of "globalization" on the scientific and political agendas. It is thus able to identify interesting developments in the different dimensions of the political power of business in the context of globalization and global governance. Together the two steps of the analysis allow a new perspective on the role of business in global governance—a perspective that draws attention to the reach and variety of political activities by business and explores their meaning and development.

The findings show that business clearly has become a pivotal political actor and highlight the need to consider it as such. At the same time, the theoretical framework provides differentiated insights regarding the facets of the role of this political actor in global governance and the most noteworthy as well as controversial trends. Specifically, the analysis suggests the following: we can identify a quantitative increase in the efforts of business to exercise instrumental power at the national level, as well as the expansion of such efforts to the transnational and supranational levels. The extent to which this growth in activities translates into a growth in influence is difficult to assess, however. We can further notice dynamics promising an increase in the agenda-setting power of business actors deriving from their ability to move capital. Yet, the empirical evidence on this agenda-setting power is not unambiguous. In contrast, we can clearly identify a substantial increase in business's rule-setting power. Finally, we can recognize a noticeable rise in the efforts of business to exercise discursive power, a dimension of power in which business has acquired a privileged but contested position in the overall political game.

In sum, the analysis demonstrates that claims about a lack of significant influence of business on politics advanced by a small but persistent group of scholars and practitioners need to be met with skepticism. At the same time, however, undifferentiated claims of corporations ruling the world, advanced by a continuously growing group of writers, fail to capture the complexities of current developments in the role of business in global governance. Unfortunately, we need to engage in the much more intricate and burdensome scrutiny of different developments in the political activities and power of business.

The Approach

Due to the nature of the topic at hand, the present analysis as a scholarly endeavor straddles a variety of disciplines and approaches.

Political science, business management, economics, sociology, and communication science all have something to contribute to the inquiry. Within political science, scholars in international relations (IR), in particular international political economy (IPE), political theory, comparative politics, and public policy, all have analyzed questions related to the research objective. In consequence, the analysis draws on a wide range of literature and approaches.

In the same manner, the analysis is both a theoretical and empirical effort. It draws on theoretical concepts to establish an appropriate foundation and framework for its inquiry, but it does not develop a new theoretical concept of power. Likewise, the inquiry draws on empirical evidence based on a systematic assessment of the relevant literature but does not itself test hypotheses based on statistical analyses or case studies. Rather, it develops a conceptual framework for analyses of the role of business in global governance and applies it to the theoretical and empirical literature on global governance and the influence of business on politics to suggest trends in this role. With this secondary-level analytic approach, the analysis responds to the weakness of the empirical global governance literature highlighted previously: the lacking perspective on the "big picture." Its starting point is the conviction that in order to gain a new level of understanding, it is necessary to first take a step back and create and then apply a framework that allows a systematic and yet comprehensive appraisal of developments in the political activities of business. We can then reconsider research findings in the light of a new perspective on their meaning and relevance.

The interest in the big picture also suggests the adoption of a bird's-eye perspective on the role of business in global governance, which emphasizes common trends rather than country-, field-, or case-specific differences. Such differences do exist (Hall and Soskice 2001). However, the analysis starts from the assumption that overarching developments in political activities by business as well as in opportunities for the pursuit of these activities can be identified. This is partly the case because of the increasing adaptability of firms to their host economies and the common determinants of business's political activities in terms of economic opportunities and threats (Hansen and Mitchell 2001; Levy and Newell 2000). The ability to identify common trends is also a function of a growing convergence in institutional settings fostered by globalization. National models are increasingly adjusting by dissolving and replacing traditional institutions with new ones and developing institutional hybrids, especially in sectors oriented toward international competition (Lütz 2003; Seeleib-Kaiser 1999). Thus, scholars find evidence of a convergence of corporate governance models toward an "information-based shareholder economy," for example (Bieling and Steinhilber 2000; Streeck and Höppner 2003).

Admittedly, generalizations about the role of business in global governance are more justified for industrialized countries largely integrated into the global economy and with broad similarities in institutional settings than for developing countries without sufficient integration or comparable political systems and regulatory frameworks. In addition, generalizations about this role apply more to large business actors operating in markets with a high degree of international competition than for small businesses in local markets. While the discussion is framed in general terms, then, the reader needs to be aware that the analysis speaks more (although not exclusively) to the situation in industrialized countries and to the role of large business actors and associations.

In addition, despite efforts to approach the subject as comprehensively as possible, the analysis cannot provide an assessment of all the business activities that are of potential political relevance. Thus, it will not consider business influence on law via courts or issues of corruption and related illegal behavior by business representatives. Moreover, the book will not consider the simultaneous employment of politicians as consultants to business actors, which may be legal though perhaps illegitimate in the public eye.

Finally, the analysis starts from the assumption that business is embedded in an institutional setting and socioeconomic and political context of both a material and nonmaterial nature and thus not an entirely autonomous player. At the same time, the approach recognizes that business plays an active role in the (re)structuring of that setting. This bi-directional dynamic is reflected in the influence of globalization on the political capacities of business and competing actors and their influence on the occurrence and shape of globalization, and it also becomes particularly relevant with respect to the discursive power of business (see Chapter 6). In the literature, this perspective has come to be associated with the label *structuration:*

> From this perspective, the course of social history results from mutually constituting agent choices and structural dispositions. ... On the one hand, structural forces largely establish the range of options that are available to actors in a given historical context. Structures also generally encourage agents to take certain steps

rather than others. At the same time, however, structures depend on an accumulation of actor decisions for their creation and subsequent perpetuation. Indeed, at moments of structural instability and flux, agents can have considerable influence in reshaping the social order. (Scholte 2000a, 91f)

Business actors, then, pursue an instrumental logic but are also subject to environmental influences and the logic of appropriateness.

The Structure of the Book

The analysis starts by establishing the empirical and conceptual setting in which the "story" unfolds: globalization and global governance. Corporate power in global governance cannot be understood without the changes in political and socioeconomic contexts brought about by globalization and global governance. If one wants to believe popular discourse and a large share of scholarly work, globalization has fundamental implications for the opportunities and constraints faced by (political) actors. Global governance, in turn, captures the changes in political practices and their conceptualization in which today's political activities of business are embedded today. Thus, Chapter 2 explores the nature, causes, and consequences of globalization and links globalization to global governance by juxtaposing views of global governance as an answer to globalization and as a consequence of globalization. In addition, the chapter explores the concept of global governance in depth and reveals the frequent neglect of questions of power in global governance research as well as their causes. On the basis of this analysis, the chapter highlights the urgent need for inquiries into the specific roles of the various actors in global governance, specifically the power they can bring to bear in the global governance "game" and the channels through which they exercise it.

Narrowing the focus to the role of business in global governance, Chapter 3 develops the conceptual framework for an examination of the political power of business and the channels through which it is being exercised. The chapter starts with a brief survey of some of the cornerstones of the research tradition on the political power of business in general and corporations in particular. The chapter then turns to the question of assessments of businesses' political power and highlights the inadequacy of the indicators traditionally used in the popular literature. As an alternative, the chapter presents instrumental, structural, and discursive perspectives of power and links them to old and new forms of political activities by business.

Chapter 4 analyzes developments in the instrumental power of business. Business exercises this power primarily via lobbying and campaign and party finance activities. At the national level, the chapter examines developments in business's political mobilization as well as changes in the access granted to business actors by politicians and bureaucrats. Moreover, it inquires into the relationship between resources and the successful exercise of instrumental power. At the supranational level, the chapter analyzes the expansion of lobbying activities by business to new targets and strategies. Specifically, it explores lobbying activities at regional and global governmental institutions, highlighting developments in business's instrumental power within the European Union (EU), for example. Here, too, the chapter considers not only changes in business strategies but also the role of access conditions, transaction costs, and the nature of competition among various interest groups. On the basis of these analyses, the chapter delineates complex developments in the exercise of instrumental power by business and emphasizes the need for global governance research to take these activities into account.

Chapter 5 turns to developments in the structural power of business. Scholars and practitioners have traditionally considered this power in the context of the ability of multinationally operating corporations to reward and punish policy choices by governments by moving investments and jobs. The chapter examines how this structural power of multinational corporations (MNCs) has developed considering changes in international financial regulation and competition for investment, as well as in the organization of production processes. Most important, however, Chapter 5 inquires into changes in the nature of the structural power of business as such. Specifically, it examines to what extent this structural power has expanded from a more passive agenda-setting power to an active rule-setting power. In this context, the chapter draws attention to the various forms of new political activities by business, such as self-regulation, PPPs, and quasi-regulation, that is, indirect rule-setting activities by specific business actors such as rating agencies, linking each to opportunities and constraints for the agenda- and rule-setting power of business.

Chapter 6, then, addresses business's exercise of power via the use and shaping of ideas—its discursive power, which is the least researched of the dimensions of business power in global governance. The chapter starts by discussing the privatization trend as a signal of the acquisition of political authority by business. After all, the literature on global governance and private authority considers privatization as providing an expansion in the political activities of business to the extent that business is taking over tasks previously provided by governments. From there, the chapter looks at the sources of this acquisition of political authority, in particular the causes of business's gaining of legitimacy as a political actor. Exploring the strengths and weaknesses of the discursive power of business, the chapter discusses the interaction of discursive power with the other dimensions of power, its vulnerability as well as the limits imposed on agency by systemic determinants of discursive power. In the end, the analysis suggests that the discursive power of business is significantly increasing, although it is far from uncontested.

Finally, Chapter 7 summarizes the analysis and discusses its implications for politics and policy as well as future research. It starts by reviewing the main argument and findings. It next ponders the implications of the core results for the general understanding of the role of business in global governance. Subsequently, the chapter extends the discussion of implications to broader political and scientific questions. Here, the chapter highlights implications for regulatory frameworks as well as for business's political self-understanding and responsibility. On the research side, the chapter points out analytical and empirical questions that can be identified as particularly worthy of further inquiry on the basis of the present analysis. The chapter concludes with a brief outlook.

Concluding Thoughts

The question of the political role of business and its implications is located in highly controversial terrain. Any study pursuing an inquiry in this field has to tread very lightly and still is likely to be accused of ideological bias. The present analysis aims at taking a balanced approach. While coming down on the side of a substantial influence of business on politics, it does not claim that business in general or TNCs in particular have complete control over the world or win every political contest. In fact, in the case of highly visible and contested short-term political struggles, civil society may well be the decisive voice. Moreover, the fate of individual business actors is subject to global competition and at the mercy of the decisions of consumers and investors, in particular institutional investors.

Simultaneously, however, business as such and corporate actors in particular do possess resources and opportunities for a significant political influence at the beginning of the twenty-first century and need to be considered crucial political actors at this point.

Clearly, business's involvement in global governance has both potential benefits and potential costs. Business actors in general and TNCs in particular have skills and resources to contribute to global problem-solving that are valuable and frequently urgently needed. Their financial, human, organizational, and technological resources in combination with their ability to promote innovation and efficiency and to support decentralized governance with a global reach make them desirable partners in the pursuit of public objectives. At the same time, private economic interests and public interests frequently do diverge. In other words, the influence of business actors on politics does not necessarily lead to general improvements in public welfare. Thus, the question arises whether developments in the political power of business require improvements in the existing regulatory framework for interest participation and what these improvements would need to be. In consequence, a differentiated understanding of developments in the political power of business is highly relevant for policy and politics today.

Note

1. The dominant label used for large business actors in the global governance literature is transnational corporations (TNCs), and therefore, this analysis will for the most part adopt this label as well. Some scholars refer to multinational corporations (MNCs) or transnational or multinational enterprises (TNEs, MNEs) instead. From a business management perspective, the major difference between TNCs and MNCs is that TNCs pursue a worldwide intra-firm division of labor, locating parts of the production process wherever it makes the most sense, whereas MNCs replicate the entire production process within different countries or regions (Wendt 1993). The early analyses in this field, which were published in the 1970s and 1980s, focused predominantly on MNCs. Recently, however, the emphasis has changed. Yet, some scholars argue that the TNC structure still does not exist as widely as the globalization and global governance literature assumes (Doremus et al. 1998). The difference between TNCs and TNEs and between MNCs and MNEs, in turn, lies in another facet of the organizational structure of the business actors analyzed. Research on TNCs and MNCs concentrates on corporate actors whereas research on TNEs and MNEs allows for other organizational structures of business actors as well.

2

Globalization and Global Governance

Corporate power in global governance cannot be examined without an understanding of globalization and global governance as such. The globalizing world, after all, provides the general empirical setting in which global governance is taking place and influences the political opportunities and constraints actors face. Global governance, in turn, represents the political empirical setting in which our research object is located. Moreover, globalization and global governance are not just empirical phenomena but also concepts used by political and scholarly observers. As such they are not merely descriptive. Rather, they are loaded with connotations and are a means to frame economic, political, and social developments. Descriptions of globalization as a natural force, irreversible trend, or tidal wave, for example, carry strong claims about the absence of political choice and responsibility (Müller 2002). In consequence, we need to scrutinize the *developments* associated with globalization and global governance as well as the *concepts* of globalization and global governance before we can assess the role of corporate power in global governance.

As an analysis of the literature on globalization and global governance immediately reveals, both are vague and at the same time highly controversial concepts. Scholars and practitioners refer to globalization to describe developments from increasing capital mobility to cultural homogenization to Internet chat rooms. They mention globalization in the context of growing job insecurity, stock market rallies, and environmental catastrophes. Accordingly, evaluations of the effects of globalization differ dramatically as well. While some observers celebrate the potential efficiency of resource allocation provided by a global market and the arrival of a borderless world, globalization has also spurred protests from Seattle to Genoa and led to the emergence of ATTAC, one of the fastest-growing protest movements of our time. Not surprisingly, some observers even argue that the term *globalization* is so vague that it should not be used anymore (Helleiner 2001).

At a first look, global governance is not as controversial as globalization. Rather, broad agreement exists on the core definition of *global governance*: multi-actor, multilevel political decisionmaking. In fact, the attention to multiple loci and new, complex forms of governance captured by this definition is the major strength of the concept, highlighting the increasing sharing of political functions by state and nonstate, substate, and suprastate actors. Upon closer look, however, the broad agreement on the definition of *global governance* only thinly veils substantial problems with assessments of the nature and implications of global governance. The political and philosophical heritage of the concept has provided it with an Achilles' heel that scholars have only recently started to consider. The attribution of an apolitical problem-solving character by many scholars and practitioners, in particular in the early phase of the global governance debate, resulted in a lack of attention to the most fundamental questions that political scientists should ask about any form of political decisionmaking: who decides, how, and in whose interest?

As both politicians and scientists would point out, such controversies about phenomena and concepts are absolutely normal. They are necessary for progress in our understanding. Moreover, such controversy can be expected in this case in particular because the developments in question are not complete. Globalization or many of the developments generally described with this term are relatively recent and ongoing, and we are still struggling to comprehend them. Nevertheless, at any point in time, we need to make judgments on the basis of the best understanding then possible. Political decisionmaking and scholarly analysis cannot wait until all of the information is finally there or a development has played itself out.

As a first step in assessing corporate power in global governance, therefore, it is sensible to try to get a good grasp of globalization and global governance. To that end, the first section of this chapter will review and disaggregate globalization accounts and spotlight implications for global governance and actors' political capacities. The section will explore the "nature" of globalization as well as the various enabling factors that have contributed to the move toward a globalizing world. In addition, the section will consider the implications of globalization in terms of equity and various dimensions of security discussed in the literature.

The second section establishes the link between globalization and global governance. It argues that the roots of the concept of global governance lie in the increasing visibility of problems requiring multilateral if not global solutions, in the end of the Cold War with its promise of a new era of cooperative world politics, and in the supposed decline of the political capacity of the state in a globalizing world. On this basis, the section juxtaposes views of global governance as an answer to globalization and as a consequence of globalization.

The third section critically examines the concept of global governance. It starts out by analyzing common elements of conceptualizations of global governance, the distinction made between global governance and global government by the majority of scholars and practitioners, and the emphasis on governance as "steering." Then, the section examines the role of questions of power in global governance research. It underlines the tendency to frame global governance as an apolitical, functional problem-solving tool and identifies the sources of this frame in the concept's political and philosophical contingencies as well as attempts to maintain the status quo in power relations. The analysis thereby highlights the urgent need for research on the role of power in global governance.

The Setting: A Globalizing World

If we can believe common judgment, we are living in a world today that is fundamentally different from what it was just thirty or forty years ago. The culprit generally identified as responsible for this crucial change is globalization. Globalization, however, means one thing to one observer of this change and a completely different thing to another. There are few terms scholars and practitioners in political science and politics use more frequently, vaguely, and inconsistently these days than *globalization*. Observers even fundamentally disagree about the nature and relevance of globalization as such. Some see globalization as the most important contemporary phenomenon, overwhelming all others (Ohmae 1996). Others consider it to be one important development among others whose scale and consequences need to be carefully assessed (Scholte 2000a). Still others claim that we witness much less fundamental change than the globalization discourse generally suggests (Krumbein 1998). Is globalization ushering in a dramatically different world on the basis of a "second" and "reflexive" modernity, or merely continuing century-old internationalization trends in a world in which the fundamentals of (inter-)societal organization remain unchanged (Beck 1997, 2002)?

Globalization, most fundamentally, is a short-hand term aggregating a vast variety of processes and practices, a meta-narrative used to describe a wide range of observations and support a similar range of arguments and claims. As Friedrich Kratochwil (2002) puts it, globalization is a "discursive formation that lumps together a variety of processes of change"; it is a term with "fuzzy boundaries" (26f). In consequence, empirical dimensions and political, social, economic, and ecological implications of globalization are highly controversial, making it a battleground for different political ideas and ideologies (Späth 2003).

From the perspective of the present analysis, we need to understand how globalization influences the behavioral options of actors. As the following section will argue, scholars disagree whether global governance is a necessary consequence of the shifts in political capacity induced by globalization or a response intentionally created to deal with the negative consequences of globalization. In any case, however, the setting for global governance clearly is this globalizing world. Globalization is creating the political, economic, social, and ecological environment for global governance and determines opportunities and constraints for the political choices and activities of actors.

The Nature of Globalization

Scholars and practitioners use the term *globalization* to refer to a whole range of phenomena. Most prevalent is the conceptualization of globalization as the perceived dramatic increase in international economic transactions. But globalization also stands for remarkable changes in information technologies and the global diffusion of values and ideas, massive population transfers, trends toward a universal world culture with a global harmonization of tastes and standards and diffusion of identical consumer goods, and the spread of certain political, social, and economic institutions, processes, and practices.

Scholars perceive both quantitative and qualitative changes due to globalization. In terms of the former, they point to rising amounts of goods, capital, and information moving around the world. In terms of the latter, they refer to an increased depth, reach, and significance in international transactions, a new character and meaning of trade due to the increasing share of intrafirm trade, or a change in the consciousness and organization of individuals and groups, for example. Many phenomena associated with globalization have both quantitative and qualitative dimensions. The value of transnational mergers and acquisitions, for instance, increased from $25 billion in 1980 to $350 billion in 1996 (Langhorne 2001, 19). Besides the mere change in numbers, however, this development also reflects the increasingly global orientation of corporate strategic planning.

Given the range of phenomena discussed under the heading of globalization and the various dimensions of these phenomena, it should come as no surprise that participants in the debate cannot agree on the nature and extent of globalization. Although the term *globalization* is present in all major languages today and we witness frequent references to globalization, global markets, and so on in everyday life, a pervasive vagueness and ambiguity paired with a high degree of emotionally and ideologically colored controversy characterize the globalization debate. The ability of *globalization* to contain multiple meanings, which has favored its rise in discourse as a commonplace term, has also created the difficulty of coming to agreement on its basic character.

One way to approach globalization in a systematic manner is to take a look at the fundamental divergence in conceptual lenses applied to the phenomenon. Scholars conceptualize globalization, for example, as internationalization, liberalization, universalization, westernization/modernization, and deterritorialization (Scholte 2000a). Thus, globalization accounts stressing the growth in transborder relations and interdependence between countries; the increasing flows of capital, goods, ideas, and people across borders; and the expanding integration of communication tend to be based on a conceptualization of globalization as internationalization. Meanwhile, conceptualizing globalization as liberalization turns the spotlight on the reduction if not removal of trade barriers and capital controls and the development of a global economy. In contrast, the universalization lens highlights the global standardization of experiences, cultural norms and tastes, and governance styles. The westernization/modernization lens, in turn, draws attention to the dominance of Western, specifically American, values and institutions in the diffusion of norms across the world and to perceptions of a cultural imperialism and threats to traditional cultures. Finally, conceptualizing globalization as deterritorialization emphasizes the increasing detachment of activities from territorial logic and constraints.

The choice of lens has fundamental implications on the perceived nature of globalization, of course. It influences what one sees as the "starting date" of globalization, for instance, as well as answers to the question whether globalization implies fundamentally new conditions or is merely a continuation of age-old trends. In this context, many observers argue that the loss of meaning of territory and borders identified by the deterritorialization lens reveals one of the most significant new traits of the globalizing world.[1] For the purposes of our analysis, moreover, the deterritorialization lens highlights substantial changes in the opportunities and constraints that actors "living" in this world face. It suggests that control over networks and flows is becoming more important than control over territory (McDowell 2006). Most fundamentally, globalization benefits actors not territorially bound.

A second option to get a grasp of globalization is to explore the globalization debate with respect to the variety of substantive foci applied by participants in the debate. We can differentiate among foci on developments in the economic arena, especially with goods and services on the one side and money and finance on the other; in the communication arena, specifically the diffusion of information and ideas; and in the demographic arena, in terms of the increasing global mobility of people as well as the pressures and societal and political consequences of migration. Some may wish to add developments in the ecological arena to this list, since the arrival of transnational and global environmental problems on the scene significantly contributed to the development of a global consciousness and calls for respective changes in governance.

A focus on the substantive foci used allows a more fine-tuned evaluation of the "extent" of globalization, which frequently is of relevance in political debates. Thus, a focus on economic developments, in particular developments in money and finance, would suggest a relatively greater extent of globalization, with speculative capital flows showing a high level of mobility. In contrast, the lack of globality of globalization becomes extremely clear when we consider the movement of people. While the cosmopolitan class may travel around the world for business deals and dream vacations, the majority of potentially mobile people from developing countries still face tough immigration laws and borders. To some extent, these borders are being undermined by illegal immigration and trafficking in people. But for the majority of potential migrants, they do exist. In the globalizing world, then, money clearly is much more mobile than people.

Finally, variances in assessments of the nature and extent of globalization also are a result of differences in geographic focus. Globalization accounts explicitly or implicitly focusing on or consciously or unconsciously drawing from the experience of industrialized countries tend to present a very different picture of globalization than globalization accounts focusing on the experience of developing countries. In fact, the latter are particularly noteworthy for critically questioning many of the claims the former make. Thus, globalization accounts that focus on developing countries highlight the difficulties of developing countries in obtaining access to world markets, for instance, pointing out that trade takes place much more between industrialized countries than with and between developing countries (Thomas 2000). Likewise, they emphasize the difference in access to global communication experienced by a large share of the population (see Figure 2.1).

These scholars would not argue, of course, that the impact of

Figure 2.1   Distribution in Access to the Internet

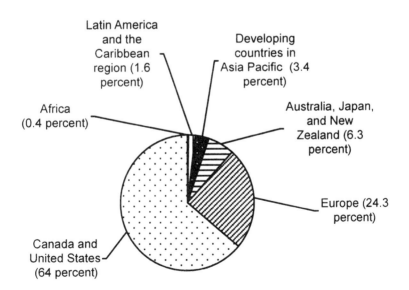

Source: Deutscher Bundestag 2002. Reprinted with permission.

globalization is not felt somehow even in the least integrated regions, be it as an influence on social conditions or on the policy choices available to governments. However, they would emphasize that huge gaps exist between industrialized and developing countries in terms of global economic, political, communicative, and social integration.[2] More important, these differences extend to the question of control over access and level of integration. In sum, exploring the nature and extent of globalization from the perspective of geographic foci of globalization accounts highlights the uneven spread of globalization. It points to the importance of access to and control over economic and informational networks.

Driving Forces

One area of controversy in the globalization debate is the identification of causes and effects of globalization. Clearly, the multitude of aspects generally combined under the concept of globalization includes both causes and effects often interacting with each other. Thus, some observers suggest that the discourse on globalization lumps together such a variety of processes of change, "each one being propelled by its own complex causal chains and interactions," that we should not think of globalization as having one cause, being a uniform cause of specific effects, or as one linear process (Kratochwil 2002, 26). Rather, we may conceptualize globalization as *simultaneous interactive cascades of change,* with each cause of further change being the effect of changes and interactions between those changes at the previous "stage."

At the same time, scholars argue that we can identify broad mutually enabling structural conditions as driving forces behind globalization (Scholte 2000a). One core enabling condition, in this respect, has been technological progress, especially in the area of communications, data processing, and transport. Developments in computer technology, satellites, microchips, and the Internet, in particular, have made possible the creation of the material infrastructure necessary for supraterritorial economic, political, and social interactions (Wriston 1992). The communications revolution and the advent of digitalization, the basis for today's quantity and speed of information exchanges, have dramatically reduced physical barriers to worldwide communication. Furthermore, these developments have created opportunities for the evolution of a global consciousness, an increasing awareness of events far away, and new and more avenues for the global diffusion of ideas and values. In addition, they have furthered the asymmetry between economic and political actors (Kobrin 1997). One indication of this asymmetry is that these technological developments have proven difficult to contain. Due to these technological changes, it has become increasingly problematic if not impossible for governments to control the population's access to outside information and resources, for instance.

Economic incentives have provided a second enabling condition for globalization often identified in the literature.[3] The intent and ability to pursue profits in increasingly open and monetized global markets has been a powerful driving force behind the global orientation and extension of economic activity. While some scholars consider business and entrepreneurship the "principal driving force behind globalization" (Biersteker 2000, 166), others point to capitalism itself—that is, the fundamental tenets of capitalist production and consumption, of ideas supporting the search for profits and of neoliberal ideology, as structural enablers and determinants of the shape of globalization (Altvater and Mahnkopf 1996, 2002).

As many scholars point out, globalization would not have been possible on the basis of technological progress and capitalist structures, however, if a third enabling condition had not existed: facilitative regulatory frameworks (Brand et al. 2000). Governments, sometimes in combination with nonstate actors or sometimes even nonstate actors themselves, have created institutional and legal frameworks that have facilitated global activities and deterritorialization. The creation and enforcement of property rights is one of the most important goods provided by governments in the enabling of global markets. In addition, regulatory frameworks for the movements of goods and capital and the standardization of technologies and procedures have contributed to the increasingly global extension of activities.

An analysis of the factors enabling and driving globalization thus highlights the important role of technology in developments. This finding, in turn, suggests that those with access to technology and control over technological development are likely to be in a better position to shape globalization and draw benefits from it than those without. In addition, this analysis reveals the important role of regulatory frameworks and those actors designing and implementing them. Finally, an analysis of the driving forces behind globalization pinpoints the particular role economic interests and incentives are playing in fostering and structuring globalization.

Effects

The discussion about globalization is perhaps most controversial with respect to its effects. The difficulty is to establish linkages between the changes at the macro level termed *globalization* and the changes witnessed in the lives of citizens, consumers, and workers (Sinclair 1999b). Whereas globalization optimists argue that globalization leads to the development of an open liberal society, to increased economic efficiency and welfare, and to the diffusion of democracy and peace, globalization pessimists claim that globalization reduces individual and global security, equity, and democracy. These differences in evaluation exist even if observers focus on the same issues. Thus, proponents of the positive evaluation of globalization emphasize that globalization brings greater income and job opportunities, while advocates of the negative view of globalization contend that globalization leads to lower wages and declining job security and welfare standards. Likewise, globalization optimists suggest that globalization provides an opportunity for the more efficient allocation and use of natural resources and therefore improved living conditions, while globalization pessimists argue that the pursuit of economic efficiency in a borderless world threatens the limits of endurance of the global ecological system(s) and humanity.

Lately, however, globalization critics have grown in number and voice, especially in the popular discourse.[4] Under the heading of "global pillage" rather than "global village," large antiglobalization protests accompany every meeting of the World Trade Organization (WTO), G8, or World Economic Forum (WEF).[5] ATTAC, which has made the fight against globalization its platform, today has groups worldwide and a membership that is growing by leaps and bounds. Protesters and antiglobalization activists are fighting for a more equitable distribution of income, more control and regulation of global capital and corporate activity, more environmental stewardship, and a host of other issues. Likewise, the ideological spectrum includes everything from Marxists to right-wing extremists. This combination of often-conflicting goals and values shows that the antiglobalization grouping is a protest movement against globalization rather than a unified movement for an alternative model. The protesters are united by their anxiety about globalization and its effects rather than by goals.

Indeed, the problems of the globalization losers should not be underestimated. Even observers generally positively inclined toward globalization currently perceive a serious risk of turmoil: "The risk of failure in the global markets and the risk of political and social violence in the face of uncontrolled power, weakened national governments and a globally unequal distribution of economic benefits, are both deadly serious" (Langhorne 2001, xv). The transformative changes generally described with the term *globalization* do have real consequences for the economic, social, and political realities of people. According to the literature, these consequences exist in two areas in particular: equity and security.

The equity debate focuses on both the national and the global distribution of income and welfare, including civil and human rights. Globalization optimists argue that liberalization and the increasingly global extension of markets will foster economic growth in particular in developing countries and therefore equality (Burtless et al. 1998). They argue that globalization means new opportunities in terms of employment, investment, and access to information and civil rights for all people, especially for those traditionally marginalized, such as inhabitants of developing countries, women, older people, and oppressed ethnic groups (Archibugi, Held, and Kohler 1998). Moreover, globalization optimists emphasize that globalization has motivated the inclusion of gender and human rights issues on the global governance agenda as well as initiatives of the International Labour Organization (ILO) to strengthen the global implementation and enforcement of labor standards. In this view, globalization will eventually foster convergence in income and welfare between countries.

Critics of globalization, in contrast, argue that globalization primarily benefits economic elites and that increasing inequality, therefore, is an inherent characteristic of globalization: "Existing evidence suggests that as governments have liberalized policies so as to integrate more fully into the world economy, almost without exception economic inequality has increased. As regards political rights and freedoms, globalization does not have a much better record" (Woods 2000, 8).

In consequence, critical observers charge that globalization in its current shape is perpetuating and strengthening social hierarchies and widening gaps in income and welfare (Falk 1999b). They suggest an increasing income stratification within and across countries, with fewer and fewer people owning more and more of the world's resources, and emphasize the concentration of economic activity within and between those states with access to production networks, investment, and knowledge (Gray 1998; see also Figure 2.2). From this perspective, economic gains from trade liberalization, in particular the Uruguay round, have accrued mostly to northern countries and investors. Within northern countries, in turn, critical observers suggest that the benefits of globalization tend to go to investors rather than workers. They point out that even if most transnational investments today remain in the Organization for Economic Cooperation and Development (OECD), they do not guarantee employment there, just like profits do not necessarily translate into job security.[6]

Between these two poles of evaluations of the impact of globalization on welfare and equity, numerous more moderate positions have appeared (Marsh and Hay 2000). These tend to acknowledge that globalization creates winners and losers and identify determinants of the costs and benefits of globalization that are modifiable. Specifically, some evaluations make the case that developing countries are able to benefit from globalization as well if they follow a certain policy advice (Rodrik 1999). Likewise, they postulate that the welfare state in many developed countries has not yet shown the signs of decline suggested by highly critical evaluations of the impact of globalization (Swank 2002).[7] Even these more moderate positions are controversial, however.

With "security" broadly defined, the debate on the effects of globalization on security also addresses the issue of material welfare,

Figure 2.2   The Increasing Gap Between Rich and Poor

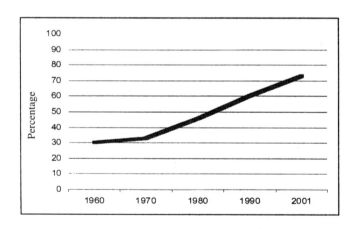

Source: Deutscher Bundestag 2002. Reprinted with permission.
Note: Percentage of difference between the income of the wealthiest 5 percent of the global population and the income of the poorest 5 percent.

of incomes and job security. In addition, the debate draws attention to the potential impact of globalization on bodily safety, ecological security, identity, social cohesion, and cultural preservation (Scholte 2000a). In general, evaluations of the impact of globalization on security again cover the whole range possible from positive effects to negative ones.

With respect to bodily safety, some scholars argue that globalization and the associated diffusion of free trade and democracy contribute to increasing security and a decline in warfare, while others suggest that we can link globalization to a rise in violence and disorder due to the social costs of economic restructuring, trafficking in people, and the growth of transnational criminal networks and new forms of crime (Mittelman and Johnston 1999). Likewise, some scholars make the case that technology transfer, improvements in living standards and the associated growth in demand for environmental quality, and the inclusion of environmental aspects in the global security agenda demonstrate a positive relationship between globalization and ecological security (Bhagwati 1993). Others, however, postulate that uncontrolled global economic activities are leading to the depletion and degradation of natural resources, and that free trade and pollution havens foster the undermining of environmental standards in developed countries (Daly and Goodland 1994).

Similarly, scholars disagree whether globalization leads to cultural and societal homogenization or differentiation, to integration or fragmentation, and to social cohesion or disintegration (Menzel 1998).[8] Whereas some see the possibility of the development of a single world culture based on consumerism, the English language, American values and lifestyles, and the mass media, along with associated threats to other cultural communities and identities, others expect and observe tendencies toward an increasing diversity and cultural differentiation as a reaction to globalization (Shapiro and Alker 1996). Likewise, euphoric reports of the development of supraterritorial communities and networks confront despairing accounts of a lower depth and stability of local networks—the loss of social connectedness and traditional societal structures and institutions. Similar controversies exist with respect to the effects of globalization on identity. Again, scholars point to the new opportunities for "identity surfing," acknowledging at the same time that this increasing scope for definition and expression of identity also means a loss in simplicity and security in defining oneself (Brock 1993).

Overall, the literature suggests that globalization has created winners and losers. Max Singer and Aaron Wildavsky (1993) speak of the subsequent advent of "zones of peace" and "zones of turmoil." Clearly, globalization has both positive and negative repercussions for equity and security, and a final judgment on its exact costs and benefits is impossible. What the discussion has shown, however, is that the potential costs of globalization suggested by a substantial share of observers are significant enough to highlight the importance of governance in a globalizing world.

From Globalization to Global Governance

Globalization, then, is a short-hand term aggregating a wide range of developments. These include economic developments such as the increasing flow of goods and capital around the globe, growing inter-dependencies, the importance of intrafirm trade, and the creation of global markets. Importantly, however, globalization goes beyond the economic sphere to include the global diffusion of ideas and norms, communicative integration, and demographic developments. Moreover, the experience of globalization differs markedly depending on one's geographic location and focus, with entire regions being "outgrated" at the same time as the economic and communicative integration among the industrialized countries is increasing. In addition, an interactive cascade of causes and consequences of globalization can be recognized, rejecting notions of a linear development while accepting technological developments, the search for economic gain, and facilitative regulatory frameworks as core enabling factors.

One of the most important aspects of globalization appears to be the trend toward deterritorialization. According to the majority of observers, deterritorialization captures the fundamentally new quality of social geography present since the latter decades of the twentieth century. The decline in importance of territorial borders in most aspects of everyday life and the collapse of space-time relations have had dramatic consequences, including, for example, an almost complete detachment of business from territorial space.

These findings contain some pertinent information about globalization's implications for global governance. First, globalization affects the political options of actors, creating new opportunities for some and new constraints for others. Thus, the preceding discussion suggests that actors not territorially bound, with access to and control over economic, financial, and informational networks and technology, are likely to be the beneficiaries of globalization. Simultaneously, actors whose resources depend on territory and who lack access to and control over networks and technology are likely to bear a larger share of the costs of globalization. Not surprisingly, then, globalization has been described as "overtaxing" the decisionmaking capacity of the state even in the traditional domains of the welfare state (Messner and Nuscheler 1996a, 3). The popular discussion has depicted global markets and economic actors as outpacing politics due to the lack in mobility and flexibility of the latter. Visions of governments held ransom by mobile capital have become familiar. To what extent such depictions of shifts in actors' political capacities overestimate the extent and implications of these shifts is controversial and will be the subject of the following chapters. Fundamentally, however, the analysis of the globalization debate presented here strongly suggests that nonstate actors, in particular large economic actors from industrialized countries, are likely to have gained political power vis-à-vis states and other nonstate actors with less access to and control over networks and mobile resources.

Second, the preceding analysis of globalization has highlighted the increasing extent of transborder activities and communication flows, which in turn can be linked to a growth in the existence and awareness of transborder if not global problems and the need for cooperation in the solving of these problems. Likewise, it has argued that the potentially negative effects of globalization on a significant share of the world population appear to be sufficiently severe to demand some form of governance intervention. In other words, both the growth in transnational, or possibly global, problems and the increasing recognition of the existence of similar economic and social problems in various countries with potential transnational causes and solutions have fostered a demand for international and supranational cooperative strategies. This demand, combined with the simultaneous arrival of powerful new actors on the scene and the territorial limits to the political capacity of the state, in turn, has made a search for new processes and practices of political decisionmaking appear desirable, if not necessary. In other words, globalization is also closely tied to the perception of a need for global governance.

Importantly, this perceived need for global governance met with the perception of dramatically improved opportunities for such governance due to developments not directly related to globalization. Thus, global governance appeared on the political agenda during the period of enthusiasm over the fall of the Berlin Wall and expectations of a potential for increasing international cooperation for the benefit of humankind. The end of the Cold War fostered expectations that common problem-solving would replace old conflicts, and visions of a new era of common pursuit of common goals flourished. Notions of the common condition of humankind, increasingly reflected in images of the "Blue Planet," for instance, were complemented by the perception of new opportunities for global cooperation. Together, they promoted images of a unified world in need of common management. In sum, the experience of globalization and the end of the Cold War led to practitioners and scholars pondering the potential for the development of a world society and the possibility of harmony and cooperation in problem-solving.

These two aspects of the implications of globalization, the shifts in actors' political capacities and the need (combined with the opportunities) for multilateral problem-solving, allow for two interpretations of the link between globalization and global governance. First, global governance can be perceived as an almost automatic consequence of globalization resulting from the shift in political capacity from state to nonstate actors. In this interpretation, newly powerful actors have expanded their political activities and assumed important roles in the political arena, thereby leading to a new kind of political decisionmaking. Second, global governance can be perceived as an intended response to globalization. In this perspective, global cooperation is identified as a promising multi-actor strategy to deal with territorial limits on state capacity and the experience of transborder ecological, economic, and political problems generally associated with globalization.

The two perspectives differ primarily in emphasis and starting point of analysis and are thus not to be seen as opposing views. Still, these differences in emphasis have important implications for the kind of global governance one is likely to see and the kinds of questions one would want to ask regarding its implications. In the second case, global governance is supposed to solve the problems created by globalization. Accordingly, global governance is a priori defined as a good thing, and the relevant questions are, How effective and how successful is global governance? Thus, this perspective entails a normative approach to global governance. This is the case even though the contributors to the global governance debate, who adopt such a perspective, claim to pursue an analytical approach rather than a normative one (Messner and Nuscheler 1996a, 1996b, 2003; Rosenau and Czempiel 1992). Yet, the a priori positive interpretation of global governance implicit in this perspective means that normative viewpoints are just below the surface of analysis.

In the first case, no such predisposition toward a positive (or negative) evaluation of global governance is implied. Global governance merely is a fact, a new kind of political decisionmaking that is taking place, in which nonstate actors assume a prominent role. In consequence, the core question regarding global governance arising from this perspective is: Who participates and decides in global governance, and in whose interest? Clearly, no perspective is ever completely free of influence from the normative viewpoints of those adopting the perspective. Scholars pursuing this perspective tend to be concerned about normative issues such as democratic legitimacy and social justice. However, this second perspective on the link between globalization and global governance avoids the direct normative framing on global governance and thereby is able to present an analytical approach to the topic.

Again, the two perspectives should not be taken as mutually exclusive. They differ in the starting point of analysis and the resulting emphasis given to certain research questions. Thus, scholars adopting the second perspective will acknowledge that some form of global governance is necessary for the solution of many transnational and global problems. But they will also point out that not every process and institution of global governance is necessarily good. Accordingly, they will highlight the need to critically analyze the role of power in global governance.

Interestingly, the normative approach has dominated much of the debate and literature on global governance. Thus, many scholars have pursued questions regarding the functioning and effectiveness of individual global governance institutions and processes. Critical analyses of the power struggles in the creation of these global governance institutions and processes and their implications for the distribution of costs and benefits and the distribution of public and private goods have been much less common. This emphasis on the normative approach and its adoption of an optimistic frame of global governance can be understood, however, if one considers the political and philosophical contingencies of its rise to prominence.

Politics in a Post–Cold War World: Global Governance

The Concept

In the early 1990s former Federal Republic of Germany chancellor Willy Brandt invited politicians and eminent individuals from twen-

ty-eight countries to Königswinter to develop visions on the functioning of the international system after the end of the Cold War.
Perceiving a need for and promise of increased possibilities for international cooperation and the pursuit of the common welfare of
humankind, the "Commission on Global Governance" met and developed proposals for reform of the international political system on the
basis of new institutions of governance and the extension of participation in governance to new actors.[9] Under the cochairmanship of
Ingvar Carlson, the Swedish prime minister, and Shridath Ramphal, a
prominent statesman from Guiana, the commission generated its
report, *Our Global Neighborhood*, containing its vision of the future
of governance in and of the post–Cold War world.

The commission defined global governance in the following way:

> Governance is the sum of the many ways individuals and institu-
> tions, public and private, manage their common affairs. It is a con-
> tinuing process through which conflicting or diverse interests may
> be accommodated and co-operative action may be taken. It includes
> formal institutions and regimes empowered to enforce compliance,
> as well as informal arrangements that people and institutions either
> have agreed to or perceive to be in their interest. ... At the global
> level, governance has been viewed primarily as intergovernmental
> relationships, but it must now be understood as also involving non-
> governmental organizations (NGOs), citizens' movements, multina-
> tional corporations, and the global capital market. Interacting with
> these are global mass media of dramatically enlarged influence. ...
> There is no single model or form of global governance, nor is there
> a single structure or set of structures. It is a broad, dynamic, com-
> plex process of interactive decision-making that is constantly
> evolving and responding to changing circumstances. ...
> Recognizing the systemic nature of these issues, it must promote
> systemic approaches in dealing with them. Effective global deci-
> sion-making thus needs to build upon and influence decisions taken
> locally, nationally, and regionally, and to draw on the skills and
> resources of a diversity of people and institutions at many levels.
> (Commission on Global Governance 1995, 2)

This definition already indicates the variety of aspects captured
by the concept of global governance. Under the heading of global
governance, scholars and practitioners describe changes in policies,
polities, and politics (Messner and Nuscheler 1996a, 2003; Schirm
2004). At the core of the debate is a focus on participation and initiative in political decisionmaking by an increasing variety of actors at
an increasing number of levels, and the resulting development of new

and complex forms of problem-solving structures and processes. In particular, global governance scholars highlight the growing participation by nonstate actors, most important among them business actors and NGOs, in political decisionmaking. These actors participate in "regimes, broad political accommodations, or discrete regulatory actions reiterated across the globe" (Latham 1999, 23). Likewise, global governance accounts stress the rising importance of subnational and supranational levels of political decisionmaking. In James Rosenau's (1995) terms, global governance includes "systems of rule at all levels of human activity—from the family to the international organization—in which the pursuit of goals through the exercise of control has transnational repercussions" (13). Capturing these developments, observers delineate a change of the international system from a state-centric to a multicentric one. They suggest that we are witnessing an expanding breadth of political decisionmaking from the global level to the local level and a multiplication of instruments used.

The changes in actors and levels of political decisionmaking depicted generally are represented as co-constitutive with changes in norms, contexts, and substance of political decisionmaking. Scholars perceive, for example, a changing nature of sovereignty, a widening of the global security agenda, and a redefinition of the use of warfare (Scholte 2000a; Thomas 2000). They argue that the international system is progressively more defined by norms and institutions as well as common interests rather than the distribution of national capabilities (Väyrynen 1999). Accordingly, they foresee more room for foreign policies pursuing the global common good, and a new multilateralism allowing the representation of different sets of interests and a broadening of the policy agenda to include more social issues (Messner and Nuscheler 1996b; O'Brien et al. 2000). Likewise, observers report a conceptual and behavioral reorientation of major institutional actors, including transnational business, NGOs, IGOs, and states, toward the regional and supranational levels (Biersteker 2000).

Governance, Not Government

A point particularly emphasized by practitioners and scholars in the global governance debate is that governance does not mean government (Pierre 2000). In *Governance Without Government*, one of the early and highly popular publications on the topic, James Rosenau and Ernst-Otto Czempiel (1992) call global governance a "fact" that needs to be recognized despite the lack of a world government. They delineate governance as a more encompassing phenomenon, including governmental institutions as well as nongovernmental mechanisms through which societal actors pursue their goals:

> Both refer to purposive behavior, to goal-oriented activities, to systems of rule; but government suggests activities that are backed by formal activities, by police powers to insure the implementation of duly constituted policies, whereas governance refers to activities backed by shared goals that may or may not derive from legal and formally prescribed responsibilities and that do not necessarily rely on police powers to overcome defiance and attain compliance. Governance, in other words, is a more encompassing phenomenon than government. It embraces governmental institutions, but it also subsumes informal, non-governmental mechanisms whereby those persons and organizations within its purview move ahead, satisfy their needs, and fulfill their wants. ... Governance is thus a system of rule that is as dependent on inter-subjective meaning as on formally sanctioned constitutions and charters. ... Thus it is possible to conceive of governance without government—of regulatory mechanisms in a sphere of activity which function effectively even though they are not endowed with formal authority. (Rosenau 1992, 4)

Likewise, the Commission on Global Governance (1995) explicitly rejects the notion that global governance could mean global government: "We are not proposing movement towards world government, for were we to travel in that direction we could find ourselves in an even less democratic world than we have—one more accommodating to power, more hospitable to hegemonic ambition, and more reinforcing of the roles of states and governments rather than the rights of people" (xvi).

The debate tends to represent global government as both undesirable and infeasible. The view of the undesirability of a world government results from fears of it developing into a (world) tyranny and bureaucratic nightmare, which, interestingly enough, were also fears raised by the opponents of a federalist United States of America (Griffin 1999). Specifically, the majority of advocates of global governance argues that a world government would be too far removed from civil society and lack democratic legitimation. Moreover, they make the case that governance at a global level is functionally similar to government at the national level (Finkelstein 1995).

Next to the undesirability of world government, practitioners and academics also postulate that such a central democratically legitimated decisionmaking body is infeasible. Thus, they raise the question whether a democracy is possible at the global level at which the ethical and sociocultural preconditions for a world demos may not exist. In this context, they stress the need for homogeneity in experience, interpretation, and values, as well as for an ability to foresee consequences of making a decision with a limited spatial and temporal range. Moreover, they point to the ability to assign responsibility as a minimum requirement.[10] Finally, another frequently cited reason for the unfeasibility of world government is the idea that the rich and powerful countries would reject the idea of a democratic world government due to the associated loss in their power.[11]

In contrast, a small but significant number of practitioners and scholars argue that world government is both desirable and feasible (Harris and Yunker 1999). In their view, global governance in the absence of a world government only means a "modification of the present world anarchy of no governance" (Martin 1999, 14). Fundamentally opposing the commission's stance, these observers claim that improvements in communication and transportation that reduce spatial and informational distances and transaction costs make global government a genuine alternative (Yunker 1999). In fact, supporters of this view postulate that global government is the best strategy to improve the fate of the world population and the only one for putting democratic ideals into practice and avoiding amoral governance by the market (Glossop 1999). They contend that the current system is inadequate from a democratic perspective and charge that the Commission on Global Governance prefers a "system of world tyranny and war enforced by the Security Council" to a "constitutional federal world government, under which the people are guaranteed the right to elect their representatives to a world parliament, which then adopts world laws by consent of the governed, with enforcement by civilian police action when necessary to apprehend individual lawbreakers rather than make war against entire populations" (Isely 1999, 99). Clearly, calls for global government assume a marginal position in the global governance debate, however.

Governance as Steering

A second point of crucial importance to the global governance debate is the conceptualization of governance as steering. The *New English Dictionary* defines *governance* as "the action or manner of governing, controlling, directing or regulating influence, control, sway, mastery; the state of being governed; the manner in which something is governed or regulated; discreet or virtuous behavior; wise self-command" (cited in Falk 1999a, 36). Note that the latter part of the definition gives governance an extremely positive connotation, while the earlier parts have a more neutral character. In the scholarly debate, Rosenau and Czempiel (1992), as early and important contributors, define governance as "activities backed by shared goals that may or may not derive from legal and formally prescribed responsibilities and that do not necessarily rely on police powers to overcome defiance and attain compliance" (4). In a later definition, Rosenau (1999) depicts governance as "mechanisms for steering social systems toward their goals" (296). These definitions have two important elements. First, they define governance as a functional tool for problem-solving or steering. Second, and more important, they attach an apolitical character to governance by starting from the assumption of "shared" or objective goals of social systems. In this perspective, then, governance is about the common pursuit of common goals.

These examples are not singular cases. Rather, they reflect a tendency by numerous scholars to define global governance as ruling or steering without consideration of questions of power, control, participation, or distributional implications. Moreover, they draw attention to the role of epistemic authority, the deference to professional and specialized knowledge, marketized institutions, and the trust placed in the infrastructural technologies of the "knowledge economy" many scholars and practitioners associate with global governance (Hewson and Sinclair 1999).

Power and Global Governance

The major problem associated with the concept of global governance arises from the frequent application of the very restrictive frame of apolitical problem-solving, in particular in the early phase of the globalization and global governance debates, and the resulting ontological biases and blind spots. On the basis of such a restrictive frame, scholars and practitioners have neglected questions of power and control. This, in turn, has allowed them to attribute an a priori positive nature and intrinsically desirable role to global governance, specifically a presumption of a democratic nature. Due to the restrictive framing of the concept, scholars and practitioners analyze what happens after "governors" have been selected and governance goals have been set, rather than exploring the politics before that stage (Latham 1999).

Given the inability to determine the need for regulation and to identify the "right" solutions objectively, however, the politics of global governance are of pivotal importance (Grande 2001a).

This apolitical framing of global governance to some extent is a function of the political and historical contingencies associated with globalization and the end of the Cold War delineated earlier. It also reflects the philosophical underpinnings of the concept, however.[12] Images of harmony, cooperation, and common problem-solving, which underlie conceptualizations of governance as an apolitical, technocratic problem-solving approach, reflect the Enlightenment tradition in which many practitioners' and scholars' concepts of global governance are grounded. They demonstrate a faith in reason and progress based on the belief in humankind's ability to learn, emphasizing cooperative social relations and the mobility and permeability of society, while excluding societal conflict and competition from the view (Mürle 1998). On the basis of such ideas and beliefs, the Commission on Global Governance arrived at recommendations that critical observers read as simply if not naively asking governments to behave fairly and observe agreed-upon standards and proposing "that primary reliance toward the objective of enhanced international security and further human progress be placed on the gradual development of properly enlightened, tolerant, humanitarian, and cosmopolitan attitudes among both the general human population and its political leaders" (Harris and Yunker 1999, viii). This faith in learning, consensus, and progress also benefited the value attached to professional, technical, and otherwise specialized knowledge in political problem-solving. The development of global governance thus would be "more or less a repetition on a global scale of the 'modernisation' of states and societies" (Björklund and Berglund 2001, 8).

In addition to political liberalism, the prevalence of the norms of economic neoliberalism also contributed to the specific conceptualization of global governance that took hold (Mathews 1997). Ideas of a reduced role of the state, trust placed in market actors to deliver societal welfare, and the associated need for and desirability of decentralized governance strongly resonate with the conceptualization of global governance as cooperative problem-solving by state and nonstate actors (Brand et al. 2000). The underlying assumption that what is in the interest of the economic actors is also in the interest of society implies that questions about asymmetries in power between these economic actors and civil society or the state need not be asked. Moreover, the persistence of low growth rates and the perception of fundamental threats to the economic stability and prosperity known in developed countries since World War II opened the door for confidence crises in the regulatory competence and capacity of governments. At the same time, the dominant political discourse has even raised doubts about the ability of states to solve global problems cooperatively (Palan 1999). Participants in the academic and popular debates have argued that problems with the capacity and willingness of governments to develop, implement, and enforce global norms in crucial areas prevent an effective and efficient pursuit of many public policy objectives in a globalized world. In this context, scholars and practitioners have come to suggest and view networks of national, regional, and international organizations, both public and private, as an alternative and promising strategy to steer globalization (Reinicke 1998).

These norms and ideas, then, further favored the strong preference given to global *governance* rather than *government*, already discussed. The choice of title for *Our Global Neighborhood* is indicative of the underlying perspective: "The term 'neighborhood' implies a small, peaceful, orderly, and inviting residential area in which people live together in serene and mutually supportive harmony" (Yunker 1999, 142). Beliefs in the benefits of individualism, decentralization, and voluntary cooperation associated with political liberalism and economic neoliberalism are a cornerstone of many global governance accounts. Such beliefs necessarily frame the "experience" that federalist structures "with an indispensable minimum of centralization" a la Kant have proven an effective system of governance for large, complex, and heterogeneous units (Messner and Nuscheler 1996a, 4). The argument of global governance advocates that governments are either incapable or untrustworthy, and that humanity's welfare is best protected through independent voluntary action by individuals and small groups, thus strongly reflects the current zeitgeist (Falk 1999a).

Faith in consensus and learning, rationality, and organization provides global governance with a promise of order and security. It suggests that the overpowering, chaotic changes associated with globalization may, in fact, be governable. According to these ideas, humankind can learn how to deal with global problems and pursue collective goals through global governance. In this manner, then, global governance also resonates with those critical of the hegemony of economic neoliberalism closer to a sociodemocratic tradition. From their perspective, global governance suggests that one can mend the crises caused by globalization and control capitalist excesses on the basis of sociodemocratic ideals, and that global governance can present an alternative to the neoliberal economic and political model.

Some assessments of global governance, in fact, suggest it as the only way to overcome the self-defeating behavior of actors in collective action situations depicted in the "tragedy of the commons" (Young 1997). They argue that global governance allows the promotion of sustained cooperation and the solution of social conflicts via social institutions instead of self-interested organizations or governments.

To some extent, the restrictive framing of the concept of global governance may not just be a function of prevalent promoting of this frame, of course (Murphy 1994). The failure to ask questions about the politics of global governance serves, in particular, the status quo in terms of the distribution of power, the institutional framework, and the dominance of certain norms and ideas. Moreover, fundamental questions about goals and values and about conflicts among different goals and values can thereby be avoided.

Thus, critical observers contend that ignoring questions of the distribution of power in global governance means ignoring the existence of a unipolar world characterized by US hegemony and an international institutional structure that favors the interests of the G7 and their corporations (Wilkin 1997), the global diffusion of only a selected set of values and social practices (Sinclair 1999b), the distributional effects of reform in the governance of markets and societies (McGinnis 1999), and the social, ecological, and gender inequities associated with global governance (Wichterich 1998; Young 1998). Moreover, they argue that the restrictive frame is intended to allow participants in the debate to ignore alternative institutional structures and processes as well as ideologies and values (Thomas 2000). Thus, critical observers charge that the restrictive lens makes it possible for the commission, in particular, to refrain from challenging the overall institutional framework:

> It is apparently unthinkable to these Commissioners that world militarism, widespread poverty and misery, massive violations of human rights, and destruction of the environment might be institutionalized within the framework itself in terms of the principles of technological domination of nature, sovereign territorial autonomy of nations in a posture of mutual hostility and economic competition toward all other nations, and worldwide economic institutions based on the principle of individual and corporate self-interest. (Martin 1999, 13)

In defense of the Commission on Global Governance, one has to point out that it did not aim at describing reality but at developing a vision of global governance. Thus, *Our Global Neighborhood* acknowledges that the current situation in global governance does not satisfy democratic and welfare ambitions for large parts of the global population. In consequence, the commission suggested a number of reforms that would need to take place to create the necessary global governance processes and institutions. Most fundamentally, the commission argued for the development of a global civil ethic based on respect for life, liberty, justice and equality, mutual respect, caring, and integrity. In addition, it called for reforms of the United Nations system and Bretton Woods institutions, proposing the establishment of a permanent rapid deployment force, the elimination of nuclear weapons and adoption and enforcement of conventions on biological and chemical weapons, the establishment of an Economic Security Council, the creation of a Forum of Civil Society in the UN and Right of Petition for individuals and groups, the creation of new competition rules created through the WTO, the implementation of improved democratic procedures for the International Monetary Fund (IMF) and World Bank, the establishment of an international tax and charge for use of the global commons, the increase of membership on the Security Council, and the creation of an International Criminal Court.

Yet, even these reform suggestions are vulnerable to some of the criticisms raised previously. Most fundamentally, critical assessments suggest that the proposed reforms ignore the political and structural causes of the current insufficiency of the global governance architecture. In the view of critics, these proposals for reform reflect the world as of 1995 and do not sufficiently challenge existing institutional structures and the ideological consensus of the international economic and political systems. Moreover, expectations regarding a future development of a common world ethic are likely to be met with substantial skepticism by critics of the dependence of the global governance concept on the Enlightenment tradition.

With or without intent, the failure to address questions of the distribution of power among the actors participating in global governance and its implications has allowed some participants in the global governance debate to apply highly optimistic assumptions of its democratic nature. Highlighting the new opportunities for the contribution of nonstate actors, in particular global civil society, to global political decisionmaking, advocates of this perspective have proclaimed the arrival of a new era of cosmopolitan democracy (Archibugi, Held, and Kohler 1998; Held 1995). They have answered concerns raised about a potential decline in public authority with the assurance that this authority was merely being redistributed among a wider range of diverse subnational, national, and supranational actors and not deteriorating.

In response, another group of scholars has started to stress the need to consider the potentially problematic implications of globalization and global governance for democracy. They emphasize the existence of power struggles among actors in governance and of a distribution of power skewed in the direction of some actors, underlining the need for skepticism toward David Held's arguments for a cosmopolitan democracy. Rather than harmonious cooperation among equals, scholars describe conflicts over power, rules, and definitions. Specifically, scholars delineate the frequent undemocratic nature and club quality of global governance arrangements:

> The disturbing side, however, is that internationalized governance seems to take place in a setting, more similar to a large club with changing, informal membership rules than to government under the law, as we teach it to our students, with accountability to the voters. The option left to use, seems to be to put our trust in the wisdom of our leaders. It is difficult not to see this as a serious step backward in the democratic sense. (Björklund and Berglund 2001, 5f)

In the view of the most critical observers, global governance even entails a "politics of disempowerment" rather than an empowerment of societal actors (Ake 1999).

Finally, critical observers point to deficits in the actual development of cooperative governance in the international system. They pinpoint, for instance, the enforcement gap in international society caused by weak ethical constraints and insufficient social pressure, as well as a lack of legal institutions with jurisdiction across state, ethnic, and religious borders (Johansen 1999). Others assert that notions of effective technocratic steering and the common pursuit of problem-solving become doubtful in the face of seemingly random agenda-setting and decisionmaking observable in global politics and the persistence of global crises.

In consequence, critical observers question an overly optimistic view of global governance as a promising solution for global problems: "Global governance should not be regarded as either necessary or beneficent. Real global governance is not in itself a political good or a solvent for the world's problems" (Hewson and Sinclair 1999, ix). They postulate that global governance in terms of multi-actor, multilevel regulatory activity does not hold the democratic reform potential promised by its advocates. In the eyes of these critics, global governance is at best a utopian vision suggested by the Commission on Global Governance and others in the hope that it will function as a model for global political developments (Brand et al. 2000). At worst, it is a tool for the hegemony of neoliberal beliefs and institutions, as well as a substantial threat to the democratic legitimacy of political decisionmaking.

More moderate positions have developed in the course of the debate. Thus, some scholars point out that global governance may foster a cosmopolitan democracy that can supplement national democracy, even if it cannot replace it (Beck 2002). In other words, cosmopolitan democracy and national democracy should be considered complementary dimensions of democracy rather than alternatives. To what extent promising conditions for the development of such a cosmopolitan democracy exist and a sufficient level of national democracy can be retained, is still subject to debate, however.

In sum, conceptualizations of global governance frequently have been associated with substantial blind spots and biases. Definitions of global governance as apolitical problem-solving in the interest of society have fostered a neglect of the intrinsic politics of global governance, specifically the question of power. These weaknesses of the analyses can be traced back to underlying belief systems of the main contributors to the debate and the historical and political contingencies at the end of the twentieth century. To some extent, scholars have started to attend to these ailments of the approach. Recent contributions, in particular, have specifically raised questions regarding the political nature of global governance and highlighted the need for more critical research on the role of power in global governance.

Concluding Thoughts

To some scholars and practitioners, global governance is an intentional response to globalization. In this perspective global governance stands for cooperation among a variety of actors across borders with the objective of solving the problems created by globalization. To others, global governance is a necessary consequence of globalization. In this view the changes in political opportunities and constraints for actors brought about by globalization mean shifts in political capacity and will therefore usher in new processes and practices of political decisionmaking with an increasing involvement of and control by the actors benefiting from globalization.

At first glance, the differences between these two perspectives may not seem substantial. Indeed, both perspectives adopt the same basic understanding of the phenomenon of global governance as multi-actor (and multilevel) political decisionmaking with an emphasis on governance rather than government. A second look, however, shows significant differences between the two perspectives in terms of the evaluation of global governance. In the first case, global governance as an intentional response to the problems of globalization appears to be desirable by definition. The main question we would tend to ask about this kind of governance is, How successful and effective is it? In the second case, no such presumption of desirability exists. If global governance is an automatic consequence of shifts in political capacity brought about by globalization, then global governance is simply taking place and needs to be carefully assessed with respect to its characteristics and implications. In this perspective, the politics of global governance immediately become central: who rules, how, and in whose interest?

Upon a third look, however, a critical observer will realize that the politics of global governance are just one step below the surface, even if we perceive global governance to be an intentional response to the problems created by globalization. After all, even in this perspective it matters who has the ability to define what the problems of globalization are that can and should be solved by governance arrangements, what the respective solutions are, who will participate in the efforts to implement solutions, and who will carry their costs, to name just a few of the political issues involved. Any political scientist taking at least three looks at global governance, therefore, will have to accept the need to assess global governance critically and to scrutinize global governance efforts and arrangements for questions of power, interests, and even the potential for dysgovernance.

The lack of attention paid to these issues has been *the* major weakness of the global governance debate, in particular of its earlier contributions, which can be best understood if its twentieth-century context, with its associated beliefs and concerns, and concurrent developments in the practice of international politics are considered. The expectation of a new era of cooperative politics due to the end of the Cold War and the recognition of common problems partly associated with globalization, challenges to the national political autonomy and capacity, and worldviews based on (neo)liberalism and the Enlightenment tradition together significantly influenced the prevalent conceptualization of global governance. Together, these political contingencies and philosophical underpinnings fostered a conceptualization of global governance as a promising political strategy based on apolitical, managerial problem-solving with a significant role assigned to nonstate actors, which laid the groundwork for its overly optimistic reception by practitioners and scholars alike: "Global governance may just fit too neatly into the global *stimmung*, or mood of the times, match too closely the rhetoric of policymakers and bureaucrats, and make us too complacent about what is at stake in structures and practices that can sometimes be oppressive" (Latham 1999, 25).

However, scholars are now realizing and voicing the urgent need to ask questions about power, rule, and agency, and about winners and losers with respect to global governance (Fach and Simonis 2000). In consequence, numerous research projects are presently starting to turn the global governance debate into a forum for discussions about political order, about loci of political influence and capacity, and about democratic legitimacy and authority in the globalizing world. These projects do promise to add important insights to our understanding of global governance.

Such research would appear to be particularly relevant with respect to the role of business in global governance. On one hand, business has provided a source of hope for global governance optimists who perceive huge benefits to be drawn from the involvement of business in the pursuit of global problem-solving. These observers emphasize the potential contribution not only of the financial resources of business but also of its know-how, decentralized organization, and pursuit of efficiency. On the other hand, business has been one of the major sources of concern for global governance pessimists who fear corporate world rule and highlight potential threats to democracy. And yet, compared to analyses of changes in the role of the state or the contribution of civil society to global governance, business has remained something of a stepchild in global governance research for a long time.

Notes

1. For an excellent discussion of the strengths and weaknesses of the deterritorialization lens, see Scholte 2000a.

2. Even within countries, the majority of globalization accounts tend to reflect more the experiences of wealthier sectors of society than those of poorer and marginalized sectors of society.

3. The triumph of economic incentives would not have been possible without the triumph of rationalism, of course. Rationalist knowledge structures based on a belief in science and the search for truth, the adherence to an instrumental, problem-solving logic, anthropocentrism, and secularism combined with the enlightenment's belief in progress, established an enabling framework for the extension of orientation and activities across the globe in quantity and depth (Scholte 2000a).

4. The failure of the Cancun meeting of the WTO and the new cohesion among the developing countries united in the G22 also shows the increasing opposition of governmental actors in developing countries to (certain aspects of) globalization in its current form.

5. The exceptions to this rule are, of course, those meetings held at particularly inaccessible locations in order to be safe from protests, such as the WTO meeting in Doha or the G8 meeting in the Canadian mountains. However, the desire of politicians and delegates to meet at such locations is an equally strong indicator of the controversial nature of globalization in its current form.

6. According to these more pessimistic assessments of the impact of globalization on the welfare in developed countries, the global "lean" corporation; job losses in the wake of mergers and acquisitions; downward pressures on wages, benefits, and safeguards; and reductions in national welfare provisions all contribute to a declining material welfare and economic security of individuals (Hirsch-Kreinsen and Wolf 1998; Strange 1998).

7. Swank's analysis identifies drastic cutbacks only for the United States and the United Kingdom. His findings and those of similar analyses will have to be reassessed in due time, of course, given current developments in many OECD countries.

8. The increasing importance of regions and regionalization frequently is discussed in this context (Roloff 2001; Schirm 2002).

9. Global governance builds on decades if not centuries of successes and failures in international cooperation, of course. In the second half of the twentieth century, in particular, one could witness a dramatic growth in international regulatory regimes and organizations and a proliferation of international decisionmaking on political, economic, and social issues with global scope. Locating a precise starting date for "global governance" is impossible under these circumstances. Some observers point to the founding of the United Nations and the creation of the Bretton Woods institutions as early examples of global governance (Brand et al. 2000), while others date the starting point back two centuries (Murphy 1994). Moreover, the multi-actor, multilevel regulatory approach, which has become the core of the global governance debate, can be recognized in the development of a new kind of interstate relationship in the wake of World War II, with direct interactions between functionally identified governmental departments and branches (see, for instance, the General Agreement on Tariffs and Trade [GATT] or European [Economic] Community) or fundamental transformations in IGO-NGO relationships (Langhorne 2001; O'Brien et al. 2000). Thus, while the

Commission on Global Governance brought the concept to the top of the political agenda, the discussion of its role here is not meant to imply that global governance started with the commission.

10. While accepting that hopes for a cosmopolitan model of democracy may be unrealistic in terms of a majoritarian conception of democratic legitimacy based on elections, other scholars, however, suggest the existence of alternative criteria (Grote and Gbikpi 2002). Scharpf (1998, 1999), for instance, highlights the importance of output legitimacy next to input legitimacy. Likewise, Steffek (2003) argues that the legitimacy of international governance may be based on the public's acceptance of justifications offered for the objectives, principles, and procedures of governance, as laid out in Habermas's notion of legitimacy deriving from justificatory discourse.

11. The choice of the term *governance* rather than *government* may also have been influenced by the intention to avoid such fears.

12. Similarly, global governance as a theoretical approach to international relations builds on the weaknesses associated with its scientific heritage: the failure of institutionalists in general, and regime theorists with their functionalist focus in particular, to pay sufficient attention to questions of power.

3

Business as an
Actor in Global Governance

The core idea of the global governance debate is that political and economic changes associated with globalization have led to shifts in political capacity. Specifically, scholars argue that various nonstate and suprastate actors have acquired important political roles. Among these, business plays a special role. In the view of many observers, business, in particular transnational corporations, is among the primary beneficiary of globalization and the associated "decline of the state" as the sole locus of political authority (Cutler, Haufler, and Porter 1999). In this context, scholars highlight "new" forms of political activity, such as self-regulation and PPPs, or the role of specific business actors such as rating agencies in establishing binding rules for business actors and society alike. Moreover, this literature delineates the increasing privatization of the public sphere, that is, the provision of goods previously considered the domain of the state by market actors, as representative of business's new political role. Due to a dominance of case studies as well as a functionalist bias toward analyses of the development and effectiveness of these private governance institutions, the literature has not offered comprehensive and systematic insights into the political power of business in today's globalizing world, however.

At the same time, the popular literature has repeatedly raised the question of the power of business. Numerous authors have voiced concerns that "corporations rule the world" (Korten 1995). These authors point to a continuing growth in power, in particular of TNCs, and a corresponding divergence in resources between business actors on the one side and the state and civil society on the other as a source of serious concern for a democratic balance in the political process. This literature does not provide, and does not aim to provide, a systematic scientific inquiry into the role of business in global governance. Yet, it offers a valuable reminder of an important question about global governance from which scholars should not shy away: the question of the power of business in global governance and its implications. In fact, looking at the "new" political activities of business from the perspective of power renders interesting insights about developments in the role of business in global governance.

This chapter sets the stage for such an inquiry. It delineates a theoretical framework for assessing different dimensions of the political power of business. On that basis, the chapter then suggests a typology linking specific forms of business political activities to these dimensions of its power. After all, the political power of interest groups in general and business in particular is difficult to capture, which is one of the reasons debates on this topic never managed to establish themselves in mainstream international relations research. But the present analysis suggests that we can get an idea of changes in the political power of business by studying developments in its political activities. Providing an overview of the interaction between forms of activities and dimensions of power, the chapter thus sets the stage for the exploration of developments in the dimensions of the power of business in global governance, which will be conducted in the following chapters.

In pursuit of its objectives, the chapter integrates macro- and micro-level arguments from the international relations and business management literatures. It thereby attempts to overcome the deficiency of much of the IR literature in terms of inquiries into perspectives of actors and their means and channels of influence in global governance. At the same time, the integrated approach aims to solve the weaknesses of the business management literature and its neglect of the larger political, economic, and social contexts and power relations shaping the perspectives, interests, and form and extent of influence of business actors.

The structure of the chapter is as follows: the next section will briefly point out some major perspectives in the history of academic interest in the political role of business in general and the corporation in particular. Additional detailed information on relevant arguments and findings regarding the various political activities of business will be provided in subsequent chapters. Drawing on the relevant theoretical and to some extent empirical literature, the second and third sections will develop the multidimensional theoretical framework of the power of business, and subsequently link the political activities of business with dimensions of its power. The final section will offer a summary and analysis.

Business and Politics

The relationship between business and politics has always interested scholars from a range of disciplines. Located at the intersection of politics, economics, sociology, and management, relevant issues have been explored by scholars of pluralism or organizations, by scholars employing policy network or public choice approaches, and by researchers drawing on new institutional economics or critical theory, among others. Within political science alone, scholars have conducted empirical analyses of issues such as lobbying and rent-seeking behavior by business actors, the role of business as a source of campaign and party finance, institutional relationships between governmental and business (and labor) actors, and the ability of business to function as an agenda-setter. Today, therefore, political aspects of business activities have been widely documented.

Studies of the relationship between business and politics can be categorized according to whether they focus on the influence of business on politics or of politics on business (some general level of interaction notwithstanding). In the former category, in turn, which is also the perspective the analysis pursues here, one can again differentiate between two different foci. First, there is the question of the extent and implications of business's influence on politics. This question has been at the core of substantial research and controversy in political science, especially in the early phase of inquiries into interest-group influence on the political process. Second, and partly because scholars failed to arrive at agreement regarding answers to the first question, they turned to narrower analyses of the situational and organizational determinants of political activities and strategies by interest groups. Lately, however, scholars have been emphasizing the need to move the broader question of the implications for democracy of business's influence on politics back to the core of political science inquiry. Since this analysis pursues a similar perspective in the context of global governance, the following brief overview of the history of scholarly interest in "business and politics" will primarily consider the respective part of the literature.

Scholars have been intensively studying the political impact of interest groups since the 1950s (Truman 1951; Almond 1963). The dominant school of thought at that time was the pluralist approach. Pluralism emphasized the desirability of participation of interest groups in the policy process. Advocates of the approach championed notions of a "marketplace of ideas" and tended to argue that competition between interests would prevent the development of political bias toward individual powerful interests and foster "rational" politics (Dahl 1961). Their optimism was fostered by the rise of citizen groups in the 1960s and based on notions of multifaceted public participation and civic engagement.

From the beginning, however, other scholars challenged the pluralists' favorable assessments of the participation of interest groups in the political process. Specifically, they argued that in order for pluralism to work as suggested by its advocates, two conditions would have to be satisfied. First, all sectors of society would have to be represented within the interest-group system or at least be in an equal position to develop an interest group easily if they wished to do so. Second, power would have to be distributed relatively equally among interest groups. Frequently, these conditions are not fulfilled, as the theoretical and empirical studies showed (Olson 1965, 1982; Schattschneider 1960). Moreover, critical observers contended that pluralism's positive evaluations of interest-group competition were only possible due to a focus on selected issues as well as a lack of attention to the issue of structural power and its role in agenda-setting (Gellhorn 1984; Lukes 1974; Pitofsky 1984). In fact, the most critical evaluations charged that pluralism fostered conservatism, rationalized disproportionate privilege, and simply justified the status quo (Lowi 1979).

Starting in the 1970s a number of scholars began to challenge and supplement the pluralist perspective from a different vantage point. Studying interest-group activity in Western European countries and Japan—motivated at least partly by the economic successes of these countries—the (neo)corporatist perspective and interest group literature demonstrated that findings from the US political system could not easily be generalized across the world (von Alemann and Heinze 1979; Schmitter 1974; Lehmbruch 1977). Specifically, the patterns of interaction between the state and interest groups in other countries often did not reflect the image of a multitude of independent interests competing for access and influence described by pluralists, but occurred within institutionalized channels of consultation and negotiation frequently created by government and dependent on government. With respect to the role of business in this process, some contributors to the literature have emphasized the ability of associations to aggregate societal interests and achieve compromise, to provide technical expertise and to facilitate the implementation of laws and regulations, thereby supporting political negotiation and problem-solving (Scharpf 1991). Moreover, they have identified the self-regulation of societal interests as a means for the state to unload some of the burden of governance on societal actors. Others, however, have pointed out the failure of corporatism to discipline capital as a political actor (Streeck 1994). Similar to more balanced assessments of pluralism, however, recent assessments have stressed that a successful and democratically acceptable integration of associations into the political arena requires the fulfillment of a range of conditions and active state support for the organization of weaker interests (Cohen and Rogers 1994). Interestingly, recent studies delineate a notable convergence of pluralist and neocorporatist systems, in particular a weakening of corporatist structures in favor of more pluralist ones (see Chapter 4).

Next to pluralist and neocorporatist perspectives, a group of methodological approaches applying economic models to political processes and explicitly relying on the assumption of business as a rational actor has greatly contributed to our understanding of the impact and implications of political activities by business (Buchanan and Tullock 1962; Mitnick 1993; Peltzman 1976; Stigler 1971). Such public choice perspectives describe particularly well why an uneven distribution of resources may be a source of concern for democratic ideals. They tend to characterize the political market as one in which interest groups invest resources to obtain favorable political decisions or nondecisions from politicians, who, in turn, pursue their self-interest by gathering resources and support. This conceptualization comes close to popular concerns about the potential of money "to buy votes" and of policies "for sale," even though most public choice scholars actually would not subscribe to such a negative view of the political process.

The Corporation and Politics

Critical analyses of the role of business in politics have focused on the role of the corporation in particular. This is not surprising, since concern about the political influence of business has always been primarily a concern about the political implications of the large size,

The Evolution of the Corporation as a Political Actor

Interestingly enough, the concern about a disproportionate influence of corporations on politics is also the reason why the corporation is an inherently political creature to begin with. Due to concerns about such "undue" influence, which even liberals such as Adam Smith held, incorporation originally was possible only on the basis of licenses granted by government, and these licenses in turn were granted only for a given period of time. This changed in the late nineteenth century, and with the first great wave of mergers starting in 1898, a dramatic increase in the number and size of corporations began to transform the US economy, as well as American politics and society.

In a noteworthy interdisciplinary study, Scott Bowman (1996) develops a critical assessment of the subsequent regulatory and discursive transformations, which provided the corporation with more political rights and a higher degree of autonomy. He argues that in order for the increase in the number and size of corporations to be compatible with American liberal ideas and norms, a number of changes had to take place, specifically changes in statutory law and judicial rulings, based on ideological justifications. First, the corporation had to "assume the guise of personhood," so that the applicability of liberalist ideas and norms could be argued (Bowman 1996, 3). Due to such anthropomorphism, the corporation came to represent not monopoly power but individual rights and freedoms in congruence with the individualist approach of liberalism. At the same time, a shift from an emphasis on shareholder control to an emphasis on the control of managers, providing them with discretion in "internal" matters, allowed corporations to exercise broad public powers in a "legally sanctioned 'private' sphere" (Bowman 1996, 80).

With rising antimonopoly sentiment in the early twentieth century, the US government started to introduce basic regulation for corporations. The resulting mix of corporate freedom and regulation, "corporate liberalism," aimed to regulate corporate power in the interest of the public, thus containing potential threats to the ideals of liberty and equal opportunity while allowing the public to reap the corporation's economic and technological benefits (Bowman 1996, 3; see also Vorländer 1997). According to Bowman, developments in politics, law, and academic discourse soon started to shift the balance in corporate liberalism to an emphasis on the rights and freedoms of the corporation, however:

> Highly critical of the dangers posed by corporate power for democratic politics, while recognizing the productive potential of the large corporations, the political activists who articulated the tenets of corporate liberalism formulated comprehensive schemes of reform designed to ensure the viability of liberal-democratic institutions and to fortify corporate autonomy against state command. Thereafter, corporate liberalism evolved from its reform-minded origins as political thinkers embraced a more sophisticated defense of the legitimacy of corporate power. In the writing of managerial theorists, the ideological precept of corporate autonomy assumed the status of an inviolable "natural" law of industrial society, whereas the legal doctrine of corporate individualism gave credence to the ideological construct of the corporate citizen. (Bowman 1996, 33)

resources, and reach of business actors, and this concern applies to the corporation most of all. Thus, some scholars have argued that the corporation as such could come to be viewed as compatible with democratic politics only after some political maneuvering, in particular the triumph of an anthropomorphic conceptualization of the corporation and the revision of liberal ideas (Bowman 1996; Korten 1995). They posit that the construction of "corporate liberalism" came to justify corporate political rights and freedoms on the basis of a balance between the "individual rights" and public regulation of the corporate enterprise, and that this balance was subsequently shifted toward an emphasis on the "natural" rights of the corporation (Bowman 1996).[1]

Again, individuals from various disciplines and walks of life have contributed to the literature on the impact of the corporation on politics and the implications thereof. Veblen provided famous critical accounts of the—in his view—extensive influence and control of corporations over governments. Managerial theorists such as Peter Drucker (1943) and John Kenneth Galbraith (1958, 1984) described the corporation's political and economic power and the extent to which its control reaches into the social realm, but they arrived at rather different evaluations of this phenomenon. Sociologists such as

C. Wright Mills (1956) and Michael Useem (1984) have critically reflected on "inner circles" of "corporate chieftains" providing a ruling elite.

In political science, critical state theorists were among the first to inquire into the political power of the corporations and the channels through which it is exercised (Miliband 1969). Moreover, critics of pluralism questioned the influence of corporations in politics, in particular, and on that basis highlighted the need for a reassessment of the pluralist perspective. Pushed by the recognition of an increasing imbalance in resources, their concerns about the difficulty of achieving a level playing field between interests grew. Charles Lindblom (1977) argued that the large private corporation did not fit with interest competition according to democratic theory and vision. Even traditional pluralist "advocates" eventually became increasingly pessimistic about the democratic implications of big business's influence on politics (Dahl 1994).

The corporation became an important object of inquiry in international relations in the 1970s and 1980s, moreover, as the recognition that an increasing number of corporations operated multinationally fostered a surge of analyses of the reasons for companies to establish production facilities abroad as well as the consequences thereof (Frieden and Lake 1991; Gilpin 1975; Kindleberger and Audretsch 1983; Vernon 1971, 1993). In particular, scholars inquired into the socioeconomic and environmental implications of the location of MNC production facilities in developing countries (Caves 1982; Wriston 1986).[2] In this context, scholars specifically explored the impact of MNCs on politics, specifically the relationship between MNCs and home and host governments. Here, the apparent role of MNCs in ousting governments in developing countries and supporting coups d'état, such as ITT's efforts to bring down the Allende government, fostered highly critical assessments of the political impact of MNCs (Barnet and Müller 1974). At the same time, however, studies made the case that foreign investors frequently were at the mercy of host country governments, especially once the investment was made (Dunning 1988).

Renewed Interest

While the influence of business in general and TNCs[3] in particular have been the object of substantial research, then, this influence has gained new momentum in the globalization and global governance debates. First, globalization has fostered a growing size of corporations and the corresponding controversial discussion about a potential associated increase in the political power of corporations vis-à-vis states and other societal actors. After all, the scale of the most recent wave of mergers and acquisitions has dwarfed that of the previous ones (Bowman 1996; see Figure 3.1). In this context, some scholars suggest that TNCs increasingly have an advantage over other actors, in particular state actors, due to their access to and control over finance and technology and their ability to simultaneously take advantage of the mobility of their own resources and the immobile resources of states (Lawton, Rosenau, and Verdun 2000; Strange 1996, 1998). Other scholars, however, maintain that the institutional characteristics of the state as well as the existing regulatory framework in countries still provide a powerful mediating force on the influence of TNCs on domestic politics and policy (Clark and Chan 1995, Garrett 1998).

Second, global governance has introduced an additional focus of scholarly inquiry on the political role of business. Thus, global gover-

Figure 3.1   Developments in Transborder Merger and Acquisition Activity

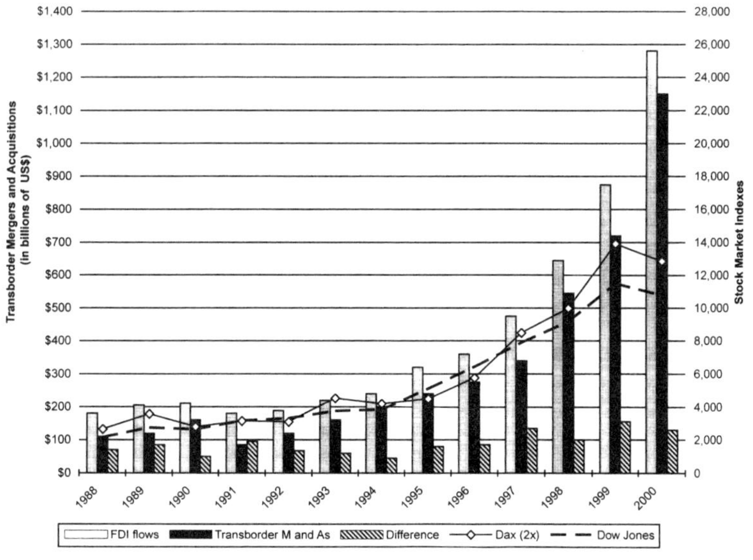

Source: Deutscher Bundestag 2002. Reprinted with permission.

nance scholars emphasize that business is increasingly pursuing a range of "new" political activities, such as self-regulation, quasi-regulation, and PPPs (Cutler, Haufler, and Porter 1999; Grande and Pauly 2005; Higgott, Underhill, and Bieler 2000).[4] Moreover, they discuss the privatization of the public realm, that is, business's increasing acquisition of functions and tasks traditionally considered the domain of the state (Brühl et al. 2001, 2004; Drache 2001).[5] The literature summarizes these developments under the topic of "private authority" or "private governance," and their implications for societal welfare and democratic legitimacy are the subject of intense debate (see Chapters 5 and 6).

In sum, the political influence of business and especially TNCs has been and continues to be the source of substantial controversy among political scientists and scholars in related disciplines, irrespective of school and approach. One side has persistently highlighted the threat of a disproportionate influence of business on politics due to its resources. In this vein, the political role of big business was viewed extremely negatively by some observers during its development in the nineteenth century and continues to be the object of highly critical assessments today. Just as long, however, observers on the other side have argued that the influence of business is matched by that of other interest groups and that any restriction on the right of business to pursue its interests would not be tolerable in a democracy. They highlight the benefits of a marketplace of interests and ideas, which, however, their opponents reject as unacceptable for the political realm. The sources of disagreement range from normative differences in perception of what political rights business should hold to methodological questions of what constitutes an adequate proof of a disproportionate influence. In addition, these differences in findings arise from a lack of systematic and comprehensive analyses of the range of political activities and dimensions of power of business in general and corporations in particular.

Analyzing Power

In the popular and academic literatures, references to the political power of business frequently are framed in terms of comparisons in resources between TNCs and other actors, in particular countries with small economies. Statements pointing out, for instance, that the fifty largest TNCs each have annual sales revenues greater than the GNP of

131 members of the UN are common in this context (Ferguson and Mansbach 1999; see also Table 3.1). Likewise, commentators often describe the power of TNCs in terms of the cornering of important global markets in certain products or services by a few companies. Thus, they highlight that more than 80 percent of the global markets in bananas, cocoa, or tea are each controlled by just three corporations, that more than 70 percent of the cereal market and tobacco production is controlled by five corporations, that three corporations control more than 70 percent of private water supply markets, that ten corporations dominate every aspect of the US media market (including newspapers and magazines, radio and television stations, movies, and book markets), and that ten companies were responsible for 84 percent of research and development expenditures and 95 percent of US patents in the past two decades, for example (Bagdikian 1997; Finger and Allouche 2002; Friends of the Earth International 1999; Thomas 2000; see also Table 3.2). Finally, another "picture" of the power of TNCs frequently mentioned by authors is the increasing ability to avoid regulations, taxes, and public scrutiny. The common referent here is the large share of intrafirm international trade as well as related accounting measures (Karliner 1997). Such information about resources, market shares, and the potential ability to avoid regulation, combined with the high mobility of capital, in turn leads some observers to argue that TNCs de facto govern both individual countries and the world today (Cox 2006; Greider 1997; Griffin 1999; Klein 2000). Accordingly, they have been calling for a global analysis of the power of business, in particular of the ways in which this power is exercised (Bonefeld and Holloway 1995; Gill and Law 1993).

The above indicators, however, can only serve as extremely rough and indirect measures of political power, if at all, because they completely ignore the question of the political process—that is, of how these numbers translate into political influence. At the same time, economically focused analyses of corporations clearly do not suffice in today's global political economy anymore, as they fail to capture the political facets and implications of their existence and activities (Harrod 2006). In consequence, systematic analyses that identify the channels and instruments of the political influence of business and link them to the question of power are urgently needed. Analyzing the power of business or the ways in which it is exercised is not an easy task, though. After all, while power is one of the core concepts in political science, it is also one of the most controversial ones. Due to the fundamental differences in frameworks applied,

Table 3.1 The Top TNCs Compared with National Economies, 2000

TNC or Country	GDP or Value-Added Sales[a] (in billions of US$)	TNC or Country	GDP or Value-Added Sales[a] (in billions of US$)
United States	9,810	Czech Republic	51
Japan	4,765	United Arab Emirates	48
Germany	1,866	Bangladesh	47
United Kingdom	1,427	Hungary	46
France	1,294	*Ford Motor*	44
China	1,080	*DaimlerChrysler*	42
Italy	1,074	Nigeria	41
Canada	701	*General Electric*	39
Brazil	595	*Toyota Motor*	38
Mexico	575	Kuwait	38
Spain	561	Romania	37
Korea, Republic of	457	*Royal Dutch/Shell*	36
India	457	Morocco	33
Australia	388	Ukraine	32
Netherlands	370	*Siemens*	32
Taiwan	309	Vietnam	31
Argentina	285	Libyan Arab Jamhiriya	31
Russian Federation	251	*BP*	30
Switzerland	239	*Wal-Mart*	30
Sweden	229	*IBM*	27
Belgium	229	*Volkswagen*	24
Turkey	200	Cuba	24
Austria	189	*Hitachi*	24
Saudi Arabia	173	*TotalFinalElf*	23
Denmark	163	*Verizon Communications*	23
Hong Kong, China	163	*Matsushita Electronics*	22
Norway	162	*Mitsui & Company*	20
Poland	158	*E.On*	20
Indonesia	153	Oman	20
South Africa	126	*Sony*	20
Thailand	122	*Mitsubishi*	20
Finland	121	Uruguay	20
Venezuela	120	Dominican Republic	20
Greece	113	Tunisia	19
Israel	110	*Philip Morris*	19
Portugal	106	Slovakia	19
Iran	105	Croatia	19
Egypt	99	Guatemala	19
Ireland	95	Luxembourg	19
Singapore	92	*SBC Communications*	19
Malaysia	90	*Itochu*	18
Colombia	81	Kazakhstan	18
Philippines	75	Slovenia	18
Chile	71	*Honda Motor*	18
ExxonMobil	63	*Eni*	18
Pakistan	62	*Nissan Motor*	18
General Motors	56	*Toshiba*	17
Peru	53	Syrian Arab Republic	17
Algeria	53	*GlaxoSmithKline*	17
New Zealand	51	*B T*	17

Source: UNCTAD 2000. © 2002 United Nations. Reprinted with permission.
Notes: a. The sales of large TNCs (shown in italics) usually are compared to the size of countries' economies. As UNCTAD (2002) points out, however, such a comparison is conceptually flawed. GDP is a value-added measure whereas sales are not. Thus, in this table the sales have been recalculated as value-added on the basis of salaries and benefits, depreciation and amortization, and pretax income.

Table 3.2   The Market Power of TNCs in the Agricultural Sector

Product	Share in Global Exports Marketed by 3–6 of the Largest TNCs in Agricultural Sector
Wheat	80–90%
Corn	85–90%
Sugar	60%
Coffee	85–90%
Rice	70%
Cocoa	85%
Tea	80%
Bananas	70–75%
Wood	90%
Cotton	85–90%
Pelts, furs, and skins	25%
Tobacco	85–90%
Caoutchouc/rubber	70–75%
Jute and jute products	85–90%

Source: Deutscher Bundestag 2002. Reprinted with permission.

there is little agreement on the definition of power or its operational-ization for empirical assessments.

Most political scientists would agree on very broad definitions of power, such as the ability of A to somehow affect the behavior of B. Likewise, Max Weber's definition of power as "the probability that one actor within a social relationship will be in a position to carry out his own will despite resistance, regardless of the basis on which this probability rests" (1978, 53) is generally cited and accepted as one of the authoritative definitions. Yet, these apparently basic definitions allow a diversity of views on the sources and exercise of power. Weber himself pointed out that the concept of power is relationally and sociologically amorphous, since "all conceivable qualities of a person and all conceivable combinations of circumstances may put him in a position to impose his will in a given situation" (53).

Moreover, studies related to IR face particular problems when analyzing questions of power. First, while comparative politics and American politics have dealt with the relationship between power and *herrschaft*, that is, legitimate rule, for a long time, the absence of a sovereign ruler in the international system frequently has caused an underestimation of the relevance of the question of legitimacy. Yet, even in the international system, questions of legitimate power and therefore authority play a major role, as the debate on global governance indicates. Second, analyses of power in the international system have focused almost exclusively on the power of states (Baldwin 2002; Schimmelfennig 1998). The sources of power and the ways in which it is used, however, are likely to be at least partially different for states than for other actors. An analysis of the power of nonstate actors in global governance thus has to rely on broader foundations of political theory, comparative politics, and sociology as well.

A few major perspectives on power dominate the discussion in political science and its subdisciplines and neighboring disciplines today. They can be differentiated into instrumental approaches based on a methodological individualism, which analyze direct observable relationships of power between actors; and structural and discursive approaches, which assume that power and its use need to be studied in the context of socioeconomic and ideational institutions and structures.[6] As David Levy and Daniel Egan (2000) have shown convincingly, a systematic assessment of the power of business in global governance needs to draw insights from all three perspectives. The strength of a three-dimensional assessment, after all, is that it combines different levels of analysis and considers actor-specific and structural dimensions of power and their material and ideational sources.

Instrumentalist Approaches

Instrumentalist approaches to power employ an actor-centered, relational concept of power based on the idea of individual voluntary action and focus on the direct influence of an actor on another actor. Robert Dahl's (1957) definition of power expresses this perspective very pointedly: "A has power over B to the extent that he can get B to do something that B would not otherwise do" (201).[7] Such perspectives on power have their origins in the "realistic approaches" that became increasingly important in Renaissance Europe and are most prominently associated with Niccolo Macchiavelli, whose approach to power exemplifies the growing interest in strategic questions regarding power that replaced concepts of an a priori determined political and social order. Instead of the common good, analyses started to focus on the acquisition and maintenance of power for its own sake. The triumph of the assumption of causality, in turn, was associated with the increasing success of the natural science perspective. Due to these developments, power came to be seen as a political actor's ability to achieve results.

In political science, instrumentalist perspectives have tended to explore how actors influence decisions by formal political decision-makers, that is, policy output. The instrumentalist approach to power has found particularly fertile ground in the behavioralists' rise to dominance in the subfield of American politics. Here, scholars have employed such an approach especially in efforts to assess interest-group influence on politicians via lobbying and campaign finance. Critical state theories use instrumentalist perspectives on power as well, but they extend the concept to refer to a broader range of specific mechanisms of business control on state policy such as "revolving doors" and social networks that facilitate lobbying and campaign finance (Miliband 1969; Poulantzas 1978).

Instrumentalist approaches to power can also be found in traditional power theories in IR, where scholars focus on the use of power by states in pursuit of national interests. Drawing on Thomas Hobbes, Hans Morgenthau's (1948) classical realism conceptualizes power as both the means and objective of states.[8] Kenneth Waltz (1979) has modified Morgenthau's approach to posit security as the objective of states, but he continues to accept power as the primary means of states to achieve it. In his neorealist approach, the relative power of a state determines its position in the international system and thereby shapes its behavioral options.[9] Subsequent theoretical developments in IR theory have moved to include other sources of power, such as interdependencies between actors, or the characteristics of a problem situation (Keohane and Nye 1977; Müller 1993).[10]

The strength of instrumentalist approaches is that they provide a framework for an assessment of the direct influence of interests on political output based on an actor's resources. Instrumentalist concepts of power also have a number of shortcomings, however, revealing their insufficiency in assessing the overall power of business. Among these weaknesses are the assumptions of mechanistic causality and of the autonomy of actors' choices of actions arising from the neglect of structural and systemic sources of the distribution of power in society. According to critics, these weaknesses have caused this "one-dimensional view of power" to capture only a small part of the picture (Lukes 1974, 2004). Moreover, instrumentalist approaches to power lack a measure of the exercise of power independent of outcome success (Caporaso and Haggard 1989). In consequence, scholars have stressed the need to consider more complex concepts of power that include structural and relational power as well as the power to influence ideas.

Structuralist Approaches

Proponents of structuralist concepts of power argue that the material structures underlying behavioral options and allocating indirect and direct decisionmaking power need to be analyzed to get a comprehensive assessment of the distribution and exercise of power. In contrast to instrumentalist approaches, then, structuralist approaches emphasize the input side of policy and politics and the predetermination of the behavioral options of political decisionmakers.

Structuralist approaches to power gained momentum in the recognition that some issues never reach the agenda and some proposals are never made because the relevant actors know that these proposals do not have a chance of being adopted. On the basis of this perspective, they examine the broader context and identify the factors that make alternatives more or less acceptable before the actual and observable bargaining starts. This is sometimes referred to as the "second face of power": "The ability of financial institutions in the City of London to transfer billions of pounds overseas in seconds may be a more powerful influence were there to be a Labour government than the representations of interest groups speaking for those financial institutions" (Wilson 1990, 12). Peter Bachrach and Morten Baratz, who first made this perspective famous with their 1962 "Two Faces of Power" article, point out:

> Of course, power is exercised when A participates in the making of decisions that affect B. Power is also exercised when A devotes his energies to creating or reinforcing social and political values and institutional practices that limit the scope of the political process to public consideration of only those issues which are comparatively innocuous to A. To the extent that A succeeds in doing this, B is prevented, for all practical purposes, from bringing to the fore any issues that might in their resolution be seriously detrimental to A's set of preferences. (Bachrach and Baratz 1970, 7)[11]

In political science, the notion of an agenda-setting power of actors took hold particularly in analyses of actors' influence on negotiations, deriving from their position in institutional processes (Shepsle 1979). Moreover, in IR theory there is a tradition of a focus on structural force (Galtung 1969). Structuralist approaches have received the most attention, however, in international political economy research in the 1970s and 1980s.[12] IPE scholars highlighted the structural dependence of state elites on private sector profitability and emphasized the bargaining power of corporations promising jobs and income on the policy agendas of host governments (Cox 1987; Frank 1978; Wallerstein 1979).

The major difficulty analyses of the agenda-setting power of actors have to face is the recognition and assessment of this power. Whereas studies on lobbying and campaign/party finance may suffer from poor data or difficulties of attributing causal influence, agenda-setting power may not "leave a trace" to begin with. The agenda-setting power of corporations provides particular difficulties in this respect, as per definition the threat to move investments and jobs should governments make unfavorable policy choices need not even be voiced. Due to these difficulties facing empirical analyses, the extent of the agenda-setting power of corporations has always been highly controversial.

Underlying economic structures and organizational procedures do not only provide actors with the ability to prevent decisions by others, however. They also may place them in the position to make decisions themselves, that is, to replace those holding the formal decisionmaking power. In today's globalized world, in particular, economic and organizational structures, processes, and interdependencies mean that actors in control of pivotal networks and resources have the capacity to adopt, implement, and enforce rules affecting the general public as well.[13] Thus, the traditional notion of structural power needs to be extended. Rather than just providing indirect agenda-setting power, positions in material structures and organizational networks may also endow actors with direct rule-setting power.[14]

In sum, structuralist approaches to power capture important aspects of power relationships that do not appear in the "first face of power." They highlight that material structures predetermine actors' behavioral options, thereby providing agenda- and rule-setting power to specific actors. In turn, a two-dimensional view of power combines analyses of decisionmaking and nondecisionmaking, de jure and de facto political issues, and influences on political output as well as input, thus widening the scope of "power politics" to be analyzed.

Even a two-dimensional analysis of power falls short of getting the whole picture, however. An analysis based on this perspective focuses only on observable conflicts of interest as well as the influence of material structures on the distribution of power. In other words, a two-dimensional concept of power still ignores the ideational and normative conditions of power located before decisions and nondecisions by actors.

Discursive Approaches

Discursive approaches adopt a sociological perspective on power relations in society and highlight the power of ideas.[15] This power is reflected in discourse, communicative practices, and cultural norms and institutions (Koller 1991). Scholars attach increasing importance to this ideational dimension of policy and politics. They identify discourse[16] as an important location for political contests[17] and highlight the need to expand Elmer Schattschneider's notion of a mobilization of bias to take into account that "some definitions of issues are organized into politics while other definitions are organized out" (Hajer 1997, 42). Discursive power shapes perceptions and identities and fosters the interpretation of situations as of one type rather than another. Thus, it influences the framing of policy problems and solutions, of actors in the political process, and of politics and the political as such.

A range of perspectives on the role of discourse in politics exists (Holzscheiter 2005). These differ in the extent of their engagement with questions of power as well as with respect to their position in the agency-structure debate. Foucauldian and Gramscian perspectives, for example, tend to emphasize the power of and in discourse, while Habermasian approaches pay more attention to the struggle for understanding. Foucauldian approaches and the systems-theory approaches building on Niklas Luhmann, moreover, see discourse as structural[18] in nature.[19] Critical and Gramscian approaches, in contrast, underline the presence of agency in discourse. Steven Lukes (1974), for instance, acknowledges that perceived needs and interests are the result of the "third face of power." He still argues, however, that this power can be used by actors in pursuit of their perceived interests:

> To put the matter sharply, *A* may exercise power over *B* by getting him to do what he does not want to do, but he also exercises power over him by influencing, shaping, or determining his very wants. Indeed, is it not the supreme exercise of power to get another or others to have the desires you want them to have—that is, to secure their compliance by controlling their thoughts and desires? (23)

The present analysis clearly focuses on the power that can be exercised through discourse. Moreover, it adopts a structuration perspective in that it assumes that both agency and structure play an important role within the context of discursive power. Actors strategically use discourse to shape norms and ideas, for instance, by employing symbols and story-lines and by strategically linking issues and actors to established norms and ideas. At the same time, discursive power does not just depend on actor characteristics but also on the system and its creation and support of certain norms and values. In other words, actors are embedded in a social setting determined by discourse, and while they may shape that discourse, they are at the same time enabled and constrained by it.[20]

Two major insights derive from a discursive perspective on power. First, power does not simply pursue interests but creates them. Second, discursive power is closely tied to legitimacy. Discursive power precedes the formation and articulation of interests in the political process due to its role in constituting and framing policies, actors, and broader societal norms and ideas. Thus, a focus on discursive power allows for an analysis of the presence and exercise of power in the absence of observable conflicts of interests and thereby provides a basis for a more comprehensive explanation of how political systems prevent demands from becoming political issues. In other words, a focus on discursive power shows that an exercise of power may not just prevent conflicts of interest from showing up on the agenda. Rather, discursive power may ensure that potential conflicts of interest will not even be perceived as such due to the influence of "soft types of power" such as authority, manipulation, positive reinforcement, or social conditioning, for example (see also Galbraith 1984). Thus, an analysis of the third face of power would consider the socialization of politicians and the public into accepting "truths" about desirable policies and political developments (Lukes 1974, 2004).

This last aspect reveals the importance of an actor's legitimacy as a source of discursive power. After all, discursive power is relational in that it relies on the willingness of recipients of messages to listen and to place a least some trust in the validity of the contents of the message.[21] In other words, in order to effectively exercise discursive power in the political process, an actor requires authority, that is, legitimacy as a political actor. Authority, in turn, can derive from a variety of sources. Public actors generally have this authority on the basis of electoral processes and the formal authority associated with political offices. Actors can also obtain authority on the basis of the trust the public places in their ability to obtain desired results as well as in their intentions. These latter sources of political legitimacy apply primarily to nonstate actors and are frequently discussed in the literature on "private authority."[22]

A number of political theorists and sociologists have emphasized links between power, authority, and legitimacy.[23] Weber (1980) relates *herrschaft* to power that is perceived as legitimate and can be expected to elicit obedience. Hannah Arendt (1970) ties power to authority by contrasting it with force, the use of which (according to her) is an indication of a lack of power and authority.[24] Likewise, a number of IR scholars have explored the role of discourse and soft power in international politics. Helen Milner (1991) has based analyses of the international system on the link between authority and legitimacy, arguing that beliefs in the validity of an order support its stability and the position of the dominant power in the international system. In addition, Joseph Nye (1991, 2002) has drawn attention to the "soft power" of actors—the power to persuade and co-opt other actors rather than coerce them along with the perception of the legitimacy of a state's aims—as a pivotal third source of power, next to military and economic power. Likewise, scholars have explored the "normative power Europe" (Diez 2005; Manners 2002). Unfortunately, these analyses primarily consider the power of state actors (or of groups of states in the case of the EU).

Within the context of globalization and global governance studies, however, scholars have paid particular attention to shifts in the political legitimacy and authority of nonstate actors in the international system. Specifically, they argue that power and authority have become dispersed and that nonstate actors now compete with state actors as sources of authority (Cutler, Haufler, and Porter 1999). Scholars speak of the development of a "new medievalism" in this context. Moreover, they show how actors use the discursive power deriving from this acquisition of authority in pursuit of their interests, for instance through "naming," "framing," and "campaigning" (Arts 2003; Holzscheiter 2005; Levy and Egan 2000; Levy and Newell 2002, 2005).

Moreover, a wealth of analyses on the strategic promotion of certain ideas, norms, and discourses exists in public policy and IR. John Kingdon (1984), for instance, is famous for drawing attention to the existence of "policy entrepreneurs," who in the presence of windows of opportunity manage to establish new definitions of policy problems and solutions.[25] Likewise, William Riker (1986, 1996) has highlighted the importance of policy entrepreneurs in structuring (procedural and discursive) decision contexts. Similarly, Martha Finnemore and Kathryn Sikkink (1998) have explored the rationally motivated creation and strategic use of norms by "norm entrepreneurs" promoting certain constructions of reality in international politics. In a related manner, Maarten Hajer (1997) has utilized story-lines and discourse coalitions as middle-range concepts to relate the role of discourse to individual strategic action in environmental policy.

In sum, the strength of analyses of the third face of power is the range of "politics" they consider. Such analyses show that the exercise of power does not have to result in the carrying out of specific actions but can also lead to the broader and more fundamental result of the acceptance of certain ideas, norms, and values. In other words, discursive approaches highlight the power resting in the definition of social and political possibilities. Thereby, they demonstrate how normative and ideational boundaries constrain and enable actions. The main difficulty associated with the third dimension of power is its identification and assessment in empirical research. Due to its reliance on persuasion, the perception of legitimacy, and voluntary compliance rather than coercion and hierarchies of legally assigned responsibility, the exercise of discursive power frequently will not even be perceived as an exercise of power and therefore not be questioned. In addition, the range and subtlety of forms through which discursive power can be exercised make its recognition as well as assessments of its impact problematic. Likewise, the difficulty of attributing intent and agency to discursive governance provides serious obstacles to assessments of any given actor's respective efforts and influence.[26] These problems will be addressed further in Chapter 6.

The Three-Dimensional Analysis of the Power of Business in Global Governance

What can we learn from applying a three-dimensional concept of power to the role of business in global governance? This analysis contends that the added value in understanding is considerable. Linking the political activities pursued by business to the three dimensions of power allows us to identify interesting relationships and developments.

The political activity through which business traditionally exercises its instrumental power is lobbying, combined with campaign and party finance. Interestingly, lobbying activities frequently do not appear in a global governance–framed focus. While case studies on specific issues in global governance tend to document considerable lobbying activity, general global governance accounts usually ignore it. However, if the case studies are correct, lobbying is still an extremely important political activity of business, especially as a complement to its structural and discursive power, and it should not be forgotten in our fascination with the "new" forms of political activities by business.

Business exercises structural power in global governance via two channels. First, given the high degree of capital mobility in today's globalized world, TNCs exercise agenda-setting power through their ability to punish and reward governments for their policy choices by moving investments and jobs. The extent of this agenda-setting power is controversial, however (see Chapter 5). This agenda-setting power of individual firms is supplemented, furthermore, by the agenda-setting power obtained through one of the "new" forms of political activities discussed in the global governance literature: rating and standard setting by coordination service firms, that is, quasi-regulation.

Importantly, however, business also exercises structural power through other "new" political activities discussed in the global governance literature: self-regulation and PPPs. These rule-setting activities provide business actors with influence on the input side of the policy process, allowing them to influence the choice of area for which rules are designed as well as the actual design, implementation, and enforcement of these rules. These forms of political activity thereby provide active structural power to business, rather than the more passive form traditionally discussed in the context of capital mobility. As pointed out previously, however, the ability of business to carry out rule-setting activities today arises from its position in the global economic structures and networks, which is why they need to be considered exercises of structural power.

The other "new" facet of business's political role discussed in the global governance literature, the privatization of the public realm, first and foremost can be linked to the third face of power: the acquisition of discursive power by business. This does not necessarily mean that privatization occurs because business demands it. Rather, privatization reflects the acquisition of discursive power by business because it demonstrates a change in attitude toward the market and market actors that has allowed business to obtain political authority. Business is being trusted to carry out tasks previously considered the domain of government. This new political authority derives from the perceived expertise of business, but it is being enhanced by business's efforts to increase its moral legitimacy, as Chapter 6 will show.

Speaking from a position of authority, then, business is increasingly able to shape ideas and norms in society.

The interactions between the forms of activities and the dimensions of power do not form such simple one-to-one relationships, of course. Each activity draws on or strengthens other dimensions of power as well. Lobbying, for instance, benefits from structural power to the extent that communication of business interests is likely to be much more successful if it is backed by the potential threat of the relocation of investment and jobs. Likewise, lobbying can be used to foster the development of structural and discursive power in terms of lobbying against capital controls, for self-regulatory arrangements (rather than governmental regulation), and for the privatization of infrastructure and other service sectors, for example. Likewise, self-/quasi-regulation and PPPs not only represent exercises of structural power but also benefit from the existence of discursive power to the extent that they draw on business's acquisition of legitimacy as a political actor. Finally, an actor's discursive power can strengthen his instrumental and structural power as well. Lobbying the public with respect to policy positions business is pursuing in lobbying activities with government can increase the pressure on government to acquiesce to business demands, for instance. Thus, the suggested categorization of the relationships between forms of activities and dimensions of power is somewhat artificial. However, it provides an effective analytical tool for the present endeavor.

Studying the full range of forms of political activities by business from the perspective of the various dimensions of its power, then, allows the complex picture of the role of business in global governance to emerge. Table 3.3 illustrates how lobbying, self-regulation, quasi-regulation, PPPs, and privatization relate to the instrumental, structural, and discursive power of business. It delineates the dominant relationships between the different forms of political activities and the dimensions of power they represent and reflect (shaded cells), as well as the various other interactions between forms of activity and dimensions of power. The dominant relationships, and to a lesser extent the others, will be discussed individually and in more depth in the following chapters. After all, having identified how the various political activities of business relate to its exercise of power, the interesting question now is what analyses of the developments in the various forms of activities reveal about developments in the instrumental, structural, and discursive power of business.

One aspect of Table 3.3 should be of particular interest: there is a

Table 3.3   **The Dimensions of Business Power and Its Political Activities**

	Lobbying	Capital Mobility, Quasi-Regulation	PPPs, Self-Regulation	Privatization
Instrumental Power	Using lobbying to influence policy output	Lobbying for liberalization of capital controls or role of ratings	Lobbying for self-regulation and PPPs	Lobbying for privatization
Structural Power	Enhancing the influence of lobbying	Implicit threat of capital mobility as agenda-setting power	Using PPPs and self-regulation to set rules	Using rule-setting power to introduce markets
Discursive Power	Enhancing the perceived legitimacy of lobbying activity and position	Enhancing the perceived legitimacy of the competition state	Enhancing the perceived legitimacy of PPPs and self-regulation	Privatization trends reflecting the acquisition of political authority by business

Note: The shaded cells depict the dominant relationships between the different forms of political activities and the dimensions of power they represent and reflect.

slight difference among the dominant relationships depicted. Two of them (instrumental power/lobbying, structural power/self-regulation) describe how the respective forms of activities represent the exercise of the respective form of power. Such a depiction of activities is not to be expected in the case of passive structural power, of course (structural power/capital mobility, quasi-regulation). In terms of consistency, however, one would expect the fourth dominant cell (discursive power/privatization) to state a similar relationship, that is, to be labeled "using privatization to acquire authority." Yet, this is not an appropriate depiction of the underlying relationship as pointed out earlier. Rather, the relationship between privatization and the acquisition of discursive power by business is more indirect. Thus, privatization *reflects* the possession of discursive power by business, rather than representing its exercise. The exercise of this power, in turn, needs to take place via different forms of political activities. In this case, therefore, further analysis is needed and will likely result in corresponding changes in the table's privatization column (see Chapter 6).

Concluding Thoughts

What can we learn from this three-dimensional perspective on the power of business in global governance and the relationships of the different dimensions of power to the various forms of political activities pursued by business? First, this discussion has highlighted that research on the role of business in global governance should not ignore the "old" political roles of business. Lobbying is likely to still be an important element in the political toolbox of business. Second, a three-dimensional perspective on the power of business in global governance stresses the need to take into account that material structures may provide business not only with agenda-setting power but also with rule-setting power. Third, such a perspective pinpoints the discursive power of business as an important facet of its power and, thereby, highlights the need to consider business activities aimed at the shaping of norms and ideas in efforts to understand its role in global governance.

In sum, a three-dimensional power-based perspective on the role of business in global governance emphasizes that business has a range of forms of political activity and dimensions of power available. It can pursue its political interests and exercise its power in global governance through micro-level processes of bargaining as well as constraints imposed by macro-level structures of socioeconomic and discursive relations. Importantly, different dimensions of power offer alternative as well as complementary means to influence people and processes, allowing business to pursue contingent multidimensional strategies if necessary. Thus, business can employ material and ideational resources at the same time. It can also use them as substitutes, however, relying on "voice" in the absence of "exit" power, for example, on increased lobbying if the structural power is weak. Likewise, business can attempt to foster the diffusion of ideas and norms, thereby reducing the need for lobbying as well as for the reliance on its structural power. In other words, business can draw on its sources of power and employ different forms of activities according to the requirements of the issue in question and its context.

The interesting question now is how these dimensions of business power are developing in the context of global governance. As suggested by the framework delineated in this chapter, such developments should be identifiable on the basis of corresponding changes in respective political activities, which, accordingly, the following three chapters will explore. The next chapter begins this analysis by delineating developments in the instrumental power of business.

Notes

1. The first regulations of corporations in the United States were administered by independent commissions. In the 1960s and 1970s, concerns about regulatory capture led to the introduction of social and environmental regulation administered directly by government.

2. Even in North America and Europe foreign MNCs have been viewed with suspicion since the beginning of this research, however. Omestad (1989), for instance, asserted that foreign MNCs presented a threat to US sovereignty.

3. Regarding the choice of TNC versus MNC as terminology, recall note 1 in Chapter 1.

4. As later chapters will demonstrate, none of these activities really is "new." However, their nature, extent, and influence have changed dramatically over the past few decades.

5. While *privatization* is the popular term used in this context, at issue is actually the *commodification* of goods and services or *marketization* of their provision. The difference between the latter and privatization becomes clear in the electricity sector, for instance. In Germany, electricity companies had been in private hands for some time but had held monopoly power in certain regions before the liberalization of the market occurred due to pressure from the EU. The same applies to the liberalization of electricity markets in the majority of US states. As shorthand for the overall trend, however, the present analysis relies on the term *privatization* since this is the terminology predominantly used for describing the phenomenon in the global governance literature.

6. A number of scholars apply similar differentiations but use different labels. Thus, Arts (2003) speaks of decisional power, regulatory power, and discursive power, for instance.

7. As Lukes (1974) shows, however, Dahl considers potential and actual power, i.e., the possession and exercise of power as well as cases of absence of conflict in his own empirical work, thus applying a more complex concept of power than the subsequent interpretation and utilization of his conceptualization of power by other scholars bear out (12).

8. Again, Hobbes's concept of power actually is more complex than its later use by other scholars suggests. Thus, his definition of power as

"present means to obtain some future apparent Good" already included the aspect of perceptions (1974, 150). As Hobbes stressed, being perceived as being powerful is a source of power.

9. See Schmidt 2005, however, on variations in realist perspectives on power.

10. Due to the different approaches contributing to regime theory (interest-based, power-based, and constructivist), arguments that regime studies uniformly fall into this category of instrumental approaches to power (and therefore neglect the broader social, economic, and political context) cannot be sustained.

11. This understanding of power draws on Schattschneider's (1960) identification of organizational bias in institutional settings, which leads to issues being systematically ignored to the benefit of certain groups and to the disadvantage of others.

12. Please note that Strange (1988, 1996) takes a different approach in her concept of structural power, as she combines aspects of the second and third faces of power.

13. Simultaneously, the existence of these technical and financial networks is limiting the scope for rule-setting by states (McDowell 2006).

14. An interaction between agenda-setting power and rule-setting power exists, of course, insofar as agendas are about rules.

15. Discursive power could or possibly even should be called systemic power, as the range of approaches to power covered here under this label has in common the idea that power is (also) located in and diffused throughout the system. However, in political science the term *systemic* automatically suggests a reference to a certain group of theoretic approaches, i.e., systems theory, and thus would lead to too much confusion.

16. Hajer (1997) defines *discourse* as "a specific ensemble of ideas, concepts, and categorizations that is produced, reproduced, and transformed in a particular set of practices and through which meaning is given to physical and social realities" (264).

17. Holzscheiter (2003) makes this point particularly clear: "Discourses, hence, work as virtual forums/spaces (arenas) for the struggle over the definition of so called 'essentially contested concepts.' They are essentially characterized by exclusionary structures, both semantic and contextual, which implies that the prevalence of a hegemonic interpretation of contested concepts rests upon a constant exclusion of a 'threatening outside'" (8).

18. The use of the term *structural* here refers to the role these authors attribute to the normative structures of social systems; it needs to be distinguished from the "structural power" deriving from material socioeconomic structures and networks discussed previously.

19. Luhmann (1975), for instance, argues that power is reflected in institutionalized rules, which regulate contingency and determine the range of desired and acceptable behavior. According to him, these rules of institutionalized power rather than acts of self-interested use of power are the dominant influences on everyday life in society. Likewise, Foucault (1980) per-

ceives power as a universal societal phenomenon that exists prior to all interests, discourse, and knowledge. It is not something an actor possesses but exists in every social act and interaction and is exercised in everyday discursive practices. One consequence of these perspectives is the difficulty of identifying agency. The institutionalization of social power structures in the system, in other words, implies the depersonalization and anonymization of power processes, which, according to some scholars, is one of the defining characteristics of modern societies. Other scholars, however, have criticized these perspectives for removing intentions of actors in the exercise of power from their focus of analysis (Koller 1991).

20. As a consequence, the effective exercise of discursive power depends both on an instrumental logic and the logic of appropriateness.

21. This aspect is also reflected in Bourdieu's notion of symbolic capital, which derives its legitimacy from the ability of its holder to persuade others of its value as a source of power.

22. It is important to note that the underlying notion here is one of output-legitimacy rather than input-legitimacy; i.e., a legitimacy focusing on results rather than notions of participatory democratic norms and procedures (Scharpf 1998).

23. In contrast, Mann (1986) differentiates between diffused and authoritative power: "Diffused power, however, spreads in a more spontaneous, unconscious, decentered way throughout a population resulting in similar social practices that embody power relations but are not explicitly commanded. It typically comprises, not command and obedience, but an understanding that these practices are natural or moral or result from self-evident common interest" (8). Most scholars studying discursive power, however, would argue that authority also does not always rest on explicit command.

24. See also Dahrendorf (1970), Deutsch (1970), and Parsons (1967).

25. See also Sabatier and Jenkins-Smith (1993) for the role of advocacy coalitions in employing and shaping norms and values.

26. Lukes suggests using counterfactual reasoning to deal with these problems in proving the impact of the "third face of power."

4

Political Mobilization

The exercise of instrumental power by business is first and foremost associated with lobbying, that is, business representatives' communication with politicians and bureaucrats in attempts to influence political and regulatory decisionmaking. Lobbying is one of the oldest forms of political activity by business as well as one of the best researched.[1] The term *lobbying* itself derives from the beginning of democracy in England, when people would wait in the lobbies of legislatures in order to try to catch and influence representatives on their way to a session. Debates about the implications of lobbying for democracy have existed almost as long as the activity itself, as practitioners and scholars weighed participatory democratic ideals against concerns about a potentially disproportionate influence of some interests.

Lobbying can be defined narrowly or broadly. The traditional scholarly definition of *lobbying* is given by Lester Milbrath (1963): "Lobbying is the stimulation and transmission of a communication, by someone other than a citizen acting on his own behalf, directed at a governmental decision maker with the hope of influencing his decision" (8). Today, lobbying activities frequently take a broad approach. After all, interest groups know that once legislation reaches the floor, it is often too late to effect significant changes (Hall 1990). Moreover, attempts to influence votes are likely to be much more visible than attempts to influence the preceding negotiations and formulations in policy texts and thus may invite more public criticism and opposition. In consequence, attempts to influence policies and regulations via lobbying nowadays frequently are combined with activities at the preparliamentary stage, with public relations strategists focusing their efforts on the shaping of the general policy agenda and process via public campaigns (see Chapter 6).

A political activity related to lobbying in interest-group participation is the provision of financial support for election campaigns and parties. By definition, lobbying does not have to involve any transfer of money. In fact, in most countries in which a regulatory framework for lobbying exists, direct attempts to exchange money for political favors would be illegal. However, it is easy to jump to the conclusion that financial support in elections will tend to increase the chances that the donor's political preferences will be heard and taken into account in the decisionmaking process. In consequence, questions of the political influence of business via lobbying and via campaign and party finance are difficult to separate.[2]

This chapter, then, explores present trends in the instrumental power of business. It considers developments in terms of business's traditional political activities both as "lobbyist" and as a source of financial support for politicians and parties. Specifically, the chapter suggests that business has expanded these activities in quantitative as well as qualitative terms. On the quantitative side, the political mobilization of business since the 1970s and the rising need of policymakers for technical and economic information, as well as financial contributions, have contributed to a growth in lobbying activity by business in general and corporate actors in particular. On the qualitative side, transnational and supranational lobbying strategies are expanding the political toolbox of business actors and the channels through which they exercise instrumental power. TNCs today do not just lobby their "home" governments, but simultaneously participate in policy processes in Washington, London, Berlin, and Delhi, for instance, as well as at the European Union or the World Bank.

When analyzing developments in interest-group activity, the following discussion will draw the major share of information from developments in the United States. Here, lobbying and campaign finance activity can be traced most easily. Due to the nature of the US electoral system and political culture, with its tradition of interest-group participation and competition, the historical extent and quantity of US political science scholarship, and the prominence of US politics as a research topic even for scholars abroad, interest-group politics in the United States are much more visible, documented, and researched than for other countries.[3] One cannot necessarily generalize from the US case to all other industrialized democracies, of course. Interestingly enough, however, other countries show evidence of trends similar to those in the United States. Although they are not as comprehensively traceable, "momentary glimpses" of lobbying and party finance opportunities and activities indicate that parallel—even if sometimes delayed—developments exist. While we may not judge the extent of the activities and the strength of their influence on the basis of the US case, the mere presence of these noticeable parallels in developments despite the differences in systems is interesting.

In addition, scholars have delineated an increasing blurring of differences between systems, as pointed out previously (Bieling and Steinhilber 2000; Lütz 2003).[4] For corporatist systems, they highlight a "dismantling or at least the disregard of structures of collective bargaining and domestic compromise" (Streeck and Schmitter 1991, 148) and the loss in monopoly of representation of associations (Backhaus-Maul and Olk 1994; Reutter and Rütters 2001), for instance. The "culprit" in these developments in the neocorporatist countries of Western Europe is at least in part the EU, which in some cases renders the national policy arena less important, while lobbying activities in Brussels exhibit more pluralist characteristics. In addition, the changes result from the increasing ability and intent of large corporations to pursue their "private" interests (see below). Furthermore, scholars contend that corporatism is also changing due to underlying changes in social structures and economic conditions in the relevant countries since the 1970s.[5] Finally, developments in global rules and regulations frequently render traditional national bargaining processes more permeable. At the same time, the partly institutionalized involvement of private interests in the development of legislation in the United States, for instance, has been known for some time and has become more common in recent years (Heclo 1978; Hula 2000).

The chapter is structured as follows: the next section will discuss quantitative and qualitative trends in business lobbying and campaign and party finance as well as developments enabling and driving these trends at the national level. The section also will explore the complex relationship between resources and the influence of lobbying activities and examine regulatory developments in this context. The second section will shift the attention to supranational lobbying activities and delineate comparable trends there. The third section will conclude the chapter by summarizing the findings and pointing out some pertinent implications.

Growing Instrumental Power at the National Level

Before 1920 only one corporation had a permanent office in Washington, D.C. By 1968 that number had risen to 175, and by the late 1990s it totalled more than 600, not counting those represented through associations (Shaiko 1998). Soft money donations reached record levels of $470.6 million in the 2001/2002 US election cycle (Common Cause 2003). Moreover, corporations outspent labor fourteen times and other interest groups sixteen times in the 2000 elections (UNDP 2002). These numbers indicate a notable increase in the lobbying and campaign/party finance activities of business in the United States. Similar trends can be shown for other countries, softened to the extent that these countries have stricter regulations on corporate political activity and frequently with a slight delay (see below).[6] This increase in lobbying and campaign/party finance activities, in turn, is to a large extent the result of two specific developments: the political mobilization of business, especially corporations, since the 1970s, and the increasing willingness of policymakers to "listen" to business. The former development indicates a deliberate response by business actors to the arrival of broad social and environmental regulations on the political agendas and business's learning of the value of being involved in the policy process. The second development results from policymakers' need for technical and economic information and expertise as well as contributions, which has fostered an expansion in the access granted to business actors in the policy process. These two developments have meant that the efforts and capacity of business to exercise instrumental power via its traditional political activities, specifically lobbying and campaign/party finance activities, have increased at the national level.

The amount of financial, organizational, technical, and human resources large business actors can draw on in efforts to influence policy outcomes itself could suggest that business may well have a disproportionate influence on politics via lobbying and campaign/party finance. Importantly, however, the relationship between resources and the successful exercise of instrumental power is not straightforward, as the following discussion points out. At the same time, the size and range of resources business has available to support its exercise of instrumental power and the value of these resources to policymakers render doubtful arguments that these resources do not matter at all. In addition, regulatory efforts with the intent of mitigating a potentially disproportionate influence of resource-rich interest groups frequently have failed to achieve their objectives and have been interspersed with attempts to gain access to additional sources of financial support by politicians.

Increasing Presence in Political Arenas

Business actors in general and corporations in particular have greatly expanded their political involvement since the 1970s, when in response to the public interest movement, business assumed a much more active role in the political process (Jacoby 1974). Among the signposts of business's new interest in US politics are the creation of the Business Roundtable, the move of hundreds of trade associations to Washington, the simultaneous establishment of a multitude of new corporate offices there, and the creation of numerous business political action committees (PACs). Lobbying work, which previously was associated with a low status in the business community, now has become the job of high-level executives with a direct line of communication to the chief executive officer (CEO). In fact, bringing the CEO to Washington and arranging private meetings has turned into one of the prime strategies of corporate lobbyists in the United States.[7] According to Jeffrey Berry (1997), the new mantra of corporate strategists is to "get into politics or get out of business" (225). The politicized corporation pursues a regular exchange of information with government and involves individuals at various levels in the corporation in political work. Moreover, it engages in the establishment of long-term relationships with politicians and bureaucrats, especially those in important positions in the political process, such as committee chairs, as Randall Kroszner and Thomas Stratmann (2000) argue. Whereas scholars in the 1960s viewed lobbyists as a service bureau for members of Congress rather than as agents of persuasion (Bauer, Pool, and Dexter 1963), the politicized corporation clearly no longer views its role that way.

Similar trends can be noticed in the neocorporatist systems in Western Europe, even though the political mobilization of business there first could be observed through an increasingly active political role of the traditional business associations. Following the example of their US counterparts, however, business actors have started to develop more pluralist patterns, as pointed out previously. In particular, corporations have begun to establish corporate offices in the national capitals to foster direct contact with government. Thus, corporations now frequently tend to lobby individually or through small

The Business Roundtable

An interesting example of the extent and success of the politicization of the corporation is provided by the Business Roundtable in
the United States, a lobbying group composed of more than 200
CEOs from the nation's largest corporations. These corporations in
turn employ more than 10 million people, and their combined sales
account for roughly 50 percent of the US gross national product
(GNP) (Bowman 1996, 145). Created in 1972, the Business
Roundtable has gained a reputation for significant influence in
Congress and the White House, lobbying, consulting, and advising
presidents, administrations, and members of Congress since the
Ford administration. Organized into issue-based task forces, the
roundtable functions both as a supra-corporate lobby and as a forum
for the development of common corporate political stances. Thus
the CEO Education Task Force in 1989 assigned 150 CEOs to discuss the "Business Roundtable Education Initiative" with the governors of the states in which the respective companies did business.
    The Business Roundtable has taken stances on domestic and
international policy issues, in particular questions of competitiveness, regulatory reform, antitrust regulation, health care, education,
information technology, and trade. Key victories of the Business
Roundtable in the 1970s included the defeat of proposals for the creation of a consumer protection agency, stricter antitrust policy, *common situs* picketing, and the Labor Law Reform Bill, as well as the
reduction in corporate income tax and capital-gains tax provided by
the 1978 Revenue Act, and the revision and elimination of deadlines
in the Clean Air Act Amendments (Bowman 1996, 147). With a
decline in activity—partly because of a more sympathetic White
House—and less cohesion among the roundtable's membership, it
failed to achieve its goals in a number of noted cases in the 1980s.
Thus, it did not succeed in obtaining regulation providing protection
from hostile takeovers, for instance. In the 1990s, however, the
roundtable reemerged as an important player again in the defeat of
the Clinton administration's health care plan (see Chapter 6).

coalitions pursuing a common goal in neocorporatist systems as well
(Kaiser 2000; Kohler-Koch 2000).
    The effect of this political mobilization of business has received
additional force from the web of organizational ties between individual business actors and the associated ability to create some level of

coherence in foci and strategies. Such organizational ties exist via business associations, of course, but, more important, also via political coalitions and common membership in directorates and governing boards, for instance. Thus, Scott Bowman (1996) has highlighted the crucial role of general business PACs such as the Business Industry Political Action Committee (BIPAC) and the US Chamber of Commerce PAC as clearing houses for business PAC contributions, which effectively distributed candidate recommendations, analyses of electoral races, and policy implications. The Business Roundtable and issue-specific coalitions of corporate actors foster the development and pursuit of common political stances as well. John Scott (1985) has pointed out the multifold existence of "interlocks"— "the social relation that is created between two enterprises when one person is a member of the board of directors in each enterprise" (1).[8]

Moreover, the effect of the political mobilization of business has been strengthened by a simultaneous decline in the cohesion, membership, and financial support of business's traditional competitors in the policy process, such as unions and environmental NGOs (Sklair 1998). According to observers, these actors no longer command the strength that provided the ground for the environmental and social reforms of the 1960s and 1970s. Thus, scholars argue that up to the 1970s, labor frequently had better lobbyists in Washington and more resources to pour into campaigns than did business, but that since the late 1970s and 1980s this situation has been reversed (Wilson 1990).

These developments suggest that business's relative capacity to exercise instrumental power has increased.[9] In fact, critical observers charge that the scales are tilted so strongly in favor of business that only business itself remains as the main potential threat to its influence:

> Business was by far the best represented sector of American society before this upsurge in lobbying and it remains in that position today. Business responded to the challenge of the public interest movement with ample resources and a fierce determination to maintain its advantages in Washington. It still faces potent competition from an array of liberal public interest groups, although its traditional rival, organized labor, is on the decline. The greatest restraint on business may not be its critics, but the divisions within and between industries. (Berry 1997, 43)

Concerns about a potential imbalance would apply in particular to corporate lobbies. After all, in order to assess the political role of corporate lobbying, one cannot only count the number of corporate offices in capitals or look at their budgets and staff. In contrast to the offices of most public-interest groups, corporate offices in capitals tend to be coordinating platforms that draw on corporate resources, such as money, personnel, or visits from the CEO, as needed. The tasks of these offices are to design and organize corporate lobbying strategies but not to carry them out themselves. Rather, they bring in experts and executives from headquarters, guide contributions, and hire law and public relations firms. The size of the office thus says little about the resources at its disposal. According to surveys, most corporate lobbyists acknowledge that they can get any resources from headquarters at any time (Berry 1997). Moreover, corporations are also represented via sectoral and general business associations, thus speaking with multiple voices. Anheuser-Busch, for instance, was represented by its Washington office and its own PAC along with four associations (the Beer Institute, National Beer Wholesalers Association, National Association of Wholesalers and Distributors, and the US Chamber of Commerce), as well as fourteen lobbying firms in 1996–1997 (Shaiko 1998).

The Increasing Value of
Informational and Financial Resources

Particularly interesting is the increase in the instrumental power of business that is fostered by its interaction with business's structural power. Thus, increasing willingness of business to be involved in politics has been paralleled by improvements in access granted by politicians and bureaucrats, whose dependence on resources and inputs from interest groups in general and business actors in particular has risen. On one hand, the increasing complexity of regulatory tasks has led to a growth in demand for technical information by governments and regulatory agencies. On the other hand, the slowing down of economic growth and struggle with high unemployment rates in many countries since the 1970s and more recent concerns about the effects of globalization have created a need for economic expertise and cooperation with business. In such circumstances the ability to provide investment and employment grants business an especially "privileged position" (Lindblom 1977; see also Chapter 6).

The latter aspect, in particular, has improved the conditions of access for business vis-à-vis competing interests. According to Paul Herrnson, Ronald Shaiko, and Clyde Wilcox (1998), the common understanding today is that leftist governments will listen to labor (and environmental) interests in addition to business interests, whereas conservative governments will listen to business but severely restrict the access of labor and environmental interests. In the United States, this improved access of business was demonstrated most visibly with the Council on Competitiveness, President Bill Clinton's "New Democrats," and Newt Gingrich's "Contract with America," for instance. The Council on Competitiveness, created during the George H.W. Bush administration and chaired by Vice President Dan Quayle, granted access only to representatives of corporations and trade associations and, according to critical observers, removed their respective lobbying activities from public view. The Clinton administration campaigned on the image of a new economically oriented and business-friendly version of the "old" Democrats. Similarly, the left-wing governments and coalitions that returned to power in many European democracies in the 1990s campaigned as the "New Left" or "Third Way," thus moving closer to business and economic interests (Hirscher and Sturm 2001). In the words of critical observers, the superior access resulting from mutual dependence allows business actors to establish long-term semicontractual relationships with members and staff of legislatures and bureaucracies (Lord 2000).

Moreover, business frequently is the predominant voice on advisory committees and delegations today. A recent study by the UNDP (2002) has revealed, for instance, that on three US trade advisory committees, individual corporations filled 92 and trade associations filled 16 seats of the total 111 seats. Labor held only two seats, while the sole seat supposed to combine the representation of consumer and environmental interests had not been filled. Likewise, Kevin Farnsworth (2004) stresses the increased institutional participation of business actors on government committees in the United Kingdom. As scholars point out, in some sectors "private interests are simultaneously the object of regulation/supervision and the chief counselors in the formulation of official policy" (Underhill 2001, 290).

Next to the increasing dependence of politicians and bureaucrats on business for information and expertise, developments in the costs of election campaigns would suggest that their dependence on financial resources also has grown. In the age of mass media, in particular TV, the costs of electoral campaigns have grown substantially. In the 2002 US elections, the most expensive races cost $17.3 million in the Senate (North Carolina) and $8.1 million in the House (West Virginia district), respectively (Common Cause 2002b). The average Senate incumbent raised $5 million for an election campaign (Common Cause 2002b). Whereas soft money donations in the 1987–1988 election cycle totalled $45 million, business interests and professionals donated more than $368 million in soft money in the 1999–2000 election cycle (Common Cause 2000, 2001). Overall campaign contributions by individual companies were as high as $7.8 million (Common Cause 2001).

The picture provided by scholarly assessments of campaign/party donations by business actors is uneven, however. Numerous studies report that corporations have significantly raised their contributions (see, for instance, Berry 1997; Herrnson, Shaiko, and Wilcox 1998; West 2000). Stephen Ansolaberehe, John de Figueiredo, and James Snyder (2003), however, make the case that campaign spending in terms of share of gross domestic product (GDP) is actually not increasing.[10] Accordingly, they argue that the "return on investment" perspective should be replaced by one viewing political contributions as a consumption good.

The high costs of US election campaigns are, of course, due to the costs of media presence and the professionalization of campaigns, in particular the hiring of public relations firms and "spin doctors." They are also a function of the increasing importance of the media presence of candidates arising from socioeconomic and cultural changes. Due to changing voting patterns, parties and candidates can no longer be as confident of getting the votes of loyal party supporters, for instance (Dalton and Wattenberg 2000).

Trends in other industrialized democracies point to an increasing need of parties for private contributions as well, even though the dependence on private donations frequently is lower due to federal funding for parties and to legal constraints for the private purchase of TV time for electoral advertisements (Naßmacher 2001, 2002). However, here too, the professionalization of election campaigns and reliance on media experts and PR agencies (even in nonelection years) have their costs (Kepplinger 1999).[11] At the same time, campaigning and media presence have become more important as well in part due to a growth in split-ticket voting and increasing shares of swing voters, similar to developments in the United States.[12] In addition, even countries with a tradition of reliance on federal funding for parties are increasingly moving toward a mixed system of public and private funding.[13]

Resources, Access, and Influence in Lobbying and Campaign/Party Finance

Scholars have identified resources along with organizational objectives and political contexts as crucial determinants of lobbying activities (Baumgartner and Leech 1998). However, the relationship between resources and influence in the policy process is not straightforward. Not all resources are similarly useful in all situations. In consequence, the capacity to mobilize one's resources and successfully convert them into advocacy tools in a given policy situation needs to be taken into account. The greater financial resources held by TNCs, for instance, may be balanced by the large membership of some NGOs. Moreover, the latter may outrun business resources due to a perception of greater legitimacy of their interests. Legitimacy is an important resource for governments as well (and may be becoming increasingly important for them in a globalizing world). Thus, the impact of resource imbalances among interest groups varies across policy issues (Heinz et al. 1993). The range of resources available to business and especially the fungibility of its financial resources, however, make it difficult to argue that they do not matter.

Moreover, from a theoretical perspective, one can argue that imbalances in financial resources make a difference, no matter whether one considers exchange or persuasion, principal-agent, or signaling models of the lobbying process.[14] Exchange models assume the political outcome to be determined through relative amounts of lobbying expenditures, as politicians with perfect information on policy issues trade private utility enhancements against aggregate welfare. Persuasion models adopt a more benign perspective on policymakers, assuming that they have incomplete information but seek to make informed policy choices and therefore require input from relevant interest groups.[15] Irrespective of whether one perceives policymakers as benign or corrupt, however, financial resources can improve the position of an interest group in the political process. In the case of exchange models and their focus on contributions, the role of financial resources is obvious. But even the ability to be informed about issues on the agenda and to provide specific information needed by politicians and bureaucrats, to gather this information and transfer it, depends on financial, organizational, and human resources. Research and analysis as well as the "signaling" of results and preferences are costly.[16] In fact, scholars argue that on average, firms spend substantially more on lobbying than on campaign/party contributions (Apollonio 2003).[17] This aspect becomes particularly clear in new approaches that model lobbying as a "legislative subsidy," as a provision of assistance to preexisting friends in legislatures who need to deal with a multitude of (actual and potential) issues on the agenda but have scarce resources (Hall and Deardorff 2006).[18]

As pointed out earlier, however, even if financial resources may frequently matter, they rarely will be the only deciding factor in a policy contest. The perceived legitimacy of NGOs or the promise of public support in terms of votes may well carry more weight than financial resources. At the same time, the sheer multitude of policy issues and costs of being informed and involved in the policy process over long periods of time, as well as the costs of the mobilization of membership, generally limit the activities of NGOs to a restricted number of issues. Thus, surveys report that environmental interest groups and even labor frequently find their resources tied up by a couple of highly controversial policy contests, while large business associations and corporations may lobby on more than 100 distinct issues in a six-month period (Baumgartner et al. 2001).[19]

Similar to the expending of resources, getting access does not necessarily mean having influence. Some scholars argue that informal interaction with public actors is primarily a function of the desire of private actors to be informed and avoid political surprises, rather than aimed at influencing policy development, for instance (Eberlein and Grande 2003). Likewise, the dependence of politicians and bureaucrats on information could, in the worst of cases from the perspective of business, mean that the latter has to provide the information, which politicians and bureaucrats then instrumentalize in pursuit of their autonomous policy preferences. The same scenario can be envisioned with respect to financial support, of course.[20]

To what extent an increase in lobbying and campaign/party finance activities translates into an increase in influence depends on another factor as well: developments in these activities by other interest groups. Thus, critics of the present depiction of developments in business's instrumental power may argue that business had to increase its activities in order to maintain a level playing field, since other interests had increased their activities as well. There is some truth to this. Business's political mobilization in the late 1960s and early 1970s was at least partly a response to the earlier growth in citizen groups pushing environmental and social concerns on the political agendas. At the same time, however, the majority of the literature suggests that the strength of these competing interests has declined markedly since those days.[21] As noted earlier, moreover, they have not benefited from similar developments in terms of access.

In sum, developments in lobbying and campaign/party finance activities suggest an increase in business's instrumental power. However, the noticeable growth in relevant activities by business cannot be assumed to reflect a similar increase in influence, due to the mitigating influence of political decisionmakers as well as competing interests. Yet some positive effect of this growth in activities on influence is plausible, due to the fungibility of resources business can bring to bear and the increasing divergence in resources between business and competing interests.

Regulatory Push and Pull

Governments have tried various means to regulate the influence of interest groups on politics and the implications of large imbalances in resources, including limits on spending and contributions, the provision of public funding for candidates and parties, requirements for the disclosure of the sources of funding of candidates and parties as well as lobbying expenditures, and constraints on the use of private media.[22] However, critical assessments contend that, for the most part, regulations aimed at structuring and controlling lobbying and campaign finance activities have proven to be half-hearted arrangements and quite ineffective (Greenwood and Thomas 1998).[23] Research on the US situation has shown, for instance, that the majority of lobbyists in Washington are not registered with Congress, even though such registration has been required since the Federal Regulation of Lobbying Act of 1946 (Berry 1997). Likewise, information on campaign donations actually appears to be used mostly by other candidates and parties (partly for purposes of identification of potential sources of money), rather than as a democratic control mechanism by the public or the governmental agencies responsible (Thomas 1998). Meanwhile, in a number of Western democracies, campaign finance scandals are becoming a familiar phenomenon.

In addition, attempts to limit the influence of interests groups in general and the business elite in particular have always been interspersed with attempts to do the opposite. In 1907, for example, legislation creating a basis for corporate gifts to candidates in the United States was adopted. Moreover, the Federal Election Campaign Act Amendments of 1974 provided corporations with full freedom in setting up committees for soliciting contributions to election campaigns, thereby providing the basis for a dramatic growth in corporate, sectoral, and general business PACs in the following years (Berry 1997). Business PACs further benefited from the Federal Election Commission giving corporations broad leeway in terms of the sourcing of PAC contributions and administration costs.[24] In addition,

Congress has at various times enacted and strengthened legislation institutionalizing business's access to specific bureaucracies.[25]

Likewise, the German legislative bodies have tried several times to remove limits on (sources of) party funding, with the German constitutional court sometimes constraining these attempts and at other times pointing to new potential sources (Kropp 2000). Changes in law in 1984, for instance, provided substantial state support for large donations to parties in the form of tax reductions and matching public contributions (von Arnim 1984). At the same time, politicians refused to follow the demands of the court regarding the disclosure of the names of sources of credit or the setting of limits on the size of loans to parties. Recently, party finance scandals associated most prominently with Helmut Kohl as well as the Christian Democrats in Hessia led to the creation of a commission on party finance reform in 2001 and revisions in party finance legislation in 2002. In spite of these reforms, however, party finance regulation in Germany continues to suffer from severe weaknesses, such as its failure to impose a limit on the size of donations and to ban donations by corporate actors to individual politicians, as well as the restriction of publication requirements to donations of more than 10,000 euro (approximately US$13,500 as of April 2007), according to Transparency International.

Expanding Instrumental Power Beyond the National Level

In addition to the increase in lobbying at the national level, developments in the instrumental power of business have resulted in an expansion of lobbying strategies to the supranational level. Studies show that the pursuit of such lobbying strategies by business actors has substantially increased. At the same time, they underline the improved capacity of business to organize internationally (Farnsworth 2004). In consequence, the role of business in global governance cannot be assessed without taking supranational lobbying into consideration. A prime example of such lobbying strategies is provided by the European Union, which therefore receives special attention in the following discussion. Evidence of supranational lobbying exists also in the context of global organizations and agreements. Again, the translation of this growth in activities into a similar growth in influence cannot be taken for granted. Some scholars document a predominance of business interests in supranational policy arenas and therefore contend that the shift in strategies toward these arenas indicates a significant strengthening of business's instrumental power. Others, however, argue that the complexities of supranational governance give the advantage to public interests and thereby limit the ability of business to exercise instrumental power successfully.

Business's Transnational and Supranational Lobbying Activities

The EU is probably the world's largest playground for interest groups, having shown the fastest recent growth in lobbying activities in any democratic system (Tenbrücken 2001). Indeed, concerns about overcrowded lobbying in combination with questions about equality of access and democratic legitimacy have become an extremely familiar theme, not just since the dissolution of the commission in 1999/2000 in the context of evidence of corruption. Stories of members of the European Parliament arriving at meetings to find all seats and all documentation taken by lobbyists are notorious. In 1992 the commission estimated that some 3,000 interest groups and 10,000 lobbyists were active at the Brussels headquarters (Nollert 1997). Other estimates count 1,400 EU-level interest groups (Greenwood 2002).

Lobbying has been an institutional part of the game in Europe since the founding of the European Coal and Steel Community.[26] Given this historical background, the current extent of lobbying activity in Brussels, Strasburg, and the respective national capitals of the EU nations cannot come as a surprise. Moreover, in recent decades, decisions made at the EU level have become increasingly important for national developments. Currently approximately 80 percent of all regulatory decisions in the member states tend to originate in corresponding regulatory developments in the EU.

The European Union is also a stark example of the degree and "market share" of lobbying activities by business actors at the supranational level. The business lobby in Brussels consists of hundreds of corporate representatives, as well as sectoral and transsectoral, national, and international associations (Fischer 1997). In fact, the representation of business interests at the EU is particularly noteworthy when compared to the representation of social, environmental, and labor interests. Seventy-five percent of all associations active at EU headquarters are business associations, for instance, whereas unions constitute less than 5 percent (Ronit and Schneider 1997). Such numbers have led critical observers to argue that the imbalance in influence between business and nonbusiness interests at the EU level is much greater than at the national one (Nollert 1997).

While business actors thus appear to be well represented in EU policymaking in general, their presence is particularly noteworthy in some areas. The trajectory of the historical development of the EU has meant that business interests are particularly well incorporated in agriculture and steel policy, for example. At the same time, business actors benefit from the specific political, economic, and technological conditions associated with some policy fields. Thus, they play a particularly prominent role in the decisionmaking processes in the fields of biotechnology and information and communication policy, according to empirical studies (Knill 2001).

Scholars have also repeatedly drawn attention to increasing activities by business lobbies in the context of global negotiations and agreements. Corporations and business associations today lobby in all international arenas and on all issues. Business associations, especially US business associations such as the US Council for International Business (USCIB) and the Organization for International Investment (OFII[27]), have been major lobbies on international investment regulation, for instance (Higgott, Underhill, and Bieler 2000). Likewise, their activities in the context of international environmental negotiations, for example in the context of the Montreal Protocol, the Kyoto Protocol, or the Basel Convention, have been widely reported (Clapp 2001; Ledgerwood and Broadhurst 2000; Susskind 1992). Corporate lobbies and business associations are present even in the international security arena, lobbying for instance on the Chemical Weapons Treaty.

Increasing lobbying efforts by TNCs have also been documented for the large IGOs, in particular the Bretton Woods triad. The World Trade Organization has a reputation for a close relationship with business lobbies in the context of the development of global trade rules (Levy and Egan 2000). It is therefore probably not surprising that scholars have identified a strong influence of the Intellectual Property Committee (IPC), a lobbying group composed of twelve US-based TNCs, on the TRIPS agreement (Sell 2000). However, recent studies report a further increase in business lobbying even within this organization (Cutler, Haufler, and Porter 1999).

In contrast to the WTO, the World Bank did not originally attribute a substantial role to business in the carrying out of its functions. Nevertheless, the World Bank is a prime example of the increasing extent of business's supranational lobbying activities.[28] According to empirical studies, business lobbies take on important roles in the design and implementation of World Bank projects today, including lobbying for the privatization of publicly owned service companies in developing countries (Finger and Allouche 2002).

In addition, scholars document both the targeting of central UN institutions such as the Secretariat and the various UN programs and committees by business lobbies.[29] Critical assessments even contend that the continuing failure of UN bodies to address the political influence of transnational corporations and develop a mandatory code of conduct for business in spite of repeated attempts to do so indicates the effectiveness of the lobbying of the UN by business (Chatterjee and Finger 1994). They link such lobbying efforts to the 1992 closing of the UN Center on Transnational Corporations (UNCTC), which had been calling for behavioral and accountability guidelines for TNCs, for example. Likewise, critical scholars credit corporate lobbies with managing to avoid any agreement on the regulation of TNCs at the UN Conference on Environment and Development (UNCED) in Rio de Janeiro, Brazil, in 2002 and to have all references to responsibilities of TNCs removed from Agenda 21 (Mintzer and Leonard 1994; Parto 1999).[30]

The gray area between private lobbying associations and official supranational governmental organizations needs to be mentioned in addition to direct lobbying activities by business actors, if one wants to assess efforts by business actors to exercise instrumental power at the supranational level. The Transatlantic Business Dialogue (TABD), for instance, whose aim is to foster the development of an integrated transatlantic market for products, investment, and services, was founded in 1995 by the US Ministry of Commerce, the European Commission, and the European Roundtable of Industrialists (ERT) (Brand et al. 2000). The TABD consists of representatives of more than 100 of the largest TNCs, interacts directly with government representatives, and is an official consultative organ of the EU. Organizations like the TABD, then, ensure an additional direct access by corporate business actors to the political decisionmaking process.

Supranational targets in terms of organizations and regulations are often combined with national lobbying strategies and channeled through national governmental actors, of course (Levy and Egan 2000). This appears to be the case especially when it comes to preventing the development of supranational regimes and regulations, in particular in the context of labor, social, and environmental issues, toward which scholars find a substantial share of business's lobbying activity to be directed (Streeck and Schmitter 1991). Efforts by the tobacco companies to undermine and block EU and World Health Organization regulation on advertising, for instance, were directed primarily at the US and German governments (Neuman, Bitton, and Glantz 2002). Likewise, scholars document the efforts of business actors to target both design and implementation of development policies and strategies through the simultaneous lobbying of the World Bank and national governments in developing countries (Finger and Allouche 2002).

Again, lobbying efforts at the EU make the orchestration of national, transnational, and supranational lobbying strategies by business actors particularly visible. Since the EU institutions are primarily involved in the early stages of the policy process, but ratification and implementation is the turf of national governments, lobbying strategies may target the European Commission and Parliament as well as the twenty-five capitals of the member states at any one time:

> Europe-wide business groupings such as the European Round-table of Industrialists of the Union of Industrial and Employers' Confederations of Europe (UNICE) assist the European Commission in agenda setting. However, the ratification process in Europe is conducted by national governments, so lobbies must focus at this stage on national capitals. The Europe-wide industry groupings noted above tend to flexibly dissolve into domestic constituents when necessary, and to reconstitute at the European level when pressure needs to be applied on the European Commission or the European Council. (Walter 2001, 55)

According to observers, the orchestration of such combined lobbying strategies promises a particularly effective pursuit of one's goals (Jordan and McLaughlin 1993).[31]

An interesting aspect of transnational and supranational lobbying by business actors is the even greater presence of corporate actors vis-à-vis other business interests.[32] This predominance of corporate actors is, of course, a function of the greater spatial reach of their interests. It is also a function of resources and access conditions, as will be shown. Moreover, the relative strength of corporate representation among business interests has been actively fostered by corporate actors themselves, according to scholars. Thus, TNCs have been undermining associational politics through individual lobbying activities.[33] Specifically, they have increasingly utilized alternative methods of organization, including small informal clubs and roundtables, due to the greater flexibility and lower costs of these organizational forms (Coen 2005; Grande 2001b, 2003).[34] Moreover, the trend goes toward "single issue maximizing," that is, the specific and timely targeting of individual policy plans and proposals in the EU based on temporary, issue-based coalitions and professional campaigns (Kohler-Koch 2000). The presence of TNCs rather than business in general, then, may actually be a major source of the relative dominance of business interests vis-à-vis labor, social, and environmental interests beyond the domestic arena. Furthermore, this situation implies that questions regarding the balance of influence between interest groups should not just be asked with respect to the influence of business vis-à-vis civil society, but also with respect to the influence of corporate actors vis-à-vis small- and medium-sized companies.

The Influence of Supranational Lobbying Activities by Business

Despite this widespread evidence on increasing supranational lobbying activities by business actors, scholars caution against overestimating the potentially associated expansion in influence. Thus, one can argue that the expansion of lobbying activity by businesses to the transnational and supranational arenas is simply a response to the increasing extent to which rules and regulations are decided at that level and simply maintains the status quo in influence. Moreover, scholars of European governance point out that the fragmented policy process and network structure of the EU create a major difficulty for the effective exercise of instrumental power by interest groups: "In such an institutional setting, it is virtually impossible for any single interest or national association to secure exclusive access to the relevant officials, let alone secure exclusive influence" (Grande 2003, 55). Furthermore, the complexity of the decisionmaking process in the EU may provide governmental actors with an opportunity to withdraw from the influence of interest groups by claiming internal ties and commitments.[35] In consequence, the Europeanization of rules and regulations may lower the risk of agency capture by business interests. In a related manner, scholars point out that an apparent concurrence between business preferences and policy outcomes may be misleading in those cases in which the European Commission pursued its policy preferences and simply utilized business lobbies in the course of that effort (Kohler-Koch 1996).

In addition, exercising instrumental power at the supranational level is likely to be associated with substantially higher costs than at the national one. The complexity of issues and of the political process in the EU, for example, means that substantial resources are necessary to acquire (or hire) the necessary know-how for the lobbying process, thus benefiting professional lobbyists rather than business interests as such. Lobbying the EU is often compared to playing three-dimensional chess. EU *comitology* and the frequent intransparency and fragmentation of the policy process mean that a comprehensive accompaniment of the policy process is difficult. Simultaneous lobbying efforts are necessary at multiple levels, as pointed out earlier. In addition, the protracted policy process means that lobbying campaigns often need to be long and enduring.

These difficulties of exercising instrumental power at the supranational level may be mitigated, however, by factors benefiting interest groups in general and business interests in particular—especially corporate interests. The most fundamental facilitator of interest-group influence at the supranational level results from the dependence of chronically underfunded IGOs and bureaucracies on information and resources. While financial contributions to politicians may be less important at that level, information and resources to design policies and carry out projects are likely to matter at least as much, if not more.[36] Thus, the relative lack of resources compared to national bureaucracies and the high complexity of policy issues has meant that EU institutions, in particular the European Commission, strongly depend on input from the business sector for the drafting of the technically demanding regulatory proposals.[37] Scholars speak of "sponsored pluralism" in this context—the commission's inviting of business associations or TNCs to contribute to working groups and committees. Critical observers charge that the result is the *do-ut-des* of EU politics: clientilist relationships based on the exchange of information, expertise, and legitimacy against influence on political decisionmaking (Nollert 1997). The European Commission itself, however, defines its role as a technocratic one, which would justify such information exchanges and render them less vulnerable to criticism, of course.[38]

In addition, business influence is likely to benefit from the emphasis in focus of many of the strongest supranational institutions. The emphasis on economic integration in the historical development of the EU, for example, has meant that business actors have been provided with better access, for a longer time, and had more expertise (for instance with respect to the harmonization of technical standards) than competing interests (Eising 2001). Likewise, scholars argue that the exercise of instrumental power by business is particularly successful in the context of the Bretton Woods triad. Levy and Egan (2000) differentiate in this respect between such "enabling institutions," which generally tend to be more sympathetic to business interests, and "regulatory" institutions supporting the diffusion of social and environmental standards, which tend to be more open to competing ideas and actors.[39]

Furthermore, the higher costs of interest representation at the supranational level may in themselves provide an advantage to business actors. While the latter have to carry these costs too, they are likely to be in a better position to do so than many competing interests.[40] The expensive video conferencing system installed by the World Economic Forum, which allows its members to communicate directly with the UN Secretary General as well as with the directors of the IMF and World Bank, for instance, illustrates the benefits of financial resources in supranational lobbying (Paul 2001).

In addition, the relative representation of corporate interests at the supranational level benefits from the difference in the ability of interests to organize (Offe and Wiesenthal 1980; Traxler and Schmitter 1994). After all, the "logic of influence" needs to be considered separately from the "logic of membership." Labor interests, in particular, suffer from difficulties of cooperating across countries due to language, ideological, socioeconomic, and organizational differences (Streeck 1994). In contrast, scholars report that producer interests, to the extent that they actually want and need to organize for collective action, tend to be characterized by a higher ability to do so (Eising and Kohler-Koch 1994). Even business associations tend to be disadvantaged vis-à-vis corporate actors in questions of organizational costs and efficiency at the EU, however, due to a general reluctance of the national members of European business groups to transfer authority and resources to the European level.[41] In consequence, associations have mainly carried out service and coordination functions rather than an autonomous lobbying function (Matthews and Pickering 2000).

Moreover, scholars argue that business interests in general and corporate interests in particular benefit from the institutional structures and processes of supranational organizations. Thus, they point out that decisionmaking processes in these organizations tend to be much more removed from the public view and scrutiny, and that they frequently lack criteria for ensuring a level playing field in the representation of interest groups. When inviting business representatives to working groups and committees, for instance, the European Commission is relatively free to choose, as no general consultation rights or territorial or functional criteria for the selection of experts have been legally defined. In this choice, then, the commission has tended to draw on individual companies that have proven their ability and willingness to deliver the necessary human and financial resources and that have shown the potential for political leadership in the past (Kohler-Koch 1996).

Other relevant characteristics of structures and processes besides the lack of transparency can be named. Scholars make the case, for instance, that the segmentation of the EU's policy process among different directorates-general biases policy choices toward specific sectoral interests rather than broader interests like consumer protection (Cadot and Webber 2002). Likewise, they show how the need to coordinate policies and accommodate interests across different institutional levels and policy areas, which is inherently associated with information and communication technology developments, in turn gives an advantage to "interface actors" (Knill 2001), among which they identify European business roundtables and associations as important players.

At the same time, regulation of lobbying activity at supranational institutions, to the extent that it exists, is minimal in scope. In the EU, for instance, the view that some control over lobbying is necessary has been voiced for a while. Among the institutional actors, the strongest call for such regulation came from the Parliament, which subsequently has pushed for the development and implementation of a code of conduct and some regulation regarding access to buildings. The European Commission, however, has favored self-regulation by lobbyists due to its reliance on input from the outside. Today, only the Parliament has introduced mandatory regulation in the form of the Ford and Nordman schemes. These regulations ban gifts and benefits that may influence votes and require Parliament members to make detailed declarations of professional activities and to report paid activities. Lobbyists, in turn, have to register and sign a code of conduct in exchange for securing a pass that provides access to the Parliament's buildings.[42] In the view of critical observers, these schemes will not help to achieve a level playing field between business and nonbusiness interests, however (Greenwood 1998).

Efforts to improve civil-society participation at the EU have been few and have arrived on the agendas only lately. In the mid-1990s, scholars still saw a high potential for the balance between business and societal interests at the EU to shift further in the direction of private, business ones, leading to further challenges to the political accountability and distributional justice of European politics and integration (Eising and Kohler-Koch 1994). Recently, however, the commission has made some efforts at leveling the playing field due to consistent criticism of the privileged position of business interests at the EU. Specifically, it has pronounced its willingness to provide more transparency and openness in access and has supported the organizational efforts of transnational societal NGOs. In consequence, there has been a substantial growth in the representation of such NGOs from the social arena in recent years. It remains to be seen to what extent the efforts of the European Commission actually will lead to an improved balance, and to what extent such efforts mainly help the commission to improve its legitimacy and silence criticism, as critical observers argue. The latter charge that the current measures are insufficient to achieve the necessary degree of change (Nollert 1997). Moreover, they document the failure of EU institutions to integrate societal interests systematically even in the most recent and fundamental decisionmaking processes, despite proclamations to the contrary (Geiger 2003).[43]

In sum, the idea that business actors in general and corporate actors in particular have not only expanded their lobbying activities to supranational arenas but can successfully exercise instrumental power at this level cannot be dismissed easily. While some conditions suggest that lobbying activities by business actors are likely to be less influential in complex supranational governance systems, a range of other conditions suggests that the effectiveness of such activities there may well be high. Moreover, one needs to differentiate between two dynamics in this respect: changes in the relationship between public actors and business interests, and changes in the relative strength of business actors vis-à-vis competing interests. Public actors may find it easier to withdraw from demands raised by business actors under certain conditions due to the complex distribution of decisionmaking capacity. From this perspective, then, an expansion of lobbying activities by business actors to the transnational and supranational level may not mean an increase in influence. At the same time, business is in a superior position in terms of its relative strength vis-à-vis competing interests at these levels, which is likely to tilt the balance in favor of business again. Importantly, however, this privileged position applies primarily to corporate actors.

Concluding Thoughts

This chapter has delineated trends in the instrumental power of business at the national, transnational, and supranational levels. At the national level, it has outlined developments both in business's general stance toward politics and in the socioeconomic and institutional settings that indicate a simultaneous rise in the value business attaches to being involved in politics and in the value policymakers attach to input from business. Moreover, the chapter has demonstrated that analyses of pluralist competition (or corporatist cooperation) at the national level need to be supplemented with a focus on the transnational exercise of instrumental power as well as the exercise of this power in supranational politics. Clearly, business activities in terms of transnational and supranational lobbying efforts have become an important complement to domestic efforts to influence policy output.

At the national level, developments in the instrumental power of business can be pinpointed in terms of its political mobilization since the 1970s, which led to a substantial growth in the presence of business actors, especially corporations and business associations, in the political process. Moreover, the increasing complexity of policy issues, concerns about economic growth, and rising campaign costs have provided business, as the actor who can provide valuable input and resources, with privileged access to policymakers. At the same time, the strength of business's traditional competitors and opponents in the policy process appears to be declining.

Next to such developments at the national level, business has expanded the range of targets of its exercise of instrumental power to the transnational and supranational levels. It expends considerable effort to influence international negotiations and agreements and to lobby supranational organizations. Again, corporate actors are particularly present in these arenas. The expansion of lobbying activities to the supranational level also means, of course, that business's efforts to exercise instrumental power may benefit from the ability to decide which level of governance to engage, or even to engage several levels simultaneously through the targeting of the national level in combination with an up-shifting and/or down-shifting of power.

Although these developments suggest that business's capacity and efforts to exercise instrumental power at the national, transnational, and supranational levels are expanding, they certainly do not provide a basis to argue that business will win every political contest or is in a position to decide every policy issue unilaterally. The relationship between activities and influence is complex. Most fundamentally, the extent to which an increase in activities translates into an increase in influence is mitigated by public actors and competing interests. The distribution of decisionmaking capacity among a large number of governmental actors and bureaucrats can help them obtain more autonomy from demands by interest groups. Moreover, policymakers at the supranational level tend to be less dependent on campaign finance. At the same time, however, one should not underestimate the dependence of chronically underfunded IGOs on informational, organizational, and financial resources. The relative strength of societal interests, the second mitigating factor, appears to have declined in national arenas and faces particular challenges with respect to transnational and supranational lobbying activity. In highly contested and visible cases, societal interests can still provide formidable opposition to business interests, even at the supranational level. Yet, while the higher costs of representation at the supranational level and the complexities and fragmentation of supranational governance make the successful exercise of instrumental power difficult for any interest group, they do advantage resource-rich interest groups over poorer ones.

Notes

1. Some scholars differentiate among lobbying, advocacy, the monitoring of compliance of governments, participation, and protest in assessments of the instrumental/decisional power of actors (Arts 2003). Such a differentiation is of limited value for the present exercise, however, and is in some cases incompatible with the definition of instrumental power. Advocacy, for instance in the context of congressional hearings or corporatist bargaining arrangements, will be considered here as a lobbying activity. Participation requires further differentiation to identify to what extent it involves actual rule-setting activities (considered here under structural power), for instance. Finally, protest, in particular protest outside of formal political arenas, actually is related to the discursive power of business.

2. The term *campaign finance* tends to be used predominantly in the US context, where donors support the campaigns of individual candidates. The focus on party finance is more common in the context of systems with a high level of party cohesion and in which parties rather than individual candidates dominate the electoral competition. In the following, the two terms will be used jointly insofar as both types of political systems are concerned.

3. The emphasis on the United States is justified for reasons other than data availability as well. The US case is particularly important for the assess-

ment of business influence on politics via lobbying and campaign/party finance because of the potential impact of relevant activities by business in the United States for the rest of the world. Many decisions taken by the US government have implications for economic, political, social, and ecological conditions in other countries. These implications arise from the transmission of economic conditions—and to some extent political, social, cultural, and ecological ones—in the United States to other countries. They are also a function of the stances taken by the US government in international negotiations, whether at the WTO or in the context of the Kyoto Protocol, for example. In other words, when business actors influence political decisionmakers in the United States, they influence more than American policies.

4. Traditional differences in interest-group activity found between more pluralistic systems such as the United States and more corporatist ones such as Germany have extended to the logics of membership and influence of interest groups, the question of access, and the formation of coalitions, for example. Scholars have shown that corporatist associations have been less autonomous in relation to the state than pluralists interest groups but have tended to be more autonomous in relation to their members due to the monopoly these associations generally enjoyed as representatives in governmental processes and the consequent de facto mandatory nature of membership (Streeck and Schmitter 1985a). The Bundesverband der deutschen Industrie (BDI, Federation of German Industries) speaks for German industry as such. In contrast, no particular lobby enjoys a monopoly in the United States, as different groups vie for the position of representatives of certain interests. The Business Roundtable, the National Association of Manufacturers, and the Chamber of Commerce all aim to be representatives of general business interests. Likewise, business representatives and lobbyists in the United States will point out that lobbying is all about getting your foot in the door and building personal relationships. In contrast, securing access is not as big an issue for the major business and labor associations in corporatist systems, as their relationships with government tend to be institutionalized, and, in fact, regulations require ministries to focus their interactions with organized interests on federal peak associations.

5. Streeck and Schmitter emphasize the increasing differentiation of social structures and collective interests as well as the rising market instability and volatility and the associated pressure on businesses to increase their flexibility in this context.

6. The United Nations Development Program has noted, for instance, that corporations were the source of approximately 80 percent of the funding of the major parties in India in 1996 (UNDP 2002).

7. A survey among corporate executives showed that 86 percent of them were able to converse directly with a member of Congress at least a couple of times a year (Verba and Orren 1985). In a similar manner, direct interaction between top management and the members of the governments has become an important element of lobbying in Germany and other European countries today (Kaiser 2000).

8. The website They Rule (www.theyrule.net) creates maps of the interlocking directorates of the top 100 companies in the United States.

9. Critical scholars contend that the imbalance is worsened by an increasing apathy of voters arising from the perception that government has become responsive to corporate interests rather than to the public (West 2000).

10. The usefulness of GDP as a "control" variable is debatable in this context, however.

11. There is some controversy whether one should speak of the professionalization or the Americanization of election campaigns in this context. In other words, scholars disagree whether it is the import of American patterns or a change in socioeconomic and technological conditions that is driving these developments (Falter and Römmele 2002).

12. See, for instance, von Alemann and Marschall 2002; von Beyme 2000; Dalton and Wattenberg 2000; Gabriel, Niedermayer, and Stöss 2002; Mair, Müller, and Plasser 1999; and Schatz, Rössler, and Nieland 2002.

13. In 1994, Germany, for example, adopted such a mixed system, with parties not only receiving federal money for the votes obtained in an election but also having a certain percentage of private donations to the parties matched by federal funds.

14. One can also differentiate among research approaches to lobbying on the basis of whether they use reduced form models and treat the policy process as a black box (both in terms of the underlying decision process of the politicians and the process of conversion of money into votes) or use microfoundational approaches and explicitly model the strategic interaction between politicians and interest groups (see, for instance, Austen-Smith 1995; Becker 1983; Grossman and Helpman 1994; Peltzman 1976; Sloof and van Winden 2000; Stigler 1971). In either case, however, resources can be shown to matter.

15. This approach allows a perception of lobbying as enhancing welfare rather than reducing it. At a second look, however, it becomes clear that even if politicians are not corrupt, imbalances in resources may corrupt the policy process as such.

16. This is the case, in particular, since politicians may be interested in information as assumed by persuasion models but still may impose "access charges" (Polk 2002).

17. Such claims about general trends say little about specific situations, however. In particularly "worthwhile" causes, individual business actors or coalitions have been known to contribute large sums in the effort to influence policy decisions. The approval of the Yucca Mountain, Nevada, storage facility for nuclear waste, for example, has been linked to $29.2 million in soft money contributions by the Nuclear Energy Institute, a policy organization whose members include nuclear energy suppliers and service companies, design and engineering firms, laboratories, and lobbying and consulting firms (Common Cause 2002a). Similarly, scholars have tied the substantial influence of the tobacco industry on congressional voting on tobacco regulation to extensive contributions to candidates and parties (Moore et al. 1994).

18. The provision of this "legislative subsidy," then, allows interest groups, politicians, and bureaucrats to promote issues and regulatory decisions favored by all. Thereby, the approach highlights that issue coalitions in the lobbying process frequently tend to involve individuals and interests both inside and outside of government.

19. Research shows, for instance, that next to broad and highly contested issues, a large share of business lobbying addresses small and particularistic issues such as tax loopholes and temporary protection from trade competition (Clawson, Neustadt, and Scott 1992; Smith 2000). As reported by Clawson, Neustadt, and Scott, when asked to describe an issue they had won, 90 percent of corporate lobbyists surveyed pointed out a tax loophole benefiting their company. Such findings resonate with research that has found that a few issues receive a lot of lobbying attention whereas a lot of issues receive only a little.

20. Such a scenario has to make very specific assumptions about the characteristics of politicians and bureaucrats on the one side and business actors on the other, however. Specifically, it has to attribute a much greater ability to strategize to the former actors than to the latter. While politicians do have room to maneuver in terms of the granting of access and obtaining of information and financial support, business has such room as well. In particular, the ability of business actors to select and frame information should not be underestimated. Moreover, if recent approaches that model lobbying as a "legislative subsidy" are correct, business is most inclined to interact with "friendly" legislators to begin with.

21. Some of this decline may be made up for by their better institutionalization, however.

22. Moreover, indirect measures (including taxation laws) and measures of self-regulation by lobbyists exist. The impact of most of these measures, however, frequently is not straightforward, as analyses of the implications of spending limits, matching funds, and the public funding of elections on campaign finance in the context of US House elections demonstrate (Goidel, Gross, and Shields 1999).

23. Even the most recent efforts in the United States to restrict the influence of wealthy interests via the McCain-Feingold Bipartisan Campaign Reform Act (BCRA), which bans parties from raising soft money, have been marked by a series of challenges and efforts to identify loopholes on the one side, and subsequent efforts to strengthen the regulation and fix the loopholes on the other. First, the Federal Election Commission substantially weakened the provisions of the new law, and then parties and interest groups scurried to create hundreds of new "issue" PACs to provide fresh channels for the banned money flows. In addition, the bill's constitutionality was challenged by the US Supreme Court after individual senators, the National Rifle Association, and the Republican National Committee filed suit. In December 2004, the Supreme Court's ruling upheld all central aspects of the BCRA, however. In the 2004 election, in turn, independent groups called "527s" (after the section of the tax code that addresses these types of political

groups) received large donations from individual contributors raising concerns about the return of "soft money." Subsequently, Senators McCain and Feingold and Representatives Shays and Meehan introduced the 527 Reform Act of 2005.

24. Specifically, the Federal Election Commission ruled that corporate PACs can solicit money from both employees and stockholders. Moreover, it allowed general corporate funds to be used to administer corporate PACs and to solicit contributions.

25. An example of such a development is the creation of a legal procedure for private firms to petition the national trade policy bureaucracy to challenge foreign trade barriers through Section 301 of the 1974 Trade Act (Shaffer 2001). This procedure was strengthened, in turn, by the 1988 Trade Act, which increased pressure on the executive branch by tightening the requirements for taking action in such cases (Noland 1999).

26. Article 18 of the treaty designed an advising committee made up of representatives of producers, employees, consumers, and retailers, and Article 46 constituted the right of the High Authority, the predecessor of the European Commission, to consult and hear governments and other interested parties as experts at any time. Likewise, business, labor, consumers, and their associations were entitled to submit comments on any question or issue relevant to them to the High Authority at any time (and continue to be in this position with respect to the commission).

27. OFII represents more than fifty affiliates of foreign TNCs in the United States.

28. The World Bank presently is formalizing avenues for corporate input into its decisionmaking processes. The same applies to the UN.

29. Taking a critical stance on such lobbying activities, Paul (2001), for example, points to Nestle's extensive lobbying of the United Nations Children's Fund (UNICEF) in an effort to prevent the latter's cooperation with NGOs in the campaign against baby formula.

30. Similarly, Hummel (2001) argues that the World Business Council for Sustainable Development was successful in its campaign for market-based approaches to ecological problems and the discrediting of command-and-control regulation at UNCED.

31. A widely shared view, for instance, appears to be that the best way to stop legislative developments in Brussels is to lobby Berlin, London, or Paris (interview with Hans Bellstedt, reported in *Das Parlament* 45, November 2, 2001).

32. Similar to the national level, corporate actors speak with multiple voices in transnational and supranational lobbying efforts. They have their individual lobbies but are part of international and sectoral associations as well (Braithwaite and Drahos 2000). Moreover, critical observers point out that the positions of the international associations, including the International Chamber of Commerce (ICC), tend to be closer to those of large corporations due to issues of organization and representation and the costs involved within the organization, a phenomenon that again mirrors

the dynamics of general business lobbies at the national level (Smith 2000).

33. Associations have tried to counter the increasing role of TNCs or their "clubs" by providing the largest business actors with more say within their associations, by having them chair central committees, and by increasing their room for decisions. However, scholars find that these measures have not reduced the emphasis on direct relationships between governmental actors and TNCs (Eising and Kohler-Koch 1994). In fact, Eising and Kohler-Koch argue that corporations frequently use the respective associations as a basis for legitimizing the pursuit of their own interests.

34. A prime example of such a "club" is the ERT, a group of forty-some CEOs of the largest European companies, founded in 1983, which critical observers credit with being the most influential lobbying organization at the EU (Brand et al. 2000). They argue that the ERT has had a strong influence on the shape of the common market as well as its pursuit of flexible labor, environmental, and social standards; the privatization and liberalization in energy, telecommunications, and transport sectors; and EU enlargement (Rhodes 1991; Sandholtz and Zysman 1989). It is controversial, however, to what extent the ERT can actually be defined as a lobbying group. Thus, one may argue that while individual members of the ERT engage in lobbying efforts and may pursue objectives in accordance with ERT deliberations in these efforts, the ERT as such exercises its power predominantly in the form of discursive power (van Apeldoorn 2002).

35. Specifically, Grande (2003) argues that three specific attributes of an EU-type of multilevel governance system constrain opportunities for an effective interest group activity: "(1) the non-hierarchical institutional design, (2) the non-majoritarian mode of decision-making, and (3) the dynamic relationship between the various decision-making levels" (47).

36. Clapp (2001) argues, for instance, that much of the business influence on the Basel Convention was achieved through effective lobbying on technical issues, such as the definition of hazardous waste.

37. This institutional set-up also means that private interests generally get involved in the policy process much earlier than (traditionally) at the national level, thereby being able to take advantage of the opportunity to participate in the definition of problems and available solutions (Grande 2001b).

38. Constituency services provided to members of Parliament by business, in terms of letter campaigns or direct services, however, are much more difficult to justify (Kohler-Koch 1996).

39. Importantly, the "enabling institutions" presently have more teeth in global governance, as Chapter 2 delineated.

40. At the same time, the lack of transparency and European media renders tools of protest and public controversies, traditionally used by social and environmental interests, less useful (Nollert 1997).

41. By refusing to transfer the necessary competencies to European peak associations, for example, business actors were also able to effectively prevent the creation of corporatist structures at the EU level (Streeck and

Schmitter 1991). At the same time, Streeck and Schmitter point out that in many instances of the pursuit of specific issues, employers and employees tacitly share the same interests, thus further reducing the need for strong European labor organizations and corporatist bargaining structures. Such a congruence in interests is not always the case, of course. Thus, the lack of a correspondingly strong organization of labor interests meant the defeat of proposals for directives on workforce participation and consultation, for example.

42. This pass also needs to be worn inside the buildings to allow the identification of lobbyists.

43. Geiger delineates the creation of working groups and Internet sites allowing NGOs to voice opinions about the desirable content of a European constitution without procedures for a consideration of these opinions and in a manner that systematically hindered their integration into the convent's deliberations.

5

Structural Power: Old and New Facets

Structural power emerges from the embedding of policy contexts in broader socioeconomic structures and interdependencies. Thus, structural power intervenes earlier in the policy process, either making alternatives more or less desirable for formally empowered decision-makers before the observable bargaining actually starts or providing other actors with de facto decisionmaking power. One may thus consider it a stronger form of power than instrumental power. Traditionally, the structural power of business has been most prominently discussed in the context of the capacity of multinationally operating corporations to influence policy agendas of (host) governments due to their ability to impose costs for certain policy choices. Especially in the 1970s and 1980s, the ability to reward or punish countries by moving investments was at the core of many debates about MNCs in the international political economy.

Today, a look at the conditions allowing corporations to acquire and exercise structural power suggests that this agenda-setting power of business may have increased. Capital mobility is greater than ever due to the increasing liberalization of the respective financial regulations as well as to changes in production structures and business organization. At the same time, more countries than ever before are competing for this capital. Moreover, a few specific business actors determine the direction of a large share of global capital flows. Importantly, however, empirical studies of trends in this passive structural power of TNCs have found that the evidence on the extent of this passive structural power is mixed.

An analysis of developments in the structural power of business in global governance, however, first and foremost reveals that the activities of business to determine policy inputs today go beyond its ability to move capital. Via self-regulation and PPPs, business actors presently do not just influence agendas and induce governments to make certain policy choices indirectly. Rather, such arrangements provide opportunities to business actors to set rules directly. They determine issues, define problems, and design, adopt, implement, and enforce "solutions" themselves. Compared to the more passive agenda-setting power described previously, this structural power of business actors is active rule-setting power. Moreover, to a substantial extent this activity takes place without public influence or control. Developments in the agenda-setting power of business thus may fade into the background, when compared to the rise in its rule-setting power.

The present chapter explores developments in the structural power of business across the various avenues for exercising this power that business and especially corporations may use today. In this endeavor, the chapter first discusses the agenda-setting power deriving from capital mobility. It then focuses on quasi-regulation by service coordination firms, in particular rating agencies, and PPPs as examples of avenues of the exercise of structural power that increasingly involve active rule-setting power. Next, the chapter turns to self-regulation as an exercise of a structural power that most clearly reflects the acquisition of rule-setting power. Among various forms of self-regulatory arrangements, in turn, codes of conduct have been a particular topic of interest and controversy in the global governance debate due to the increasing use of this rule-setting device. In consequence, the second major part of this chapter examines developments in codes of conduct and delineates the controversy associated with them. The final section summarizes the findings and lays out some relevant implications.

Channels of the Structural Power of Business

Mobile Capital: The Agenda-Setting Power of TNCs

The structural power of business actors, in particular corporations, traditionally discussed in the literature derives from the capacity of MNCs to punish one country and reward another for their policy choices by moving jobs and investment across territorial borders (Frank 1978; Wallerstein 1979). According to observers, the extent of this power is shown by corporations that do not even need to voice their preferences; governments will comply with them in *vorauseilen-dem gehorsam*—that is, on the basis of the anticipated reaction of MNCs, due to governments' structural dependence on economic growth, employment, and investment. In other words, the structural power of corporations to a large extent traditionally has been seen as a passive influence on governmental agenda-setting and policy choices.

On the basis of their analyses, structuralists initially arrived at rather extreme assessments of a lack of state power relative to that of corporations. Such results have subsequently been criticized and challenged by other scholars, however. Their studies have found, for instance, that corporations often fail to impose demands on host states (Palan 1992). Rational choice and cost-based approaches, in turn, have argued that the relative bargaining power of corporations and host governments is contingent upon the distribution of assets and capabilities between the respective actors (Fagre and Wells 1982). On that basis, one can stress the difference in extent and impact of this power across sectors as well as the stages in the investment cycle. TNCs in extractive industries, for instance, face a substantial reduction in their structural power once (expensive) investments in physical capital have been made.

In environmental policy analyses, the structural power argument has led to a focus on the concept of pollution havens—the linking of the need of governments to attract investment to a race to the bottom in environmental (and social) standards. Again, respective claims can be challenged on the basis that factors such as market size,[1] access to natural resources, or human capital frequently matter as much if not more in locational decisions of corporations than environmental and social policies and standards adopted by countries (Thompson and Strohm 1996). At the same time, environmental costs are high in some industries, and environmental standards and charges frequently are linked to competitiveness concerns in political debates. Moreover, scholars have found that the result of the structural power of capital may not be a race to the bottom but a ratcheting up to some common minimum level and involve disincentives for individual countries to rise above that minimum level (Braithwaite and Drahos 2000).

The "traditional" structural power argument has acquired new momentum in the context of the globalization and global governance debates. Numerous scholars and practitioners contend that recent developments are leading to further expansion in the ability of corporations to divide the world into national states and subnational units competing on the basis of taxes as well as institutional, environmental, social, and moral standards (e.g., Altvater and Mahnkopf 1996; Gill 1995; Strange 1998). They point out that the number of states competing for investment in the international system has markedly increased since the 1970s. Not only have more and more developing countries changed their economic regimes and liberalized their investment regulations, but the entire post-Soviet bloc has entered the market for private capital as well. Furthermore, scholars report increasing competition between substate and subregional authorities for investment (Walter 1998). In consequence, scholars make the case that countries increasingly need to engage in image building and investment service activities to attract corporations rather than regulate them (Wells and Wint 1993). In addition, they delineate strategies of capital to further shape the world in a way that would provide even more structural power (Beck 2002). In the perspective of supporters of the structural power argument, such strategies also include the efforts to obtain a Multilateral Agreement on Investment (MAI), as these efforts appear to document the continuing corporate pursuit of an international investment regime that would secure maximum operating flexibility in host countries.

Furthermore, scholars argue that structural power increasingly influences not only national policy choices but also international ones. While supranational institutions tend to be more insulated from structural pressures, business may exercise structural power in international arenas through national and regional governments.[2] Peter Newell and Matthew Paterson (1998) demonstrate, for instance, the extent to which the stances taken by governments in the international negotiations for a climate change regime were a function of the structural power exercised by "national" corporations.

Assumptions about the increasing structural power are underlying much of the debate on the "decline of the state" in the globalization and global governance literature (Ohmae 1996; Strange 1996). Indeed, the controversy surrounding this debate reflects the controversy associated with assessments of developments in business's structural power. Contrary to the argument that the structural power of business has grown substantially, some scholars claim that globalization imposes fewer constraints on the political autonomy of the nation state than popular and academic discourses tend to suggest (Hirst and Thompson 1996). Others contend that the role of the state is even being enhanced in some areas, in particular as a promoter of national economic competitiveness (Schirm 2001).

Many scholars, even among those not agreeing with the decline of the state hypothesis, accept that capital mobility is influencing the state's policy choices to a certain degree, however. They differ in their evaluations of the extent as well as the implications of this influence. Thus, globalization induces a transformation from the welfare state to the competition state or from a positive state to a regulatory state, according to some observers (Cerny 1990, 1997; Majone 1996). Yet the state may still retain policy choices, in this role, as the influence of party politics or national institutional preferences can be shown (Busch 2003; Garrett 1998, 2000).

Critical observers point out, however, that the constraints on policy choice faced by the competition state are crucial. According to these scholars, an investment-friendly environment generally is associated with reductions in wage levels and social benefits, and a decline if not removal in public sector guarantees of education, health care, housing, and minimum wages, as well as progressive taxation regimes. In other words, the new state orientation toward supranational constituencies, in particular global capital, associated with this move toward the competition state actually fits well with the structural power argument (Hewson and Sinclair 1999).

Likewise, some of the original criticisms of the structural power argument can be challenged today. In recent decades, finance capital has acquired increasing importance vis-à-vis productive capital in the international economic system, for instance (Brand et al. 2000). In contrast to traditional productive capital, this finance capital does possess an "exit" option. Moreover, even production processes and their capital bases have changed. Nike is probably the most famous example of a TNC that does not *own* production sites in any particular country but flexibly shifts short-term production contracts among local subcontractors. Most fundamentally, outsourcing trends increasingly have allowed the transfer of risk to groups dependent on TNCs and vulnerable to their exertion of structural power (Amoore 2006). At the same time, the growing role of knowledge-intensive production and innovation-based competition has furthered the importance of knowledge relative to capital as a basis of structural power, which in turn is largely "owned" by corporations (Mytelka 2000).

Empirically, developments in the passive structural power of business are difficult to assess. Accordingly, it cannot come as a surprise that the results of the existing empirical studies are ambiguous. Studies looking at developments in taxation levels and standards, for instance, arrive at diverging results. Clearly, average corporate tax rates in OECD countries have substantially declined in recent years (see Figure 5.1). Analyzing the driving forces behind this development, some scholars argue that the data indicate that competition for investment is causing this convergence in corporate tax rates at lower levels (Ganghof 2005; Webb 2006).[3] Others, however, postulate that the empirical data cannot prove trends toward the reduction in the size of the welfare state or decline in state income from taxes on capital that structural power arguments would suggest (Bernauer 2000). Other scholars claim that competition among firms and collective action problems in oligopolistic market structures limit the structural power of TNCs resulting from the high mobility of capital (Walter 2000). In addition, they make the case that institutional factors, in particular the number of veto players, provide a stronger determinant of tax reforms than the structural power of business (Wagschal 1999, 2003).

At the same time, the influence of competition for investment on policy decisions may be more subtle and difficult to prove (and disprove) than many quantitative studies using macro-level data have assumed. First, it is necessary to differentiate between output (tax

Figure 5.1   The Average Corporate Tax Rate in OECD Countries

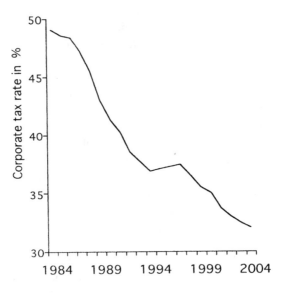

Source: Ganghof 2005. Reprinted with permission.

rates) and outcome (tax income) data as dependent variables, as the latter is likely to be influenced by a range of factors. In addition, analyses need to differentiate between corporate tax rates and income taxes, as only the former relate to capital mobility in a direct manner. Applying these criteria, Steffen Ganghof's (2005) finding that global competition for capital is the primary source of declining corporate tax rates appears much more convincing than the diverging results of other studies.[4] In addition, some of the effects will take a while to play out, given that politics in general tends to react slowly and politicians are likely to tinker with less obvious and politically controversial answers to globalization pressures as long as possible.[5] Most fundamentally, the economic and political relationships captured in the respective data are so complex that individual causal relationships frequently are difficult to isolate.

In addition, findings showing that factors besides labor and environmental standards or taxes matter in locational decisions of corporations would surprise few supporters of the structural power argument and fail to prove that these standards and factors do not matter. Such findings, at the most, serve to soften structural power arguments but do not disqualify them. Moreover, recent studies of the structural power of corporations themselves extend the arenas for competition for investment among states to include education, transport, and communication policies as well as ethical standards, while at the same time acknowledging that institutional and economic characteristics of countries and firms influence their relative bargaining power (Gill and Law 1993; Kobrin 1997).[6]

In sum, an intuitive examination of current trends in capital mobility and the competition for capital as well as with the organization of corporate production would suggest that the "traditional" structural power of capital is increasing. At the same time, however, empirical findings on the extent of this power vary. Lately, persuasive empirical evidence suggesting an increase in the passive structural power of business has appeared. But analyses of the role of business in global governance will have to further explore and carefully assess developments in this structural power.

Quasi-Regulation: The Agenda- (and Rule-) Setting Power of Coordination Service Firms

Quasi-regulation provides the second mechanism through which business actors, in this case specific business actors, exercise passive structural power in global governance today. Quasi-regulation, in the context of the present analysis, refers to the ability of coordination service firms to indirectly set standards for policies and practices worldwide. At the core of this debate is the role of rating agencies and their ability to determine the acceptability of national policies. The quasi-regulation exercised by these specific business actors is similar to the passive structural power exercised by corporations vis-à-vis national governments (delineated earlier). The only difference is that rating agencies do not threaten that one company will move its investment out of a country. Rather they influence the investment decisions of the entire global financial market. Thus, by rating countries in terms of their policies and politics, rating agencies exercise structural power on the policy and institutional choices made by governments and voters. To the extent that the standards applied by the rating agencies in this context are made explicit, moreover, this passive structural power comes close to an active one.

Three major rating agencies, Standard & Poor's, Moody's, and Fitch ICBA, dominate the market and influence about 80 percent of world financial flows (Hillebrand 2001). In combination with the increasing dependence of developing countries on private rather than public capital, this dominant position grants the three companies a substantial impact on the access of countries to financial markets and therefore a major role in the shaping of countries' economic, fiscal, and social policies. In consequence, they and the standards they apply to evaluate countries' policies and politics have become more important for developing countries' capital inflows than the IMF or World Bank, according to observers (Kerwer 2002).[7]

Rating agencies have been the focus of substantial criticism, in particular since the East Asian financial crisis of 1997, which was triggered in part by a downgrading of the rating of the respective economies (Sinclair 1999a). The major complaint against rating agencies was not that they conducted this downgrading, of course. Rather, the criticism was that they failed to see the crisis coming, the underlying assumption being that an earlier downgrading would have prevented the crisis or at least reduced its extent. This raised the question of the reliability of the ratings themselves. Subsequently, critical observers have pointed out that rating agencies actually have little experience in evaluating political criteria and have insufficient data for many countries in this respect. In fact, the situation is rather perverse in that the data are poor and the experience is weak for those ratings that are most important to developing countries (Hillebrand

2001). Moreover, rating agencies are charged with not sufficiently considering environmental and social aspects in their ratings. The most fundamental criticism regarding rating agencies, however, concerns their implications for democracy. Critical observers decry the ability of rating agencies as economic actors to "dictate" policies to democratically elected governments (Boyer and Drache 1996).

The structural power exercised by quasi-regulation does not only focus on countries' policy choices directly, however. A range of coordination service firms exercises structural power on other business actors, thereby influencing corporate conduct and, indirectly, economic and societal organization. Financial actors such as banks and institutional investors are the ones named most frequently in this respect. The pressure exercised on business to externalize environmental and social costs in the interest of good quarterly reports has been a mainstay in the debate, for instance. Clearly, hedge funds and private equity firms deserve much more attention in this context. Likewise, multinational law and accounting firms as well as management consultants exercise transnational rule-setting power by determining and enforcing standards for the behavior of business companies. Systematic research on the processes through which these actors exercise power and the implications of this exercise of power is only starting to come forth. For the present analysis, however, it is important to note that these actors exercise structural power on other business actors, but via that route also on the political choice set of countries.

With respect to social and environmental objectives, the power exercised by coordination service firms can cut both ways. On one hand, the pressures for cost savings mentioned earlier clearly exist. As Andreas Nölke (2005) has pointed out, even the changes in accounting standards promoted by the large accounting firms, whom one would not necessarily think of as holders of power in this respect, are forcing the social provisions associated with the Rhenish capitalism out of the market. On the other hand, consultancies and financial actors are also interested in reducing the environmental and social liabilities of firms. A growing interest of investors in ethical investment opportunities thus is starting to exercise pressure on the sustainability conduct of companies. Recent political activism by pension funds is providing further impetus in this respect. However, the market for ethical investments currently is still a niche market, and most sustainability audits and ratings are extremely shallow (partly due to a lack of resources and access to information).

In sum, the influence of coordination service firms on policies and the socioeconomic organization of societies presents an additional form of structural power exercised by business. Importantly, this power does not apply to business in general but to certain sectors and types of actors in particular. Thus, it draws special attention to the role of financial actors, accountants, and management consultants in global governance.

Public-Private and Private-Private Partnerships: Participation in Rule-Setting

Public-private and private-private partnerships present an additional means for the exercise of active structural power by business insofar as they allow business to influence agenda-setting directly and to set rules and regulations. PPPs draw on the cooperation between business and governmental actors or civil society in the pursuit of specific or broad policy objectives.[8] Specifically, the aim of PPPs is to foster participatory governance and promote the use of private resources to gain public policy objectives (Mayntz 2002). As mentioned previously, PPPs actually are not a new phenomenon. Scholars have pointed out a long tradition of governance on the basis of formal and informal cooperation between public and private actors, in particular in the modern democratic welfare state (Rosenau 2000). In fact, corporatist arrangements constitute PPPs in the broadest sense.[9] The recent increase in reliance on such arrangements, in particular at the global level, and the prominence of some of these arrangements, however, have drawn the attention of the global governance literature to PPPs.

The most prominent example of a public-private partnership at the global level is the Global Compact created in July 2000 by UN Secretary General Kofi Annan, a voluntary initiative simultaneously pursuing improvements in corporate conduct and in global problem-solving. Under the Global Compact, participating corporations commit themselves to complying with ten global norms, including especially human rights norms but also workers' rights, environmental rights, and anticorruption standards.[10] Moreover, the compact aims to foster learning and the diffusion of best practice in corporate conduct among participants (Brinkmann 2004). In turn, corporations benefit from the publicity and legitimacy provided by the UN.

Not surprisingly, the Global Compact has both strengths and weaknesses (May 2006b). Some scholars and practitioners laud its ability to draw on corporate resources to increase the legitimacy and effectiveness of global problem-solving and emphasize its ability to contribute to social learning and the diffusion of best practice (Ruggie 2001). Other observers criticize that the compact may allow corporations to gain prestige from cooperation with the UN and the use of the UN logo for their image campaigns without achieving substantial improvement in their environmental and social practices (Bennis 2001). They point out that the compact involves no official evaluation of actual corporate compliance with the Global Compact's principles. In the most extreme case, they fear a selling out of the UN system and resulting threats to the legitimacy of the UN (Paul 2001). More moderate evaluations postulate that voluntary cooperative agreements like the compact can make a modest contribution to global governance under specific conditions, inducing a concurrence between public and private interests (Kell and Ruggie 2001).[11]

The UN secretary general is not the only one promoting public-private partnerships at the global level today, however. The World Health Organization has been cooperating with the pharmaceutical corporation Merck in a successful effort to eradicate river blindness, a major public health threat in Central and West Africa. Likewise, the IMF and the World Bank both promote public-private partnerships as an instrument to improve global governance. Similarly, the World Commission on Dams provides a tripartite effort to ensure the sustainability of activities in that area (Ottoway 2001).

Many public-private partnerships, however, face the same potential benefits and costs as the Global Compact. Under promising conditions, they offer an opportunity to pool public and private resources in the pursuit of public objectives. In the ideal case, they also provide a tool allowing business actors to appreciate their potential contribution to global problem-solving (Kollman 2003). Under less promising conditions, public-private partnerships are unlikely to provide much progress toward the effective pursuit of public objectives and in the worst case would allow the utilization of public resources in the pursuit of private interests. Such conditions exist, in particular, if public actors actually depend on the contribution of private resources and if the respective policy processes are opaque and removed from societal control (Rosenau 2000).

A highly noted example of a private-private partnership is the Forest Stewardship Council (FSC).[12] The FSC aims to improve the sustainability of forest management through the creation of a certification system for businesses along the timber product chain on the basis of environmental, social, and economic criteria. Among the FSC's core principles are the voluntary nature of the initiative, the creation of acceptance through participation and transparency, certification through independent auditors, the adaptation of its global principles to local conditions, and the certification of the entire product chain. In addition, the FSC defines ten principles of responsible forest management, including legal compliance, the consideration of long-term tenure and use rights as well as the rights of indigenous people, the maintenance and enhancement of the social and economic well-being for forest workers and local communities, the conservation of biological diversity and associated ecological functions, the development of an appropriate management plan, monitoring and assessment of forest conditions, yields, the chain of custody, and relevant social and environmental impacts, and the maintenance of high conservation value forests.

Next to the advantages typically cited for PPPs such as the efficiency of decentralized governance, the FSC's particular strength is the definition of relatively stringent standards, including performance standards. Moreover, the FSC has filled a policy vacuum, as governmental negotiations on a forest convention had been failing for years. For these reasons, the FSC has achieved much acclaim.

At the same time, however, the FSC has also become a prime example of business interest in weak private governance. Perceiving FSC standards as too stringent, timber industries in several countries have created weaker, competing labels, which has led to a marginalization of the FSC standard in the market (Fuchs 2006a, 2006b). At this point, only about 4 percent of global forests have been FSC certified, and the further diffusion of the FSC certificate is at risk, as most consumers lack the information to distinguish between the different environmental labels for timber products. Indirectly, the FSC may well serve as evidence for business's interest in using private-private partnerships in image campaigns without substantial changes in conduct.

In sum, PPPs provide business with an avenue to exercise active structural power. In PPPs, business actors directly participate in decisions on rules and regulations. The extent of this power, however, differs across PPPs. While in some public-private partnerships, for instance, business may dictate agenda- and rule-setting, public actors enforce strict limits on the decision room of business actors in others. Moreover, public actors still are in control to the extent that they can decide with whom they want to sit at the table. This may be more so in the national arena, however. In the international arena, PPPs can provide large business actors with considerable leeway in agenda-

and rule-setting due to resource scarcity among public actors as well as civil society and a frequent lack of transparency in decisionmaking processes.

Self-Regulation: Increasingly Autonomous Rule-Setting Power

Self-regulation provides the most prominent new channel for the exercise of structural power by business. In self-regulatory arrangements, business actors today design, adopt, implement, and enforce their own rules. Self-regulation, therefore, is the furthest reaching example of the extension of business's structural power from passive agenda-setting power to active rule-setting power.

Self-regulatory arrangements presently exist in many shapes and forms. They range from formal arrangements involving written agreements and highly regulated cooperation to loose and informal modes of communication and cooperation. Moreover, they differ in terms of the role played by government and, correspondingly, the autonomy of business in rule-setting. Some self-regulatory arrangements are developed voluntarily by business actors, without public input and control. Others are developed at the behest of government and strictly monitored by public authorities for their fulfillment of given tasks. Finally, a third group of self-regulatory arrangements exists that falls somewhere in between the other two.

Self-regulation is not a "new" phenomenon, of course, despite the surge in interest in it in the global governance literature. Self-regulation by private actors played an important role in the Middle Ages, for instance in maritime law and the self-regulation of guilds (Cutler 1999, 2000). *Lex mercatoria,* the transnational trade law, is a form of self-regulation by business that was developed over centuries to facilitate commercial activity. In fact, there is a considerable tradition of interfirm cooperation in the development of regulatory frameworks in efforts to reduce transaction costs, stabilize expectations, and increase information flows. Such regulatory cooperation can also be seen in the development of self-supervisory mechanisms in the stock markets, global banking and insurance industries, and the Internet (Langhorne 2001). In the context of rapid technological development and the emergence of new market sectors, in particular, cooperation in the development of regulatory frameworks can help firms establish some level of order in turbulent markets. As scholars have pointed out, such cooperation is most likely in the case of the existence of learning processes, complex knowledge and technology, and repeated interaction (Cutler, Haufler, and Porter 1999).

Moreover, corporatist institutions in the Western democratic welfare state, particularly in sectors close to the state such as infrastructure and health care, frequently have relied on self-regulation by private actors as a complement to and partial substitute for state regulation (Mayntz and Schneider 1995). Here, the question of the governability of complex systems led to arguments for the potential contribution "private interest government" could make to social order (Streeck and Schmitter 1985a).[13] Even in international politics, analyses of the role of "legislative nongovernmental organizations" already existed in the early 1960s (Ronit and Schneider 2000).

The fact that self-regulation draws such attention in the global governance debate despite its long tradition is partly the result of the increasing replacement of traditional private authority by public authority in the late nineteenth and early twentieth centuries (Haufler 2006), the use of a dichotomous conceptualization of "states" versus "markets" in many policy analyses (Lederer 2002), and the lack of familiarity of some global governance scholars with corporatist arrangements, as well as the lack of visibility and transparency of the latter. These aspects fostered the perception of public authority as the norm.

Partly, however, the rise in interest results from the dramatic increase in quantity and influence of self-regulatory arrangements as well as new facets to self-regulatory practices. Private actors today define regulations across a wide range of policy arenas, including environmental issues, human rights, and the international financial system. Developments are particularly noteworthy in the area of standards and codes of conduct, which now exist at the level of individual companies such as Levi-Strauss and Karstadt; at the sectoral level such as the Responsible Care Program of the Chemical Industry; and at the global level, such as the regulation of transport of dangerous goods by the International Air Transport Association, the International Standards Organization (ISO) 14000 or SA 8000 standards for environmental management and social accountability (see pp. 120–121), or the advertising code of conduct developed by the International Chamber of Commerce. Importantly, much of this activity extends beyond core activities of business.

A further reason for the attention paid to self-regulation in the global governance literature is that self-regulatory arrangements today frequently develop without input from and control by public authorities, a characteristic that makes them very different from self-regulatory arrangements known under corporatism, for instance. The latter, in fact, were only possible on the basis of coexisting public authority, which delegated regulatory authority. Moreover, they existed in the shadow of hierarchy, as a threat of state intervention always existed in cases of the failure of self-regulatory arrangements or their lack of consideration of public interests (Lütz 1995). The necessary public authority for this shadow of hierarchy, however, does not exist in a similar manner at the global level, and changes in self-regulatory practices there frequently induce corresponding changes in self-regulation at the national level. In consequence, it appears that business has acquired an important new role as an autonomous actor in rule-setting.

Not surprisingly, this new role of business actors is highly controversial. On the positive side, of course, is the potential contribution of business's organizational, technical, and financial resources to governance. In this context, some scholars and practitioners highlight the benefits of decentralization, flexibility, and efficiency in problem-solving.[14] They argue that successful governance in today's complex environments depends on the deconstruction of the traditional hierarchical regulatory relationships and the increasing reliance on societal capacities for self-regulation (Scharpf 1991; Willke 1992). In addition, they point out that the potentially negative impact of self-regulation should not be overestimated, since holders of public authority could take that authority back should private authority fail or a crisis develop.

On the negative side, scholars and practitioners criticize the ability of private actors to set rules without input or control from public actors. They claim that in many cases there is an unavoidable tension between private interests and public welfare (Altvater and Mahnkopf 2002). Moreover, they criticize the lack of transparency and accountability of many self-regulatory arrangements, arguing that private regulatory authority frequently is hidden from public view. Furthermore, scholars and practitioners complain about the cartel-like functioning of many examples of self-regulation, advantaging members and raising barriers to entry for others. Finally, due to the absence of a global public authority, the lack of political will and capacity on the part of governments, and the diffuse nature of private regulatory authority, critical observers question the optimistic view that public actors would actually be able to retake authority from private actors in the event of crisis or private regulatory failure. In other words, they argue that the shadow of authority may have disappeared.

Particular controversy is associated with the self-regulation of actors in areas that are or should be considered public spaces according to some observers (Drache 2001). This pertains in particular to voluntary regulations in the areas of environmental and social welfare, which, therefore, will be discussed in detail in the following section. It also pertains to the delegation of public authority to private actors in the context of the regulation of the Internet and the international financial system, however. Scholars highlight problems associated with private governance in information technology and telecommunications sectors, for instance, arising from its ability to impose negative externalities on other sectors and society as such (Arthurs 2001; Schneider 2002). Likewise, they perceive threats to democracy and public welfare arising from the private capture of public goods such as the monetary and financial order and stability, and from the lack of ability of public authorities to even carry out the fundamental framework functions of supervision and crisis management:

> In supervision and risk management, in the new environment, the principal result has been the emergence of "market-based" approaches to supervision, wherein firms are responsible for risk management through complex mathematical models implemented under the approval of supervisory agencies. The problem becomes, who defines the criteria for the regulation and supervision of the markets, and in what consists the public interest?
>
> Crucial information and expertise for the process remains the proprietary domain of firms, which supervisors admit they cannot match. In a highly competitive environment there is also an intense need for firms to remain relatively free, in terms of product innovation and corporate strategy. Level playing field concerns abound. This relative disarmament of public authorities carries with it the very real risk that private market interests increasingly define supervisory criteria. This would mean that this crucial aspect of public policy, the safety and stability of the financial system, is dominated by the preferences of those very private market agents who profit from it most. Public authorities are potentially reduced to crisis management and (costly) lender-of-last-resort functions. The implications for moral hazards in crisis management should not go unnoticed. The mix of public and private is always a problem in any regulatory context, but the marketization of the global financial system brings this dilemma sharply into focus. (Underhill 2001, 287f)

Self-regulation is associated with potential costs and benefits, then. Many scholars today would argue that self-regulatory arrangements need to be tied to basic democratic norms and fair procedures and require effective supervision and sanctioning mechanisms if they are to function as valuable supplements or alternatives to public regulation. What is clear, however, is that self-regulatory arrangements, with their increase in numbers and autonomy from state delegation of authority and supervision provide an important new channel for business to set rules actively and thereby suggest an expansion in its structural power. In fact, self-regulatory activities are political instruments that most directly translate into influence. The extent of this influence can differ vastly, of course, depending on the range of actors affected by the self-regulation. Moreover, most observers would evaluate the extent and meaning of the influence of self-regulatory activities differently depending on whether they serve to add to existing regulation or, in the worst case, to undermine or prevent public regulation. In this context, it is important to note that studies find that governments increasingly take self-regulation into account in the design and implementation of national policies (Nadvi and Wältring 2002). Thus, the combination of ISO 14000 certification with regulatory relief is being tried in a number of developed and developing countries (Clapp 2001).[15] It is still too early, however, to draw broad generalizations regarding the actual influence and meaning of rule-setting activities by business from these individual cases. In the end, then, an overall evaluation of the influence of business's active structural power will be intimately tied to questions of the motivation behind this self-regulation, its interaction with public regulation, and its strengths and weaknesses as a contributor to (global) political problem-solving.

Codes of Conduct as Structural Power

"If companies really have adopted a new bottom line, then all to the good, self-regulation is an appropriate way forward for environmental policy-making and the poacher may be employed as a gamekeeper. If, on the other hand, companies have not modified their bottom line, as unfortunately most of the available evidence tends to suggest, then the risk is that the poacher is still a poacher" (Garrod 1998, 57). Codes of conduct and private voluntary standards deserve particular attention in the context of analyses of new channels of the exercise of structural power by business for two reasons. First, the number and influence of such codes and standards has skyrocketed in recent years. Second, the voluntary nature of and exclusively private control over many of these codes and standards means that they most plainly reflect both the costs and benefits of self-regulatory arrangements perceived by scholars and practitioners.

The Rise of Codes of Conduct

Codes of conduct provide a "soft-law," nonbinding form of governance of the behavior of business actors.[16] They delineate roles and responsibilities of management and accounting systems and regulate the provision of resources for implementation as well as monitoring, auditing, certification, and labeling programs demonstrating the performance of the industry or company to the outside world. Business actors have developed or participated in the development of standards, especially in the context of national and international standard-setting organizations, for a long time (Genschel 1995). In particular, they have been involved in the design and promotion of technological standards defining physical characteristics of a product or service in order to facilitate trade or foster the reputation of an industry. Since the 1980s, however, business actors have increased their activities in standard development in areas beyond their traditional sphere enormously (Weiser and Zadek 2000).

Today, a wide net of corporate, sectoral, and global codes of conduct exists, the range of which the early predominance of case studies in this field had hidden (Hodess 2001). In a 1998 study, the OECD identified and analyzed 233 corporate codes of conduct. Eighty-five percent of the largest 100 US corporations had a company code of conduct in 1990 (van Liemt 1998).[17] When Levi-Strauss published its Global Sourcing and Operating Guidelines in 1991, it was one of the first companies in the textile industry to do so. Today, codes of conduct are the norm for corporations in this sector. Moreover, the textile sector as well as numerous other sectors, such as the chemical, insurance, banking, and advertising industries, have since developed sector-wide codes of conduct. Likewise, the adoption of global codes of conduct has grown considerably. The ISO 14000[18] environmental management standard, for instance, witnessed a 79 percent increase in the number of certified plants between 1998 and 1999, with more than 13,000 plants in seventy-five countries having been certified by the end of 1999 (Clapp 2001; Nadvi and Wältring 2002). A number of corporations are seeking certification for all their sites worldwide.

Moreover, codes of conduct span a wide subject area from social and human rights to environmental ones. At the global level, the social accountability standard (SA 8000[19]), for instance, defines principles for corporate conduct in terms of child labor, forced and slave labor, worker safety, and freedom of association. Likewise, numerous company and sectoral codes focus on social issues and especially human rights protection. As mentioned previously, the ISO 14000 standard, in turn, delineates global environmental principles for management systems, while other codes define company- or sector-specific environmental objectives and measures. Increasingly, codes of conduct combine environmental, social, and human rights objectives.

While business actors initially defined the respective codes of conduct by themselves, lately they have cooperated with civil society in such efforts in a number of cases, as for example in the Forest Stewardship Council discussed earlier. Khalid Nadvi and Frank Wältring (2002) identify a development over five generations of standards in this respect, from company codes of conduct to tripartite generic social standards (see Table 5.1). In other words, business individually and in collaboration increasingly sets rules for human rights protection and social and environmental regulation and thereby contributes to the shape of transnational and global politics and policy in the respective areas.

Engines Behind the Rise of Codes of Conduct

What explains the rise in extent and influence of business-owned codes of conduct and voluntary standards? Scholars argue that risk and learning provide the main sources of momentum in this respect. Risk, in this context, relates to both the economic risk of consumer boycott and the political risk of public regulation. Starting in the late 1980s, reports of twenty-hour workdays for children in Honduras for Wal-Mart or the production of shoes in sweat shops in Vietnam for Nike created substantial public pressure on corporations. Likewise, the environmental disasters of Bhopal, India, and the Exxon *Valdez* brought environmental carelessness and misconduct by business actors into the limelight and resulted in mounting pressures on governments for more stringent regulation of corporate behavior. This was the case, in particular, as the visibility of such scandals increased markedly in the era of global media and the Internet.

Codes of conduct have provided an answer to these risks by allowing companies, industry sectors, and business as such to efficiently convey information about environmental and social matters to

Table 5.1   Five Generations of Codes and Labels

Generation	Examples/ Contents	Actors Involved	Key Drivers	Influence on International Trade	Certification
1st generation Company codes of conduct	Nike, Reebok, Karstadt: self-obligations of TNCs on the firm and supplier level, internal formulation and implementation	TNCs and their suppliers	TNCs as lead firms of supply chains	Existence of a large number of firm codes, focused on some brand-name companies in consumer-near sectors and in buyer-driven chains	1st-party self-monitoring; setting process easy, legitimacy weak
2nd generation Business-defined sector codes and labels	ICC, Eco-tex, AVE: sector-specific codes and labels formulated and implemented by enterprise associations	Enterprise associations, chambers, suppliers	Enterprise associations	Sporadic, but with more comprehensive influence according to the sector approach	2nd-party monitoring through sector association: setting quite easy, still weak legitimacy
3rd generation Business-defined international standards	ISO 14000: environmental management standards (using the model of ISO 9000)	ISO, national standardiza-tion bodies, business mainly from industrialized countries	Business	Not necessary, but gets increasing influence especially in natural resource–intensive sector	3rd-party monitoring through market-based certification bodies, setting more difficult, legitimacy high

(continues)

governments, the public, and each other, and to demonstrate the willingness and capacity to improve their behavior. Indeed, the development of codes and standards frequently can be traced to specific
crises and scandals. Thus, Shell revised and widely advertised its
code of conduct after the scandals over Brent Spar as well as its operations in Nigeria.

Table 5.1 continued

Generation	Examples/ Contents	Actors Involved	Key Drivers	Influence on International Trade	Certification
4th generation Business and NGO-defined sector-specific codes and labels	Transfair, FSC, Rug-mark: NGO-fostered sector-specific codes and labels, formulated and implemented mainly through NGO and business partnerships with independent monitoring procedures and civil society participation	NGOs, religious associations, solidarity groups, minority groups, unions, large retailers	NGOs	Gain increasing importance according to new strategies of NGOs and retailers	3rd-party monitoring through certification bodies or NGOs, setting difficult, keeping legitimacy requires constant negotiation
5th generation Tripartite-defined generic social standards	SA 8000, FLA, ETI: tripartite social minimum standards to harmonize the diverse number of codes and to increase legitimacy, transparency and traceability (existence of divergent approaches)	Social NGOs, unions, TNCs (buyers and producers), certification bodies, government	Public-sector NGOs	Increasing influence despite disagreements between special actors involved in the formulation of the standards	3rd-party monitoring through certification bodies

Source: Nadvi and Wältring 2002. Reprinted with permission.

Likewise, the Responsible Care Program of the Chemical Industry goes back to Union Carbide's accidental release of forty tons of lethal chemicals in Bhopal in 1984, which led to the deaths of thousands of people. After this accident, the Canadian Chemical Association adopted the Responsible Care Program to forestall restrictive government regulation, ideas for which had already been developed after the 1976 explosion at a chemical factory in Seveso, Italy.[20] Today, the program has been adopted by more than forty national associations and is being overseen by the International Council of Chemical Associations.[21]

In general and not surprisingly, codes of conduct have been particularly widely employed in highly globalized sectors that are labor intensive and/or involve substantial environmental risks, such as petrochemicals, mining, agriculture, forestry, chemicals, textiles, carpets, and the clothing and footwear industries (Nadvi and Wältring 2002). Likewise, they play an important role in buyer-driven sectors in which ethical, social, and environmental performance may turn into a key component of competition and become important in the perceptions of consumers. Moreover, codes and standards have been pushed by insurance and banking industries, actors particularly concerned about the reduction in risk of their clients and investments (Adams 1998).[22]

At the same time, scholars argue that learning has fostered the development and adoption of codes and standards and the associated cooperation and consensus among business actors substantially (Harrison 1999; Prakash 2000). They make the case that transnational epistemological communities of managers, accountants, and certifiers have developed, which fosters the awareness of problems and the transfer of successful business practices (Kollman 2003).[23] Moreover, they suggest that the diffusion of and compliance with international codes and standards is a function of the embedding of these codes and standards in routine practices (Porter 2005).[24] Thus, some scholars contend that learning has led to a cultural change in terms of a new consciousness and developments in basic norms and practices defining "appropriate behavior" in the business community (Nash and Ehrenfeld 1997).

In association with risk and learning as driving forces for the growth in codes of conduct, scholars emphasize the opportunity and need for self-regulation by business actors caused by gaps in global governance arising from the failure of state efforts to regulate corporate conduct and the "invisibility" of the corporation in international law (Cutler 2006; Landfried 2001).[25] Efforts to establish global regulations for corporate conduct had already started in the 1970s, when scandals such as the involvement of ITT in Chile led developing countries to call for the development of general codes of conduct for corporate actors. In 1974 the Economic and Social Council (ECOSOC) of the UN established the UNCTC and asked it to develop a code of conduct for multinationally operating business actors that would address issues such as the respect of national sovereignty and human rights, disclosure requirements for relevant information, and transfer pricing. The resulting negotiations were highly contested, with developing countries demanding a mandatory code for corporate actors rather than host governments, and developed countries desiring a voluntary code applying to both host governments and corporations. Moreover, questions of nationalization and compensation caused intense struggle. The negotiations had made little progress when the general attitude toward regulation and support for developing countries shifted with the triumph of conservative parties and ideas in the 1980s. The subsequent negotiations, accordingly, forced developing countries to soften their demands considerably. Even the development of a more modest code, on 80 percent of which a consensus had been achieved by 1992, however, did not succeed, as the UNCTC was closed down before the negotiations had been completed.

The OECD and the ILO both developed respective codes and standards as well. In 1976 the OECD published its Guidelines for Multinational Enterprises, defining principles on issues such as finances, taxation, employment, and environmental protection (the Guidelines were revised and strengthened in 2000). The ILO developed a tripartite Declaration of Principles Concerning Multinational Enterprises and Social Policy, likewise addressing employment, training, working conditions, and industrial relations. Importantly, both codes defined principles for governments to voluntarily apply to the private sector. Scholars have argued that neither the OECD guidelines nor the ILO declaration had much "direct and measurable" effect, however (Haufler 2001, 17). In sum, a regulatory void existed in this area.

An additional source of opportunity for self-regulation by business arose due to the desire of activists to use the potential influence of corporate actors in pursuit of public policy objectives. A number of codes and standards, especially in the social and human rights arena, were initiated by civil society actors with this explicit purpose. The FSC and SA 8000 are relevant examples. Likewise, the Sullivan principles were developed by civil society (specifically the Reverend Leon Sullivan) as an attempt to undermine apartheid policies of the South African government through changes in the way foreign corporations conducted their operations there.[26] These principles are now becoming global guidelines and reflect the idea of drawing on economic actors and their resources in the pursuit of broader social principles.

In sum, business has had both the opportunity and ample incentives to engage in the design and implementation of codes of conduct and private standards.

The Contribution to Global Political Problem-Solving

The fundamental question is, of course, what the implications of business's rule-setting activities through voluntary self-regulatory arrangements are for global problem-solving. It is here that scholars and practitioners fervently disagree. While some perceive codes of conduct and private regulatory standards as sincere efforts on the part of companies, sectors, and the business community as such to monitor and improve their social and environmental performance, others claim that business actors use these codes primarily as superficial window-dressing measures in order to secure and increase profits and avoid public regulation. Overall, these evaluations reflect many of the hopes and concerns noted earlier with respect to PPPs and self-regulation, only these hopes and concerns are at their most extreme here.

On the positive side, scholars emphasize the contribution that codes of conduct and private standards can make to the pursuit of public policy objectives, especially due to the potential influence of consumers and investors and their drawing on corporate resources rather than increasingly scarce public resources. In addition, scholars point out that the diffusion of global codes and standards is particularly valuable, since these cannot be evaded by footloose capital if they become the de facto norm for business practices (Messner 2002). Furthermore, observers argue that this involvement of economic actors in governance is desirable from the perspective both of the public, with its increasing unwillingness to trust governments alone, and of governments themselves (Ledgerwood and Broadhurst 2000). For the latter, such self-regulatory arrangements can provide a tool to promote investment and environmental and social standards at the same time, as well as an instrument to promote "soft" foreign policy goals (Haufler 2001). Surveys show that opinion leaders in countries frequently view corporate codes as a desirable and important instrument for addressing social and environmental issues (Kolk and van Tulder 2002). In addition, scholars make the case that such self-regulatory arrangements provide businesses with an opportunity and incentive for proactive behavior (Sharma and Vredenburg 1998).

Finally, advocates point out that these forms of self-regulation work through the market rather than against it, as they allow businesses themselves to choose their suppliers or clients consciously on the basis of the latter's adherence to the desired standards. In other words, the arrangements are expected to allow the achievement of the desired environmental and social objectives in an economically efficient and cost-effective manner. Scholars and practitioners emphasize that the decentralized decisionmaking by those actors with the most expertise and information reduces the costs, incoherence, and ineffectiveness of traditional public regulatory measures (Wylynko 1999). Moreover, observers underline the ability of codes of conduct to integrate environmental and social problem-solving strategies along the entire supply chain, to involve all stakeholders, and to generate transparency (Müller 1995). A number of codes, such as ISO 14000, in fact, require communication with suppliers and customers about such issues for certification. In addition, the fact that business "owns" such self-designed rules and regulations, along with the perceived legitimacy of regulation by one's peers, may allow a degree of compliance that traditional public regulation in the absence of stringent (and costly) enforcement would not achieve.

In contrast to accounts stressing the positive impact of codes of conduct and private voluntary standards, however, numerous practitioners and scholars voice concerns. They claim that such codes and standards frequently represent marketing ploys and attempts to preempt public regulation rather than sincere commitments to broader public policy objectives (Braun 2001). Specifically, critics charge that such codes signify attempts by business actors to "greenwash" or "whitewash" themselves via the utilization of environmental or social standards respectively, that is, to represent a pretense at environmentally or socially responsible behavior in the absence of any real improvement. As evidence, observers point out that even the most prominent proponents of codes of conduct among companies have been shown to be quite lax in their implementation and sometimes even have led to worse results (Haufler 2001; von Mirbach 1999).[27] Likewise, even supposed "success stories" such as the Responsible Care Program of the Chemical Industry may fail to live up to their promises when looked at closely. Scholars thus have documented that there is no evidence of a positive influence of the Responsible Care Program and membership on the rate of environmental improvement among its members, while at the same time dirtier firms are actually more likely to participate in the program (King and Lenox 2000).

In addition, critics stress that the reach of voluntary measures is still limited, as many companies continue to ignore the need to invest in activities to improve their environmental and social conduct. Moreover, the conduct even of the leaders in this respect needs to be critically evaluated. As Scott Pegg (2006) shows, supposed leaders in corporate social responsibility (CSR) activities frequently undermine and prevent the development of regional and global CSR initiatives. Furthermore, critics stress that the selectivity of measures and standards adopted by businesses suggests limits to the interest of corporate actors in environmental, social, and human rights objectives. They point out that companies have been very selective in their inclusion of social rights in their codes of conduct, for instance.[28] Thus, few social standards address issues of worker representation and organization, or the right to a living wage. In fact, a few codes, such as the one of Sara Lee Knit Products,[29] explicitly speak out against the organization of their workers in unions. The limited success of SA 8000, which addresses these issues, thus does not come as a surprise to critics.

Likewise, critics suggest that limits to arguments about a fundamental change in business culture with respect to environmental and social issues can be seen in the fact that some of the most widely adopted codes of conduct are also the weakest. The ISO 14000 standard, for instance, does not entail actual environmental performance requirements beyond compliance with local laws. Likewise, other more ambitious requirements, such as the principle to adopt the best available technology, which had originally been pushed by some actors in the development of ISO 14000 standards, were quickly abandoned (Parto 1999). Without such specific requirements in terms of performance and practice, however, companies can specify their own goals and set them at extremely low levels while still obtaining certification (Krut and Gleckman 1998).

In sum, empirical studies demonstrate that social and environmental responsibility frequently functions as an add-on to business activity, being employed when beneficial and lacking integration into general business operation (Yosie and Herbst 1998). Critical analyses of the impact of codes of conduct and private standards frequently find that the latter tend to address only select issues by select companies in an insufficient manner. In consequence, they contend that arguments of a sea change in business values or claims that compliance with environmental and social objectives has become an unavoidable condition of economic success today need to be met with considerable skepticism.

Indeed, an immediate concurrence between the logics of business and society exists only under certain circumstances, for instance with respect to issues in the public eyes, in market segments with less of a dependence on price-based competition, and in areas where improvements in ethical conduct mean opportunities for profits (Hummel 2001).[30] After all, environmental and social improvements frequently are associated with very real costs for business actors. In addition, efforts to improve the environmental and social conduct of business actors at the global level face difficulties even in the best of circumstances. Complex interactions between the national and international economic and political levels can render the extension of best practices difficult for corporations (Broadhurst 2000). Similarly, difficulties may arise from increased outsourcing and network organization of business activities. Even corporate actors sincere about the implementation of environmental and/or social codes of conduct, for instance, frequently have difficulty knowing about the relevant conditions in pre– and post–house production processes.

Some of the potential "loopholes" of codes and standards could be overcome by effective public scrutiny. In fact, advocates of codes of conduct emphasize the ability of the public, especially consumers and investors, to hold companies accountable for their commitments. Moreover, public pressure could force companies to increase such commitments to a meaningful level if the public considered the existing goals too low or selective. Yet, public monitoring and enforcement of codes of conduct is extremely difficult due to the high costs of such monitoring and information-gathering activities. These problems are further multiplied by the growing number of codes and standards, which frequently confuse rather than inform consumers and investors and thereby reduce their ability to influence business conduct.[31] In addition, the privatization of regulation reflected by these codes has actually prevented direct public involvement and scrutiny for a long time, according to critical observers (Heinelt 2002b; Muldoon and Nadarajah 1999).

Increasingly, business is attempting to answer criticisms of "greenwashing" or "whitewashing" by cooperating with NGOs in the development and implementation of codes and standards (Utting 2004). As Table 5.1 shows, fourth- and fifth-generation codes of conduct and labels are based on such collaborative arrangements. Such an approach will only silence critics to a certain point, however. They point out that business tends to control the respective processes and, most fundamentally, can select "friendly" NGOs with whom to cooperate (Gibson 1999). In consequence, the existence of private-private partnerships should not be seen as reflecting an equal extent of rule-setting power by business and civil society. In fact, the FSC (discussed earlier) indicates the asymmetry in this power well, as it highlights the role of business's influence on the spread of private standards and certificates. Thus, stringent standards and certificates created in partnership with civil society may be easily marginalized in the market by weaker business-created standards and certificates. The potential improvement in the internal effectiveness (stringency) of standards created by private-private partnership compared to self-regulation frequently is diluted by their lack of external effectiveness, or spread (Fuchs 2006b). In other words, the extent of civil society's role in private-private partnerships depends on business's preferences regarding the contents of private standards to a substantial extent.

An additional criticism of voluntary standards and codes is that participation in the development of standards and codes is not distributed "democratically," even in the business community. Large firms from industrialized countries dominate in the design of such codes and standards (Muchlinsky 1997).[32] Moreover, these codes and standards tend to further favor large firms due to the substantial costs associated with certification measures and the tendency toward centralization in supplier structures induced by the need to be informed about pre–house production processes (Messner 2002).[33]

Clearly, the active role business plays in the setting of rules and regulations via codes and standards has both advantages and disadvantages. Studies identify both "green" and "greenwashing" motives in the development and adoption of voluntary environmental commitments, and the same applies to social ones (Arts 2003; Fluck and Schmitt 1998). Research finds both examples of companies taking a sincere proactive role going beyond compliance with public regulations, as well as companies merely reacting if forced by scandals or threatening new public legal requirements (Hildebrandt 1995; Schwarz 1995). Likewise, corporate "leadership" has been linked to both the promotion and hindrance of improvements in environmental and social stewardship (de Bruijn and Tukker 2002; Garcia-Johnson 2000).

Due to the range of potential weaknesses of codes of conduct and private voluntary standards, however, critical observers are likely to continue to stress the insufficiency of these self-regulatory institutions for the solution of global environmental problems or the universal implementation of human and basic social rights. The absence of a mandatory and comprehensive nature of these rules and standards, the lack of sufficient public scrutiny, and the failure to establish a level playing field suggest to them an informalization of regulatory politics that may undermine rather than further the pursuit of broader societal objectives. From this perspective, then, the effectiveness of codes of conduct in the pursuit of societal objectives requires public involvement in their design, effective internal and external monitoring and enforcement mechanisms, and compliance with democratic norms and procedures.

Concluding Thoughts

This chapter has explored developments in the structural power of business. Traditionally, the power of business discussed in the context of structural power is passive agenda-setting power deriving from the dependence of politicians on private-sector profitability. Pointing to the shift from productive to finance capital, the increasing reliance on subcontracting and outsourcing in the organization of productions processes, and the general trend toward a liberalization of financial markets on one hand, and the increasing number of countries and subnational units competing for investments on the other, the chapter has depicted trends suggesting an increase in this passive agenda-setting power. At the same time, however, the chapter has highlighted the need for further empirical evidence of this trend.

More important, the chapter has outlined the increasing expansion of the structural power of business from this more passive agenda-setting power to active rule-setting power. Quasi-regulation still embodies more characteristics of the agenda-setting power, strengthened by the fact that politicians are forced to anticipate the reaction of 80 percent of global financial flows directed by a small number of companies, for instance, rather than just the investment decisions of one corporation. PPPs expand the structural power of business clearly into the active rule-setting arena, although the extent to which business controls this rule-setting vis-à-vis public sector and civil society participants varies widely across PPPs. Finally, self-regulation is the most visible embodiment of active rule-setting power. Here too, some self-regulatory arrangements still exist in the shadow of public authority. Increasingly, self-regulation is designed, implemented, and enforced solely by private actors, however, with no public involvement and control. The latter types of self-regulation—voluntary regulation autonomously developed and controlled by business actors—deserve particular attention.

Why should one consider these rule-setting activities by business as exercises of its power? After all, one could argue that codes of conduct, for instance, constrain rather than enable business actors; that in the end they make TNCs more accountable, socially responsible, and less autonomous. In other words, is not business an object rather than a subject of power here? Moreover, many scholars and practitioners argue that rule-setting by business fills governance gaps public actors have left due to a lack of political will or capacity; they thus highlight its benefits rather than costs.

Nevertheless, three reasons exist why the increase in rule-setting activities by business actors matters from a power-theory perspective. First, the exercise of power by business actors is relevant even if it is (only) directed at (other) business actors. The design and implementation of these rules tend to be dominated by corporate actors, while medium- and small-sized firms as well as firms from developing countries frequently are underrepresented but have to bear the costs of the rules and standards as well. Second, the distributional consequences of business-set rules also affect employees and consumers and therefore societies.

Third, and perhaps most important from the perspective of critical observers, rule-setting by business actors may prevent or undermine (more stringent and effective) rule-setting by public actors; this again highlights the link between business's rule-setting and agenda-setting powers. Indeed, some self-regulatory institutions, such as the Responsible Care Program of the Chemical Industry, have been created in response to major scandals and the associated perception that public regulation would be forthcoming. In other cases, such threats of public regulation have been more diffuse, arising from the general presence of public skepticism regarding corporations rather than a foreshadowing of concrete plans for public regulation of business (which, after all, has a history of failure in the international arena).

Developments in the structural power of business, especially in its active rule-setting power, then, are an important facet of business power in global governance. Based on these developments, legal scholars have identified corporations as an authentic source of global law that is increasingly competing with public sources (Robé 1997; Teubner 1997). In other words, the expansion of the structural power of business delineates most visibly the potential of business-made law to replace state law-making.

The increasing rule-setting activities by business carry the potential for both substantial benefits and costs. The active involvement of businesses, especially TNCs, in the design, implementation, and enforcement of environmental and social regulations and rules, for example, is a positive development insofar as public regulation of corporate conduct in this area is insufficient. Moreover, observers laud the inclusion of business's organizational, technological, and financial resources in the pursuit of public policy objectives as well as the benefits of decentralized governance mechanisms, along with improvements in the "rationality" and "efficiency" of regulation. At the same time, however, critical observers highlight the voluntary nature and frequently limited objectives of regulatory arrangements resulting from the exercise of active structural power by business and voice fears that private, voluntary, informal, and weak regulation may avoid or replace public, mandatory, formal, more stringent, or better-enforced regulation.

In the end, rules and standards developed and controlled by business do hold a significant promise to the extent that they expand in global coverage and include serious commitments to performance. If standards with sufficiently stringent regulations for environmental and social conduct were to become the de facto norm for business practice, footloose capital could no longer avoid them. In this case, international governmental regulation would indeed be unnecessary, and in fact, active structural power by business would reduce passive structural power.

One final remark regarding the structural power of business, especially its active structural power, is necessary. The expansion of the political activities and power of business in this area would not be possible to the extent that they are occurring without the increasing perception of business as a legitimate political actor. In other words, this expansion in structural power is substantially enabled by the expansion in the discursive power of business, which Chapter 6 will explore.

Notes

1. The "California effect" generally is cited as an example of the ability of governments deciding the rules for attractive markets not only to set these rules more stringently than competing markets but also to force the adaptation of other markets to their rules. Thus, the California legislature was able to adopt stringent standards for car emissions, thereby inducing car

producers to improve emissions for their entire fleet, since it would not have been cost-effective for them to run separate production lines. However, the impact of this phenomenon should not be overestimated. It applies only to sufficiently large and attractive markets, and car manufacturers, in fact, had managed to delay the new regulations in California again and again before the legislature finally adopted them.

2. As Levy and Egan (2000) point out, the fact that international organizations cannot be held directly accountable for employment, investment, or fuel or food prices has generally meant less structural leverage over these actors. Both the contestation of IGOs in terms of legitimacy as well as dependence on business resources may increase the structural dependence of IGOs on corporations, however.

3. See also Farnsworth (2004) for an excellent in-depth analysis of the increased structural power of TNCs in UK social policy.

4. Similarly, only an appropriate research design will be able to show if competition for investment does force a weakening or abandonment of standards and regulations but prevents their strengthening. Next to the work by Braithwaite and Drahos (2000) cited above, such dynamics have been revealed with respect to general regulations on investment, for instance. While demonstrating that not every country studied has adopted policies liberalizing regulations regarding capital flows, Walter's (2000) data, for example, indicate that most measures that have been carried out are in the direction of liberalization.

5. Initial answers to these pressures in some countries have involved the privatization of public assets or larger public deficits, for instance.

6. Beck (2002) argues that the ability of the state to make ethical decisions about innovation and risk has declined due to competition for capital, raising the specter of a downward spiral in ethical standards and moral dumping.

7. From an economic point of view, rating agencies merely provide a service to companies, allowing the individual company to save the costs and time of the research it would otherwise have to do itself. Having these special business actors fulfill such tasks rather than individual companies becomes a question of cost savings and efficiency improvements, then. While the economic logic of this argument is absolutely correct, this does not mean that the rating agencies do not exercise substantial power as a by-product of their activities.

8. The literature also tends to speak of PPPs in the context of cooperation between the state and NGOs, which will not be considered here.

9. Moreover, one could argue that the informal transnational policy networks on which the European Commission relies in the implementation of European regulatory activities may be called PPPs to the extent that they include the relevant market actors (Eberlein and Grande 2003).

10. Scholars argue, however, that the Global Compact should be seen less as a code of conduct than as a frame of reference, a benchmark of best practice (Kell and Ruggie 2001).

11. Representatives of Daimler Chrysler, for instance, acknowledge that

their initial efforts with respect to HIV/AIDS in communities close to the company's production sites in South Africa were in the company's economic interest, as the high death rate among its workforce meant increasing costs of recruitment and training. Recognizing such limits to individual corporate activities, corporations now have started a Global Business Coalition on HIV/AIDS.

12. The FSC is governed by three chambers with equal rights: an environmental chamber, a social chamber, and an economic chamber.

13. Examples for this reliance on self-regulation (with a larger or smaller role of the state) named by Streeck and Schmitter (1985b) include accounting standards in the UK, advertising self-regulation in industrialized countries, and quality regulation in the pharmaceutical industry.

14. Not surprisingly, self-regulation on the basis of delegation of public authority frequently occurs in areas requiring the development of technical standards in highly dynamic environments, which raises the benefits of decentralized governance (Reinicke 1998).

15. This phenomenon is also associated with the role of the WTO. ISO 14000 standards were on the horizon when in 1994 the Technical Barriers to Trade (TBT) agreement was being developed under the GATT (Clapp 2001). In consequence, the agreement considers them as legitimate and conforming with global trade rules. More stringent standards for environmental management subsequently run the risk of being challenged under WTO rules, however.

16. Scholars use different terminologies in analyses of developments in this field. Cashore (2002), for instance, speaks of nonstate market-driven governance systems while Gibson (1999) subsumes them under voluntary nonregulatory initiatives. Gibson's categorization also nicely shows that next to codes of conduct, other regulatory approaches relying on voluntary activities by business exist (especially in environmental policy) that also provide business with considerable rule-setting power (for a differentiated list of such measures, see Moffet and Bregha 1999).

17. For European countries the numbers still were substantially lower, but trends were pointing in the same direction.

18. The standard according to which firms can be certified is actually ISO 14001, while the other parts of the ISO 14000 series develop the broader framework and provide information. In the literature, scholars use both labels, ISO 14000 and ISO 14001, to refer to the respective standard.

19. The standard is administered by Social Accountability International, an NGO that also trains and certifies auditors.

20. Likewise, the pharmaceutical industry's development of a code of conduct has been described by scholars as a successful attempt to avoid public regulation of its marketing practices (Ronit and Schneider 1999).

21. Similarly, the Exxon *Valdez* oil spill led to the creation of the Coalition for Environmentally Responsible Economies (CERES) and the CERES Principles (formerly Valdez Principles), under which a number of Fortune 500 companies signed on to guidelines for corporate behavior.

22. The growing market for ethical ratings of investment opportunities

signals the increasing importance of ethical conduct and private governance for business's economic well-being as well. Ethical rating still covers only a small share of overall investment flows, and the rating practices clearly require substantial improvement, as such ratings still suffer severely from the lack of time the analyst has for each company (approximately one day) and the associated need to rely on company reports to a large extent. Yet, recent decisions of British pension funds to adjust their investment schemes to ethical criteria demonstrate the growth in volume and significance that this market is experiencing.

23. DiMaggio and Powell (1991) speak of mimetic isomorphism in this context, i.e., the modeling of organizations after other (successful) organizations as a means to reduce uncertainty and decisionmaking complexity and benefit from the legitimacy provided by the new norm. Cutler, Haufler, and Porter (1999), in turn, argue that the development of cooperation among firms in these "new" forms of political activities is similar to the development of epistemic communities.

24. Success, in this case, can mean social or environmental success, as in the solution of the respective problems. It can also mean economic success, as in the creation of comparative advantage and business value on the basis of the marketing of environmental and social conduct and information (Porter and van der Linde 1995; Nelson 1998).

25. Braun (2001) speaks of a gap in responsibility and accountability in global governance into which companies are forced and into which they are forcing themselves in this context.

26. The MacBride principles for Northern Ireland are a similar case.

27. Thus, Clapp (2001) argues that ISO 14000 standards have "tended to reinforce, rather than reduce, the gap in regulations on hazardous waste and production processes between rich and poor countries" (19).

28. Even within individual companies, studies have shown differences in the handling of social and environmental commitments. Kolk and van Tulder (2004), for instance, suggest that the majority of corporations is not following universal strategies in the adoption and implementation of ethical norms, especially in the context of child labor, but rather relativist multidomestic ones.

29. Interestingly, the Sara Lee Corporation publishes "Global Business Practices," which seemingly speak out strongly in favor of workers organizing.

30. Karliner (1994) and Clapp (2001) show, for instance, that a large share of environmental investment in developing countries and of the technology transferred in the context of international environmental treaties as well as the ISO 14000 standard has been focused on "clean-up" technology rather than "clean" technology. Likewise, the certification processes for codes of conduct has led to a notable growth in the auditing and accounting sector.

31. To combat this development in the environmental arena, for example, the United Nations Environmental Program (UNEP) has developed the

Global Reporting Initiative (GRI) together with business associations and NGOs to standardize the format for environmental reporting.

32. Altvater and Mahnkopf (2002) argue, for instance, that the increasing share of contracts relying on "alternative dispute resolution" outside of public institutions is a function of the pressure large corporations exert on their suppliers, customers, and employees rather than consensus on the superiority of such measures.

33. Likewise, the proliferation of different (private and public) standards and the need to monitor developments constantly in order to be able to comply with the necessary standards involves substantial costs but relatively little influence for developing countries (Messner and Nuscheler 2003).

6

The Power of Ideas

Discursive power is the capacity to influence policies and the political process as such through the shaping of norms and ideas. Scholars attach increasing importance to this discursive dimension of the political process. They point out that policy decisions to a growing extent are a function of discursive contests over frames of policies and attempts to assign problems to one category or another by linking them to specific fundamental norms and values (Kooiman 2002). On that basis, they highlight the importance of shifts in dominant dimensions of policy issues, symbols, and story lines, as well as the importance of the provision of "effective" evidence and compelling arguments in the public debate (Hojnacki and Kimball 1998).[1] Likewise, scholars draw attention to the construction of identities of target groups and the strategic framing of their own identities and interests by actors (West and Loomis 1999). Finally, scholars examine the ability of actors to influence the definition of fundamental norms of politics and society as such in particular with respect to recent developments (Beck 2002; Drache 2001). Such arguments and findings regarding the role of discourse clarify that the policy contest starts earlier and at a broader level than traditional analyses of interest group activity assumed. Moreover, these "political" efforts are directed at the public and thereby aim to shape policy and politics in a less direct way.

It should not come as a surprise, then, that recent studies of interest group behavior find that interest groups today are spending increasingly more time and resources on efforts to shape perceptions of problems and to define and redefine issues (Cigler and Loomis

1995). In fact, a number of authors argue that the power of resource-rich interest groups in the political process primarily originates in their ability to create and repeatedly send messages shaping the public debate (West and Loomis 1999). In other words, developments in this discursive power rather than changes in instrumental and structural power may be the crucial determinants of the increasing political influence of business.

In consequence, developments in the discursive power of business clearly deserve attention in efforts to explore the role of business in global governance. Unfortunately, discursive power is the least researched of the three dimensions of the power of business, so that there is a lack of empirical studies in this field.[2] Only recently, case studies have started to invest more time and effort in analyzing the discursive power of business in global governance. In consequence, all the present chapter can do is investigate some of the relevant developments identified by the case study literature and point out how changes in the discursive power of business shine through the general global governance literature, even if they frequently are not sufficiently explicitly discussed there. Likewise, it will examine activities with which business actors are securing and expanding their discursive power. Moreover, the chapter will identify some of the difficult questions in this field that require further conceptual and empirical clarification.

The chapter starts by delineating the privatization trend and discussing its relationship to the discursive power of business. It links this privatization trend to business's acquisition of political authority and its sources in the perceived expertise of business, as well as business's activities that may allow it to improve its position in terms of its moral legitimacy. Based on this analysis, the second section of the chapter discusses challenges and limits to this discursive power, highlighting in particular the strengths and weaknesses of business in a contest for political legitimacy. The chapter ends by outlining some implications of an expansion in the discursive power of business.

Expanding Discursive Power

Signals of Expansion

A substantial share of the global governance literature focuses on changes in the political role of business due to privatization and liberalization trends. This literature highlights the contraction of the public domain due to the expansion of the market domain: "Governments everywhere continue to privatize, deregulate, and out-source the business of government to business" (Drache 2001, 6). In other words, privatization indicates a change in the political power of business insofar as business is increasingly carrying out functions previously considered the task of public actors.

The trends toward privatization and liberalization are not new and have not come up only as a topic of research and discussion in the context of the global governance debate. Rather, scholars have pointed out a change in attitude toward the desirability of market-mechanisms as instruments of societal organization since the 1980s. Today, however, these developments have reached an amazing extent and led to the "renaissance of the market economy as the dominant socio-institutional system of resource allocation" (Dunning 1997, 1). Moreover, they imply that global corporations play an increasingly important role not just in the economic realm but in society as such.[3]

Since the 1980s the privatization trend and the underlying concerns about efficiency objectives have been reaching more and more policy areas. At the present time, a large variety of goods and services previously considered part of the public domain and sufficiently sensitive to require provision and control by government are traded in the market (Arthurs 2001). This development could be seen early on in transport and telecommunications infrastructure and energy provision. Infrastructure has increasingly come to be viewed as a private rather than a public good, and governments have privatized, liberalized, and deregulated public transport as well as telecommunications sectors (Grayson 2001; Kaul 2001).[4] Likewise, energy markets and other public services are being liberalized in pursuit of more efficiency and cost-effectiveness in provision (Arentsen and Künneke 2003; Finger 2002; Midttun 1997). In addition, privatization is also increasingly permeating the health and education sectors and even security policy.

Scholars point out that today there are hardly any areas in Western and Eastern Europe as well as other OECD countries that are not shaped by privatization and liberalization trends. Even in countries in which scholars had identified the occurrence of "symbolic" privatization and half-hearted attempts at reforms (Esser 1994), recent studies have shown that significant changes have indeed taken place (Grande and Eberlein 1999). At the same time, the provision of "public services" has become a major growth sector from the perspective of business. Presently, twenty-six of the top 200 Fortune 500 companies are public services TNCs—that is, they earn their money predominantly from the provision of public services (Finger and Allouche 2002).

The privatization of security is especially noteworthy and, not surprisingly, receives particular attention in the global governance literature (Leander 2005).[5] Security, after all, was once considered one of the best examples of a public good and the prime prerogative of the state.[6] Since the 1990s, however, there has been a noticeable trend toward privatization in the security sector, with private firms taking over police and military functions. Today a global security market exists and continues to grow (Eppler 2002).[7] Private security firms such as Executive Outcomes, Sandline International, Gurkha Security Guards, Defense Systems Limited, and Military Professional Resources Inc. provide police and military consulting, militarized plant security, and even mercenary services. In fact, commercial security forces are outnumbering public ones in many areas of the world.[8] Even in countries with a tradition of relying on the market as the dominant societal organizing mechanism, this privatization of security represents a major step.

The border between public and private has been moving throughout history as a consequence of changes in political and economic circumstances and the struggle between competing interests, of course (Ferguson 2001; Haufler 2006). Since World War II, however, nonmarket coordinating mechanisms had been intentionally employed in many industrialized countries in an attempt to simultaneously foster economic growth and social welfare (Lehmbruch and Schmitter 1982; Shonfield 1965). In consequence, the present redefinition of the public interest and domain is extremely visible and suggests a fundamental change in the nature of societal organization.

At the same time, however, the dynamics frequently are somewhat more complex than suggested in a large share of the literature highly critical of this privatization trend, due to the failure of the latter to differentiate between formal and material privatization. Thus, the privatization of public services and assets, especially in Europe, in many cases has not been associated with a full withdrawal of the state from its traditional responsibilities and regulatory ambition. Rather, while no longer providing certain public goods and services itself, the state has retained its overall responsibility for their provision even in some of the formally privatized sectors (Eberlein and Grande 2003). In consequence, privatization frequently has been accompanied by the creation of new actors and institutions for regulatory oversight and control.

However, one should also not underestimate the implications of the privatization trend. After all, the pattern of the state's retention of regulatory oversight and responsibility is uneven. Moreover, critical observers often lament the insufficiency or in-built bias of the remaining regulatory control. Experience shows that re-regulation often faces a conflict between the necessary focus on issues of market access, competition, and efficiency objectives on one side, and social and environmental regulatory objectives on the other. In consequence, even a re-regulated privatized sector may well exhibit a fundamental change in the level and pattern of provision of public goods and services.

To some extent, the privatization trend does point to a significant change in the political role of business and especially its discursive power. It highlights noteworthy developments in attitudes toward the ability of the market and market actors to provide public goods and services. Associated with this change in attitude toward the relevant actors is a shift in objectives toward an increasing emphasis on efficiency vis-à-vis notions of social justice or public access, for instance; in other words, toward objectives in the pursuit of which private actors are supposed to be superior to public actors. Thereby, privatization draws attention to the increasing occupancy of core positions in today's societal organization by business and its privileged position in dominant underlying norms. These positions grant business authority and thus provide it with the "right to speak" on political issues, thus strengthening its discursive power.

Sources of Expanding Discursive Power

The acquisition of authority by nonstate actors, that is, business actors as well as NGOs, has been one of the major topics in the global governance debate. Defining *authority* as "decision-making power over an issue area that is generally regarded as legitimate by participants," Claire Cutler, Virginia Haufler, and Tony Porter (1999, 362) argue that authority should no longer be considered as an attribute of public actors alone. In their view, private actors increasingly are acquiring authority—which is to say, a position in the political arena infusing their relationships with other actors with an "obligatory quality" (ibid.).[9] This acquisition of private authority, in turn, is of fundamental importance for a comprehensive appraisal of the role of business in global governance because it increases the discursive power of business actors.

As pointed out earlier, authority, that is, perceived legitimacy as a political actor, can derive from a variety of sources. The authority of state actors generally derives from formal institutions and positions. Nonstate actors draw legitimacy as political actors from the public's trust in their ability to deliver desired results as well as in their intentions. Scholars refer to pragmatic or moral legitimacy, for instance, in this context (Cashore 2002). Business has particularly benefited from the former source of trust, as its resources and economic expertise have come to be viewed as a valuable and necessary basis for the solving of societal problems. The increasing emphasis on efficiency, competitiveness, and growth, for instance, in the last three decades of the twentieth century has turned business into *the* politico-economic expert, the primary actor considered able to provide and guarantee the provision of the desired goods. As the previous chapters have already argued, due to business's possession of superior information and expertise, in combination with the view that complex and fast-changing technological and economic environments require decentralized governance and flexibility in reaction, business has come to be perceived as the better regulator (Reinicke 1998). Parallel to this rise of faith in business actors, trust in government has declined (Ledgerwood and Broadhurst 2000). In the popular debate, public regulation frequently has come to be seen as the main villain for an increasing range of economic and social problems, suggesting that companies react to faulty signals rather than cause problems themselves (Schwartz 1985).[10] In sum, the reemergence of a widespread trust in market actors and their capabilities in terms of the solving of broader societal and political as well as economic problems has been one of the sources of the acquisition of political authority by business and the corresponding expansion in its discursive power.

At the same time, business increasingly has had to face the issue of its moral legitimacy as well, due to its expanding societal and political roles and public debates about their appropriateness. As a consequence, one can notice a rise in business investment in activities allowing it to obtain moral legitimacy or at least to protect itself against threats to its legitimacy resulting from the perception of "moral," in particular environmental or social, misconduct. Studies have identified a dual strategy adopted by business actors in this respect: business has tried to gain access to new sources of legitimacy for itself while simultaneously challenging the presumed legitimacy of competing actors.

For the former strategy, business has been engaging in and promoting new discourses that permit it to improve its own moral identity. As Scott Bowman (1996) writes, "Beginning in the early 1970s, numerous corporations initiated a variety of advertising and public relations campaigns designed to shape public opinion. As part of this effort, an estimated $1 billion are spent annually by firms to sell an image of the responsible corporation" (149).[11] Such activities have been particularly prominent in the context of concerns about the environmental conduct of business, but they extend to other policy issues as well.[12] In the environmental arena, business has participated in, supported, and shaped discourses such as "greening of industry," "green and competitive," "ecological modernization," and "corporate environmental responsibility."[13] These perspectives have since been expanded to the legitimizing discourses of "corporate citizenship" and "corporate social responsibility" (CSR) in general, thus combining social and environmental aspects (Ougaard 2006). The US Chamber of Commerce, for instance, has established a Corporate Citizenship Center that hosts conferences and conducts information and public relations campaigns.

In addition, business increasingly has sought coalitions with NGOs as a source of legitimacy.[14] The support of civil society is especially important, since public opinion can play a determinative role in politics. Studies have shown that differences in public opinion and the preferences of the business community are typically resolved in favor of the former, in the case of highly visible policy contests (Smith 2000). It is not surprising, therefore, that scholars find that business frequently builds coalitions with civil society actors in the context of specific issues and negotiations as well as in efforts to improve its general image.[15] Whether business seriously considers and implements input from NGOs or just instrumentalizes these coalitions is controversial. Critical observers contend, in this context, that business co-opts and adapts "other voices" while continuing with business as usual (Rutherford 2003).[16] Such critical assessments receive ammunition from studies that find that business actors and coalitions sometimes even create "their own" NGOs when civil society partners for coalitions do not exist: "Where partners in civil society cannot be located, one industry tactic has been to establish organizations ostensibly representing private citizens in order to give the impression of grass roots lobbying, an activity termed 'astroturf organizing'" (Levy and Newell 2002, 96). In fact, business-created NGOs often are extremely difficult to tell apart from societal ones due to the similarities in name and self-presentation to societal NGOs aligned on the other side of a policy issue. The most prominent example of this strategy is probably the Global Climate Coalition formed to prevent international agreements on climate change policy.

The second type of strategy business actors have employed to improve their position in the "distribution" of moral legitimacy and to win discursive policy contests according to the literature is to challenge the presumed legitimacy of other actors. Thus, critical observers charge that business has fostered the diffusion of images of government and politicians as incompetent if not capricious (Smith 2000; Yergin and Stanislaw 1998). Likewise, studies show that business campaigns have challenged IGOs as undemocratic, costly, and inefficient actors. They delineate campaigns by the tobacco industry, for instance, which aimed to discredit both the UN and WHO because of their information and legislation initiatives regarding the health threats of smoking (Ong and Glantz 2000).[17] Similarly, an option in policy contests with NGOs is, of course, the discrediting of the latter on the basis of their own lack of accountability and representativeness.

Other activities by business can contribute to the gaining and securing of its moral legitimacy as well. Corporate philanthropy is an important means of business to prove itself as a valuable societal actor. In fact, scholars point out that companies frequently give more to charity than to politics (Milyo, Primo, and Groseclose 2000). Critical observers, however, suggest that corporate philanthropy is a means of high-level advertising for little overall improvement (Bennis 2001). Taking a more balanced view, Himmelstein (1997) argues that corporations struggle between "looking good" and "doing good" in this context.[18]

In sum, the discursive power of business is tied to its increasing acquisition of political authority. This political authority, to some extent, derives from perceived legitimacy of business as a politico-economic expert. Increasingly, however, it also is a function of a range of activities by business allowing it to improve and/or secure its moral legitimacy. Together these sources of authority provide business with growing discursive power.

The Power of the Discursive Power of Business?

The discursive power of actors is an important dimension of their political power. One could mischievously call discursive power a particularly "powerful" power. First, by preceding interest formation, discursive power intervenes at the earliest point and in the broadest possible way in the political process. Second, it is a diffuse, pervasive, and socially comprehensive power:

> It is not power in the sense of prevailing in overt conflict ... or possessing structural indispensability. Instead it involves a more subtle and perhaps smaller-scale kind of power than any of these—a presence at multiple levels in society and a place in multiple conversations, which allows a set of voices to be heard and a set of interests to be taken seriously almost everywhere. This is power as a discursive presence. (Himmelstein 1997, 143)

Third, discursive power relies on persuasion, the perception of legitimacy, and voluntary compliance rather than coercion and hierarchies assigning legal responsibility. Together these characteristics mean that it is difficult to recognize and assess the exercise of discursive power by actors and to hold these actors accountable (Dugger 1989; Hurd 1999).

A fourth reason why discursive power can be viewed as a particularly powerful power is that its exercise can enhance an actor's instrumental and structural power, and even his or her discursive power. Thus, the discursive power of business can enhance its instrumental power in that the framing of policy issues in efforts to "lobby the public" can serve to generate public support for business's policy objectives and thereby increase pressure on policymakers.[19] In such efforts, business has been found to employ media campaigns, for instance, to fund studies, and to conduct conferences and discussions to shape public values, attitudes, and knowledge (Berry 1997).[20] Studies have delineated numerous examples of public opinion campaigns by business with respect to specific policy issues.[21] Bowman (1996), for instance, links the defeat of the Clinton administration's health care plan to a $45 million media campaign against the initiative conducted by the Business Roundtable and the major insurance lobbies. Likewise, David Levy and Daniel Egan (2000) highlight the Global Climate Coalition's advertising and "education" campaigns, which emphasized scientific uncertainty and images of attacks on the American values of freedom and prosperity in the context of the climate change negotiations. As part of this campaign, business actors established NGOs such as the Information Council for the Environment, which ran media campaigns specifically targeted at selected sectors of society, produced newsletters such as the "World Climate Review" (mailed to all members of the Society of Environmental

Journalists), produced the video *The Greening of Planet Earth*, commissioned studies to support its interests and claims, and created expert groups with scientists (Levy and Egan 2000, 147).[22]

The framing of actors, in turn, can enhance the structural power of business, in particular its rule-setting power. The communication of business about its societal achievements as a "corporate citizen," for instance, contributes to the popular perception of a certain identity of business actors. Thereby, such communication adds legitimacy to self-regulation.

Finally, the exercise of discursive power by business can enhance this discursive power itself by shaping constitutive norms of society and societal organization. Through its discursive power, business can influence the definition of the public and the private domains, for example. Most fundamentally, it has an effect on societal notions about politics, the political, and legitimacy as such. In a discursive polity, after all, political order can no longer be taken as given but is subject to redefinition by those with discursive power (Hajer 2003). In the words of Ulrich Beck (2002), business's new authority is giving it the revolutionary privilege to change the rules of the game.

While discursive power can thus be a particularly strong source of influence, it simultaneously is the most fragile dimension of an actor's power as well as the most dangerous one if undermined. A decline or disappearance of a business's political legitimacy would not only lead to a dramatic reduction in its discursive power but cause challenges to its rule-setting and instrumental power as well. If business loses its legitimacy as a political actor in the eyes of the public, self-regulation, for instance, will become very difficult to justify. The precariousness of the situation becomes clear when one considers how vulnerable the discursive power of business actually is. In fact, the question of legitimacy in politics presently is the site of a particular struggle among business, civil society, and the state.

The legitimacy of business as a political actor can face challenges on two accounts. First, the legitimacy and discursive power of business in general and TNCs in particular are vulnerable to scandals and crashes in market power, which in turn can render NGOs powerful enemies, especially in the time of worldwide mass media. This is particularly the case now, as environmental and social NGOs have adapted their strategies due to their decreasing success in influencing governments since the late 1970s and early 1980s. Thus, the exposure in the media of "black sheep," highly visible lawsuits, and the creation of pressure and negative publicity in shareholder meetings have become important tools of NGOs in targeting the legitimacy of business. National and transnational NGOs such as Corporate Watch, Multinational Monitor, and Corporate Europe Observatory have made it their task to monitor corporate conduct and constantly threaten exposure and scandals.

In this context, business benefits from the lack of resources and difficulties and costs of gathering the necessary information by NGOs. If TNCs find it difficult to be informed about the production practices of their suppliers, NGOs face even larger hurdles. Due to these difficulties and costs, the ability of NGOs to continuously, thoroughly, and comprehensively monitor business conduct should not be overestimated. Furthermore, this ability tends to be limited to the largest and most visible business actors. Finally, information overload, the public's short attention span, and its general acclimation to scandals constrain the ability of NGOs to use publicity as a tool to challenge the legitimacy of business actors.

The legitimacy of business today is extremely precarious, moreover, because its political activities have not only increased but also become more noticed. The political power of corporations, in particular, has become contested in the context of the (anti-)globalization discourse (Gill 2002; Helleiner 2001).[23] Global surveys currently reveal high levels of suspicion of and aversion to corporations (Gallup International 1999). Likewise, numerous books in the popular literature lamenting the power of corporate actors have appeared in recent years.[24]

Discourses and activities under the CSR label can only help to soften this criticism to a limited extent. As critical observers point out, there is such a heterogeneity and vagueness in CSR activities that they frequently provide little evidence of a systematically improved environmental and social conduct of companies (Ougaard 2006). At the same time, the heterogeneity and vagueness make assessments of performance difficult, of course, and thus may well be intended to diffuse possibilities for evaluation and criticism. It remains to be seen how long such a strategy will work. In the long term, a widespread failure of private governance efforts is likely to undermine the legitimacy of business as a political actor.

These developments are related to the second potential source of challenges to the political legitimacy and discursive power of business actors: changes in dominant societal norms and ideas. As pointed out earlier, discursive power depends not only on actors' characteristics and resources but also on the social context in which they are embedded. Specifically, the new authority gained by business is, to a considerable extent, a function of the privileged position the neoliberal discourse grants it (Tooze 2000). Large business actors or groupings, such as the WEF, frequently act as prominent public advocates of corresponding norms (Hewson and Sinclair 1999). Likewise, scholars have found that the European Roundtable of Industrialists has played a pivotal role in the framing of the debate in the EU in terms of competitiveness and the constraints imposed by global markets on politics (Mazey and Richardson 1997).[25] Yet, business depends on nonbusiness actors supporting these norms as well. A change in societal values away from neoliberal norms, therefore, would bring about substantial changes in business's political role as well. Already, some scholars argue that the dominance of neoliberal ideas in global politics is drawing to a close, as they perceive social justice norms and frames to be regaining importance (Falk 1999b; Florio 2002).

At the same time, the diffuse nature of discursive power as such makes its contestation difficult, as noted earlier.[26] Moreover, even though discursive power does not necessarily and certainly does not solely depend on material power, in the age of the (private) mass media, material resources can facilitate its exercise. The prevalence and coherence of discourses depend on the constant reproduction and reconfirmation of the respective norms and ideas in speech situations, after all, and the ability to buy media space and time clearly can help in this regard.[27]

In fact, the potential breadth and density of business's communication via media space and time probably should not be underestimated.[28] Official statements in the context of election campaigns or on a given policy issue, advertorials and public relations announcements intended to create a favorable environment for the pursuit of one's goals, and even advertisements and films can all be considered part of the exercise of discursive power by business in the broadest sense. From a critical perspective, therefore, the attribution of rights of political speech to corporations becomes *the* crucial issue:

> Corporate individualism continues to be the most important ideological weapon in the arsenal of corporate power. Through modern methods of advertising—especially television commercials—the corporate persona regularly advertises, entertains, and indoctrinates a captive audience. Recent Supreme Court rulings concerning corporate political and commercial speech have provided constitutional protection for this practice. This is not to say that corporations

are necessarily irresponsible, only that they spend huge sums of money and countless hours year-round trying to convince the public that they are good citizens. The corporate individual simply has no rival in the world of appearance, in the corporate-created universe of high-tech sounds and images of glitter and fads, of mass conformity hawked as the latest style. (Bowman 1996, 182)

While the discursive power exercised through the advertising and entertainment channels is of a more general and subtle nature than the one typically assessed in political analyses, its communication of values, identities, and lifestyles does, in the end, relate to the shaping of public views on politics and societal organization. Critical accounts, in fact, associate this discursive power with particularly fundamental effects, such as the diffusion of individualistic and materialistic values of a consumer society and the commercialization and depoliticization of the global public (Linder 2003; Reljiç 2001; Schmidt 1998; Solomon 2003). From their perspective, arguments of the limited effect of advertising due to the cancellation effect of competing firms, which Richard Posner (1974) makes, capture only one facet of the effect. Thus, one can argue that the cancellation effect is likely to exist in terms of the direct commercial impact of advertising, but that the similarity in the underlying ideological frames would mean that competition does not necessarily reduce the broader societal and political effects.

In addition, critical observers charge that business interests indirectly also affect news reporting as well as the reporting on specific policy issues. They argue that the dependence of the private media on the sale of advertising time and high ratings means that news and reports to some extent are framed by commercial needs as well.[29] In support of such perspectives, critical observers point to the increasing power of marketing departments within the media. Analyses of news reporting show, in turn, how event management, the strategic selection and spotlighting of "newsworthy" events, and the reduction of political complexity in the news influence the public perception of political and societal developments (Bergsdorf 1980; Kepplinger 1998).[30] Evaluations of the potential influence of business-sponsoring of news content should not forget the extent to which the interests between sponsors and the media diverge and the associated principal-agent problems, however.

The breadth and variety of business's political communication via the mass media makes the exercise of discursive power difficult to assess. Moreover, the subtlety of messages renders simplistic evaluations of the exercise of discursive power by business and its intent highly problematic. One of the few more easily accessible indicators in this respect is the proliferation of advertorials in recent years reported by empirical studies (Brown and Waltzer 2002; Kollman 1998; Schlozman and Tierney 1983). The actual effectiveness of the media in the exercise of discursive power, however, is extremely difficult to measure again. In fact, scholars have strongly disagreed about the ability of the media to influence public opinion over time.[31] According to Hans-Bernd Brosius (1997), three broad phases of perspectives of the influence of the media on public opinion can be identified. Assumptions of a strong media influence up to about 1940 were followed by a dominant perception of a relatively limited influence of the media until about 1970. Then a third wave of research started arguing that the mass media have a clear but selective influence on public opinion.[32]

Specifically, the state of the art on political communication research tells us that the effect of media and therefore the exercise of discursive power by business via media space and time is complex. Thus, researchers have demonstrated that the mass media substantially influence the evaluation of the importance of issues: "[the press] may not be successful much of the time in telling people what to think, but it is stunningly successful in telling its readers what to think about" (Cohen 1963, 13). This research identified the media as agenda-setters and gatekeepers (McCombs and Shaw 1972; Noelle-Neumann 1973). Subsequent studies have documented a link between the perceived salience of issues and the evaluations of politicians, highlighting the broader implications of the priming ability of the media (Brettschneider 1997; Iyengar and Simon 1993). At the same time, however, empirical studies have not been able to prove that advertorials affect the public's opinion of the interest groups running them, for instance (Cooper and Nownes 2003).

More fundamentally, the ability to buy media space and time does not automatically decide policy contests. Civil society actors sometimes are able to contest the discursive power of business with messages lower in volume but that draw on the greater moral legitimacy of these actors. Actors with fewer resources can win contests over policy frames, for example, if their arguments are superior in terms of their resonance with broadly held cultural values. After all, it may take just one compelling argument or story line. Even the most extensive use of resources cannot undermine some arguments and perspectives, especially since such frames tend to be "sticky." As

Frank Baumgartner and his coauthors suggest, policy punctuations arising from the introduction of new frames to the debate actually are rare, since the various dimensions of an issue typically are well-known to all the participants and therefore "not subject to dramatic redefinitions at any given time" (Baumgartner et al. 2001, 7). Thus, economic power cannot guarantee the ability to dominate the framing of policy issues (Mucciaroni 1995).

Yet, the resources business has available to facilitate the exercise of its discursive power are not useless either. While the redefinition of policy frames may be difficult, resources do help in terms of getting new issues on the agenda and in maintaining the status quo in old issues (Baumgartner et al. 2001). Next to the ability to buy media space and time, financial resources can improve one's ability to support messages with scientific evidence by funding research on topics of interest, for example.[33] In addition, the ability to hire public relations firms as needed aids resource-rich actors in exercising discursive power, that is, in the translating of financial resources into persuasive arguments and frames.

In sum, the discursive power of business is not a secure power. The legitimacy of business in general and TNCs in particular as political actors is especially highly contested. Current trends are both "empowering" and "enfeebling" TNCs (Prakash 2002, 514). While business is "riding the wave" of dominant societal discourses granting it strong discursive power at this point, it could also find itself entrapped in a different discourse at some time in the future. The resources available to large business actors suggest that they are privileged in the shaping of discourses. Yet, they guarantee neither control over discursive frames nor impermeable protection against broader normative changes in society.

Concluding Thoughts

Business increasingly is gaining political authority, or, in other words, legitimacy as a political actor. This legitimacy derives from the present focus on competitiveness, economic growth, and efficiency in the political arenas, which make business the primary expert in the provision of the desired "goods." At the same time, business's efforts to improve its position on moral legitimacy, its traditional weak point, can be identified. Its political authority, in turn, provides business with discursive power.

This discursive power appears to be a particularly strong source of potential influence for business. After all, the diffuse and socially comprehensive nature of discursive power allows the earliest and broadest intervention possible in the political process through the definition and shaping of basic norms and ideas. Moreover, this diffuse and comprehensive nature in combination with its reliance on persuasion rather than coercion makes discursive power difficult to contest. In addition, discursive power is particularly valuable to political actors because it can be used to enhance one's instrumental, structural, and discursive power. Thus, business can employ its discursive power to enhance its instrumental power by supporting its policy stances and providing a justification for improved access to policymakers. Likewise, business can utilize its discursive power in attempts to expand its structural and discursive power by influencing the definition of the public and private spheres as well as the identities and characteristics of actors, and by thereby strengthening the perceived legitimacy of self-regulation and reaffirming the legitimacy of business as a political actor.

However, the discursive power of business is particularly vulnerable and dangerous if undermined. Scandals and market crashes can easily create fundamental threats to business's political legitimacy and therefore discursive power. Moreover, the present extent of the discursive power of business depends on the prominence of neoliberal norms and ideas. A shift in societal support for these norms would damage business's political legitimacy and discursive power as well. Importantly, a challenge of business's political legitimacy from either side would affect not only its discursive but also its structural and instrumental power.

In the competition for discursive power, business holds an advantaged position due to its preponderance of resources and structural linkages between private mass media and general business interests, as well as the overall difficulty of contesting discursive power. While financial resources clearly do not win every political contest in terms of the framing of issues, actors, and societal organization, they can provide an advantage in achieving the necessary density of messages, establishing scientific evidence, and identifying and effectively communicating persuasive arguments. Yet, these resources cannot guarantee the maintenance of business's discursive power either. Future developments with respect to changes in societal norms and the perceived legitimacy of business therefore will be particularly interesting to watch.

Notes

1. As Baumgartner et al. (2001) argue, all policy issues are potentially multidimensional. Likewise, Hajer (1997) points out that today's policy problems involve many different discourses.

2. See, however, Paul Du Gay and Michael Pryke's (2002) interesting analysis of the *Cultural Economy*.

3. As Farnsworth (2004) nicely shows, direct corporate social provision allowing business actors to determine the shape and extent of welfare receipts among both employees and other citizens also provides a form of political power.

4. Efforts to liberalize trade in services under the General Agreement of Trade in Services (GATS) demonstrate that privatization trends also occur and are being pushed at the global level. Likewise, the World Bank has been actively pursuing the privatization of public services in developing countries. Since 1994 it has argued that privatization is a superior choice to impediments provided by inefficient governments, in particular due to changes in technology, environmental pressures, management problems in the public sector, and new insights developed by economic theory (Finger and Allouche 2002).

5. The second example of privatization that is particularly remarkable and receives substantial attention in this context is the privatization of information (Roberts 2001).

6. And yet a prominent role of private security is not unprecedented, and, in fact, used to be quite normal from the seventeenth to the nineteenth centuries: "The various East-Indian companies held private police and military forces with up to 300,000 members in some regions" (Lock 2001, 209). In the context of the consolidation of the rule of law in Western democracies, however, we have gotten used to the notion of security being a public good provided by the state.

7. In accord with the working of a "market," this increase in the private security sector is being driven by both demand and supply. On the supply side, the downsizing and lack of sufficient payment of military forces in the former Eastern bloc, combined with the early retirement of military personnel in general, provides a large supply of recruits for private security companies. On the demand side, key demanders are governments, corporations, and international aid agencies. The potential effect that a supply-side driven market for private security may have on security levels is a stark indicator of the extent to which governments today are willing to rely on the private supply of goods previously considered to be in the public domain. Critical observers charge that the privatization of security has already been a major cause of a rising number of crises since the end of the Cold War. Specifically, the dynamic in which the providers of security have both an incentive and opportunity to increase the demand for security can almost be called perverse (Lock 2001). Scholars even report that in some cases the same private security company has been working for both sides in a conflict (Leander 2001).

8. In the United States, for instance, three members of private security forces exist for every police officer (Lock 2001).

9. In a similar manner, other scholars have emphasized the need to differentiate between authority and jurisdiction, arguing that "non-state actors increasingly have the capacity to get things done without the legal competence to command that they be done" (Czempiel 1992, 250).

10. Attempts of private actors to sabotage public regulation have been ignored in this context, according to critical observers (Adams and Brock 1987).

11. See also Clapp 2001, Hornung 1999, King and Lennox 2000, Moffet and Bregha 1999, and Stewart 2001 for critical assessments of the potential for a strategic use of these discourses.

12. Thus, scholars claim that individual members of the initial anticlimate coalition, such as Shell and BP, carried out complete turns in the debate in efforts to improve their image and secure their legitimacy (Rowlands 2000).

13. Academics, NGOs, and politicians have also contributed to these discourses, of course (e.g., Bansal and Roth 2000, Brink 2002, Charter and Tischner 2001, Fischer and Schot 1993, Hart 1997, Hart and Ahuja 1996, Mol 2001, Nelson 1998, Porter and van der Linde 1995, Prakash 2000, and Smart 1992).

14. In a similar manner, TNCs increasingly are contracting with regionally based firms, who tend to enjoy higher levels of popular legitimacy and political acceptability, and who receive favorable local treatments (Langhorne 2001). This development has led to a renaissance of small- to medium-sized firms simultaneous with the present wave of global mergers.

15. In a similar manner and with a similar motivation, TNCs increasingly incorporate consumer incentives in their lobbying efforts at the European Union, according to Coen (2005).

16. Beck (2002) speaks of the melting of identities of capital with the state in this respect, and one could easily add the notion of the melting of identities with civil society. Dugger (1989) refers to the respective activities as subreption, contamination, emulation, and mystification: "Subreption ties all institutions together so that noncorporate institutions are used as means to corporate ends. Contamination puts corporate role motives into noncorporate roles. Emulation allows corporate leaders to gain acceptance, even respect, in noncorporate leadership roles. And mystification covers the corporate hegemony with a protective (magic) cloak of the most-valued American symbols" (139).

17. See also the report of the Committee of Experts on Tobacco Industry Documents (2000). Likewise, critical observers claim that the military industry has sought to undermine the UN in order to derail its efforts at disarmament (Paul 2001).

18. Interestingly, scholars find that the philosophy behind corporate philanthropy resembles that behind party and campaign finance, in some sense. Thus, "pragmatists" tend to support a diversity of interests in return

for access and communication, while "conservatives" seek to shape society by limiting support to "friendly" organizations.

19. Differences between strategies in different systems exist in terms of the level at which lobbying strategies will try to generate public support. In party-dominated systems, public lobbying campaigns tend to target primarily the national level, while the local level also receives a substantial share of attention in systems in which individual campaigns play a more important role.

20. In an interesting study, Katzenstein and Tsujinaka (1995) have shown how such efforts take place transnationally. They delineate how Japanese corporations spend large amounts of resources in attempts to create a favorable image in the United States, conducting public relations campaigns, sponsoring research, and donating to charities.

21. In addition, scholars have reported that business utilizes canvassing methods, i.e., surveys testing the persuasiveness of different arguments, in order to identify the most effective arguments to influence public opinion. Scherrer (1999) argues that such canvassing methods led businesses in the United States to portray trade liberalization measures in conjunction with the right to leadership rather than on the basis of economic benefit, for instance.

22. Critical observers charged, however, that these experts all had received research funding from the fossil fuel industries (Levy and Egan 2000).

23. Smythe (2000) argues, for instance, that the failure of the MAI is indicative of business's lack of sufficient legitimacy and power. Other studies emphasize the lack of consensus on objectives among business actors as well as OECD governments, however (Lederer 1998).

24. See, for instance, Balanyá et al. 2000, Cox 2006, Greider 1997, Keat 2000, Klein 2000, Korten 1995, Kurbjuweit 2003, Kuttner 1997, Luttwak 1999, and Suter 2005.

25. Similarly, critical observers contend that business uses the "monster of global competition" to actively promote ideas of economic determinism and the desirability of a neoliberal economic order (Marazzi 1995; Schmidt 1998; Sparrow 2000).

26. Historically, efforts by relevant groups to promote certain norms and ideas have often been difficult to recognize. Examples of such groups include the Trilateral Commission, the World Economic Forum, the Rhodes/Milner group, the Bilderberg conferences, and the Mont-Pèlerin Society, and reach back to the medieval masons and lodges (Plehwe and Walpen 1998). Of the various groups, only the WEF has received substantial public attention. In contrast, relatively little information about the Trilateral Commission's activities reaches the public in spite of the considerable influence some observers attach to its policy stances and activities (van der Pijl 2001).

27. Noelle-Neumann (1996) delineates a *schweigespirale* (spiral of silence) if communicative asymmetry exists. New telecommunication technologies frequently are expected to lead to greater balance in the abilities of

actors to shape public opinion as these technologies allow communication in both directions and carry substantially lower costs. Yet, studies show that these new communication channels worldwide are used primarily for private economic interests too (Reljiç 2001).

28. Members of the mass media itself would appear to form a group of special actors in the context of discursive power. Their particular position raises some questions about their greater or lesser discursive power in global governance compared to other business actors. In particular, the relationship between the power of the media, the influence of economic interests, and the influence of politics is highly complex and controversial (Mast 1996). On one hand, one could argue that the private media, in particular the private media conglomerates that have developed over the last couple of decades, are particularly powerful and autonomous shapers of discourse. They directly decide the contents of their programs and publications. On the other hand, one could argue that they are dependent on other business actors, in particular corporations, providing the media with income and profits through advertising, which, in turn, varies with the size and nature of the expected audience. In consequence, the question of the relative discursive power of the private media vis-à-vis other business actors cannot be answered as easily as it may seem at first glance.

29. In a more direct manner, i.e., via sponsoring, business interests also affect a large share of the variety of so-called reports and lifestyle magazines. Most noteworthy, in this respect, is the pervasiveness of "reports" on branches with restrictions in advertising such as cosmetic surgery.

30. Expectations of such an influence had led to heated debates about the introduction of private media in countries with a tradition of public media to begin with (Glotz 1980).

31. Findings are even more varied with respect to the new telecommunication technologies.

32. At the same time, views that the political influence of the media generally is limited continue to exist. Carmines and Huckfeldt (1996) argue, for example, that the conflict between the information and orientational function of the media will substantially constrain their effect on public opinion formation.

33. In this context, business-created think tanks such as the American Enterprise Institute (founded in 1970), the American Council for Capital Formation (1973), and the Center for the Study of American Business (1975) play an important role.

7

Interpreting the Power of Business in Global Governance

Globalization has both benefits and costs. Clearly, its costs for some parts of the global population are sufficiently severe to require governance intervention as a means to shape globalization, specifically the distribution of costs and benefits deriving from the changing economic, political, social, and ecological dynamics in a globalizing world. Political discontent among large sections of the global population, who perceive themselves as globalization losers, can easily turn into a fundamental threat to democracy, security, and welfare, even for those (sectors of) societies that benefit from globalization. Thus, the need for governance increases rather than decreases in a globalizing world. In this context, it is important to remember that globalization is not a "natural" phenomenon. On the contrary, globalization can be shaped, and its current form is a function of regulatory choices actors have made.

Importantly, governance is being carried out by state and nonstate actors, and by suprastate and substate actors, today. The political and scientific debates on global governance, in particular, have emphasized the new political capacities acquired by nonstate and suprastate actors. There are two possible ways to evaluate this development. On one hand, one can assume that nonstate and suprastate actors cooperate with traditional political actors in harmonious global problem solving and laud their contributions to the global provision of public goods, which is what much of the early global governance literature did. On the other hand, one can critically inquire into the implications of these changes in governance institutions and the underlying shifts in political capacities. The latter perspective by necessity then will ask questions about who rules, how, and in whose interest, today. Accordingly, it will induce inquiries into the actual and potential capacities of various actors to pursue their interests in governance.[1]

Business is the actor particularly deserving of attention in this respect. A large number of popular and scientific publications in recent years have identified TNCs as the major beneficiary of globalization in terms of increasing political power. At the same time, scientific research for a long time tended to pay attention mostly to the fate of the state in a globalizing world as well as the new political opportunities and activities of civil society. Business began to come into the limelight in global governance research only in the late 1990s. Even then, case studies of self-regulation by business and PPPs have dominated the field (as is the case with the global governance literature in general), and more comprehensive and systematic efforts to understand shifts in the political capacities of business have been rare. The political power of business in a globalizing world has received considerable attention in the popular literature, of course. Here, however, authors have tended to rely on indicators of this power, such as firm size or market shares. Yet, such indicators ignore the political process and, accordingly, fail to answer questions regarding the actual and potential channels and extent of business influence in politics.

Against this background, the present analysis has aimed to contribute to a systematic understanding of the role of business in global governance. It has suggested a new cut at this role, an approach that allows an encompassing and yet differentiated assessment of the political activities by business and their meaning in terms of power. Specifically, the analysis has proposed a typology linking the forms of business's political activities in global governance to the exercise of different dimensions of its power. In addition, it has delineated specific developments in the different dimensions of this power on the basis of corresponding developments in the various activities and changes in opportunities and constraints associated with them.

The present chapter summarizes the discussion and findings and ponders their implications. The chapter is structured as follows: the first section will point out core findings and discuss their implications for the general understanding of the power business can bring to bear in global governance. Moreover, the section will discuss the interaction between the different dimensions of power as well as existing constraints on the power of business. Section two will explore the implications for policy and politics for both (traditional) regulators and business itself. Section three will discuss the implications of the analysis for future scientific research, and the final section concludes the chapter with a brief outlook.

The Role of Business in Global Governance

In order to move the understanding of business power in global governance ahead, the present analysis has linked the range of political activities pursued by business in a globalizing world to different dimensions of power. Thereby, the analysis has highlighted that assessments of the role of business in global governance must pay attention to all facets of this role, including lobbying and campaign finance activities, power deriving from the ability to move investments and jobs, rule-setting activities, and the participation in contests over the frames of policy issues, actors, and societal norms in the public debate. In other words, assessments of the role of business in global governance need to take into account material, institutional, and ideational sources of its power and explore its power in its direct and indirect, concentrated, and diffuse manifestations. The interactions between the various forms of political activity of business and the dimensions of its power are depicted in Table 7.1.

From this perspective on the role of business in global governance, then, the analysis has been able to delineate quantitative and qualitative developments in the different dimensions of the political power of business in general, and corporate actors in particular, that general claims of an expansion in this power tend to miss. Specifically, the analysis has shown the following:

- Business has increased efforts to exercise instrumental power at the national level and extended them to the transnational and supranational levels.
- The dynamics accompanying this increase in efforts are complex, including both enhancing and weakening trends.
- General trends suggest an expansion in the passive structural power of business deriving from its ability to move capital.
- The empirical evidence on the effectiveness of this structural power is somewhat ambiguous, however.
- Business has expanded its active structural power, that is, its rule-setting power.
- Business increasingly is focusing on the expansion and exercise of its discursive power.
- This discursive power is contested.

Table 7.1   The Dimensions of Business Power and Its Political Activities Revised

	Lobbying	Capital Mobility, Quasi-Regulation	PPPs, Self-Regulation	Political Communication
Instrumental Power	1. Using national, transnational, and supranational lobbying activities to influence policies	2. Lobbying for liberalization of capital controls	3. Lobbying for self-regulation and PPPs	4. Lobbying for a legal framework allowing broad and effective use of political communication
Structural Power	5. Capital mobility and competition for capital enhance the effect of lobbying	6. Implicit threat of capital mobility as agenda-setting power	7. Using active structural power to set rules	8. Using self-regulation to promote discursive capacities
Discursive Power	9. Enhancing the perceived legitimacy of lobbying activities and positions	10. Enhancing the perceived legitimacy of the competition state	11. Enhancing the perceived legitimacy of PPPs and self-regulation	12. Using political communication to shape policy- and actor-specific, as well as broader societal, norms and ideas

In terms of instrumental power, the political mobilization of business since the 1970s indicates rising efforts by business to engage in lobbying and campaign/party finance activities, as Chapter 4 has shown (see cell 1 in Table 7.1). Likewise, the incentives for political decisionmakers to provide business actors with privileged access arising from the increasing complexity of policy issues, concerns about economic growth, and rising campaign costs can be linked to improvements in the opportunities for business to exercise instrumental power. At the same time, one can notice evidence of increasing lobbying activities of business actors at supranational institutions and in international negotiations.

To what extent can a growth in the respective activities and opportunities be assumed to translate into a similar growth in influence? After all, an increase in the expenditure of resources and an improvement in access may simply mean the maintaining of the status quo if competing interests face similar developments or public actors increase their autonomy from interest groups. Yet, evidence of a decline in the relative strength of competing interests and of limits in their ability to match the financial resources of business with their "moral" legitimacy, especially at the transnational and supranational levels, exists. At the same time, public actors' increasing dependence on information and financial resources may indeed be mitigated in part by their greater ability to withdraw from interest-group influence due to the partial transfer of decisionmaking capacity to international and supranational arenas and the complex distribution of this capacity in these arenas. In consequence, it is important to differentiate between developments in the relative instrumental power of business vis-à-vis competing interests and the probability of an effective exercise of this power vis-à-vis public actors.

With respect to business's structural power, one can identify an expansion from the more passive *agenda-setting power* of mobile capital to an active *rule-setting power* of business actors, as Chapter 5 has delineated. In terms of the former (cell 6), recent trends indicate a shift from productive to finance capital, an increasing reliance on subcontracting and outsourcing in the organization of productions processes, liberalization trends in the regulation of financial markets, and substantial growth in the number of countries and subnational units competing for investment. These trends would suggest a rise in this form of the structural power of business. The empirical evidence on respective developments for a long time remained inconclusive, however, since a number of studies failed to find sufficient proof of expected changes in fiscal policy, for example. Only recently, sophisticated quantitative and qualitative studies have appeared providing clear evidence of political effects of the competition for private capital between national (and subnational) units.

With regard to business's active structural power, trends clearly delineate an increase in the quantity and shift in the quality of rule-setting by business via PPPs and self-regulation (cell 7). The degree of business control over rule-setting vis-à-vis public sector and civil society participants varies across PPPs. Likewise, some self-regulatory arrangements exist in the shadow of public authority. Yet, business actors design, implement, and enforce rules and regulations to an increasing extent. PPPs and self-regulatory arrangements most visibly demonstrate that business has become a pivotal participant in global governance and an important source of global rules and regulations.

Clearly, there are benefits to be gained from business taking on responsibility and providing resources in areas in which public regulation is insufficient and in an era in which public resources are particularly scarce. Moreover, decentralized governance mechanisms can have substantial advantages in terms of improvements in the efficiency of regulation. At the same time, however, the potential costs deriving from the voluntary nature and frequently limited objectives of self-regulatory arrangements cannot be ignored. They are particularly worrisome, should soft and voluntary regulation be used to preempt or undermine superior public regulation. It is this rise in rule-setting power, then, that most visibly signals the potential of business in general and TNCs in particular to compete with and replace public law-making, in the eyes of critical observers.

Finally, business's exercise of discursive power can be noticed in the political communication activities in which business engages.[2] The expansion in this discursive power, which Chapter 6 described, can be linked to an increasing perception of business as a legitimate political actor and its associated acquisition of political authority (cell 12). The perception of business's political legitimacy to a considerable extent derives from the present focus on competitiveness, economic growth, and efficiency in the political arenas, which make business the "expert" in the political debate. At the same time, business is trying to improve its position on moral legitimacy, for example through coalitions with (and the creation of) civil society actors.

Business employs its discursive power in efforts to lobby the public, thereby framing policy issues and actors as well as underlying societal norms and ideas. These activities show that the discursive power of business is a particularly "powerful" type of power. Its diffuse and socially comprehensive nature allows an early and broad intervention in the political process through the definition and shaping of basic ideas and norms while making its contestation difficult. At the same time, however, the legitimacy of business is not uncontested and, accordingly, its discursive power is fragile. In this context, one has to acknowledge advantages of business in the contest for legitimacy arising from its preponderance of resources, structural linkages between private mass-media and general business interests, and the difficulty of contesting such a diffuse and pervasive power. Financial resources do not win every political contest over the framing of issues, actors, and societal organization, however, even though they certainly can provide an advantage in achieving the necessary density of messages, establishing scientific evidence, and identifying and effectively selling persuasive arguments.

In sum, the analysis has highlighted both differentiated trends toward an expansion in the power of business in global governance and constraints on the effective exercise of this power. A number of interesting questions arise from these developments in activities and power that have not been dealt with sufficiently yet. What is the interaction among the three dimensions of power? Can we identify a hierarchy of power, that is, is one form of power more important and useful than the others? And what are the primary constraints on the exercise of business's overall political power?

Interaction and Hierarchy

With respect to the interaction among the three dimensions of power, arguments raised in Chapters 4, 5, and 6 have implied that the three dimensions of power can be mutually reinforcing. In other words, activities representing the exercise of one dimension of power can be aimed at strengthening another dimension of power. The discussions in those chapters have pointed to lobbying activities on behalf of deregulation or advertising activities (cells 2, 3, and 4 in Table 7.1), the ability of passive structural power to back lobbying activities (cell 5), the introduction of self-regulation in advertising or specific political communication activities in an effort to preempt more stringent public regulation (cell 8), and political communication efforts by business in pursuit of the shaping of norms relating to the legitimacy of lobbying activities and positions as well as self-regulation and PPPs (cells 9, 10, and 11), for example. In fact, the various dimensions of power clearly can be and are likely to be combined in the development and application of multidimensional strategies in the pursuit of individual political objectives by business. In other words, we should be able to locate each political strategy pursued by business actors somewhere in the triangle between the three dimensions of power.

However, if the three dimensions of power can be mutually rein-forcing, they also can be mutually constraining. The close association of the discursive power of business with the popularity of neoliberal ideas, for instance, means that lobbying efforts by business to achieve protection against free trade are difficult. More fundamentally, any major challenge to the legitimacy of business as a political actor is likely to not only affect its discursive power but also damage its structural and instrumental power.

This latter dynamic has to influence evaluations of a potential hierarchy of power as well. At first glance, discursive power may appear superior to instrumental and structural power, since it inter-venes in the political process in the broadest possible way and yet is difficult to identify due to its diffuse nature. As Steven Lukes (1974) had already asked, what is more powerful than making the opponent believe that what is in one's own interest is also in the interest of this opponent? Moreover, discursive power can be used as a fall-back option, if instrumental power and structural power fail to achieve the desired policy objectives, a dynamic that does not work in the oppo-site way. Direct lobbying is less likely to reach the intended result if corresponding attempts to influence public opinion (or establish self-regulatory arrangements or threaten the withdrawal of investment) have failed already.

At the same time, however, the discursive power of business may also be the most vulnerable point of the political power of business. As was delineated in Chapter 6, business's discursive power depends on its perceived legitimacy as a political actor in a much more direct manner than its instrumental and structural power. However, this legitimacy is still contested, and major environmental, social, or political scandals or dramatic economic downturns can destroy it. A decline or disappearance of the perception of this legitimacy, in turn, immediately would lead to challenges to business's rule-setting power and would affect its instrumental power as well. If business loses its legitimacy as a political actor in the eyes of the public, PPPs and self-regulation will become very difficult to justify. Thus, the dis-cursive power of business is also intimately tied to constraints on its overall power.

Constraints on Business's Political Power

A number of constraints on the political power of business can be identified. As pointed out earlier, today's political power of business to a substantial extent depends on business being perceived as a legitimate political actor. This legitimacy, however, is far from secure. In fact, one of the major political contests today evolves around to what extent the increasing political role of business is legitimate.

Aware of this vulnerability, business actors actively engage in efforts to secure and, if possible, increase their political legitimacy. Thus, they are attempting to improve their moral legitimacy or at least to protect themselves against threats to this legitimacy resulting from the perception of "moral," in particular environmental or social, misconduct (as Chapters 5 and 6 have delineated). Many of the strategies employed to this end, however, carry inherent risks. With respect to the promotion of CSR or self-regulation, for instance, it is unclear whether images of the "greening" or "greenwashing" of industry are winning the day. Similarly, prominent PPPs such as the Global Compact are lauded by some for business's contribution to global problem solving and criticized by others for allowing business actors to use them as superficial window-dressing measures. Should self-regulation and PPPs be widely perceived as governance failures at some point in the future, business's legitimacy as a political actor clearly would be damaged.

In addition, business's legitimacy as a political actor is vulnerable to the appearance of too extensive an influence of business on politics. The public still tends to react strongly to signals of business's abuse of its power: likewise, opinion polls reflect substantial support for critical views on business's political power. The threat of perceptions of an abuse of power, then, may be one of the most potent constraints on the political power of business.

Another major constraint on the political power of business has only been touched on in the present analysis. This constraint is business itself. After all, on many political issues, business interests will be lined up on both sides, and most policy decisions have winners and losers within the business community.[3] The deregulation and liberalization of sectors, for instance, create new opportunities for some business actors but involve costs for some of the established ones as well. Likewise, globalization has provided advantages to those business actors with global networks and mobile resources (in particular corporations and especially coordination service firms) and disadvantaged small- and middle-range firms with strong locational ties, a dependence on rather than control over (global) networks, and fewer and less mobile resources.[4] Moreover, one can argue that the competition among business actors has increased, as policy decisions have moved up to the international and supranational levels at which "national champions" now have to confront other "national champions." In sum, one major constraint on the political power of individual business actors is the political power of other business actors.

This constraint is mitigated somewhat by the existence of conditions under which business actors are able to exert strong influence on politics either individually or collectively. From a structural power perspective, business does not need to organize itself as a political actor, for the aggregation of actions of individual companies by itself has a powerful political effect, frequently in the form of uncoordinated, unintended politics as a by-product. In addition, a large number of policy decisions may be controversial among business actors, but an equally large number is small and particularistic, directly affecting only one specific company or sector. Moreover, the organizational ties between corporations as well as roundtables and informal communication and coordination activities (discussed in Chapter 4) can facilitate consensus-building on general political objectives and strategies among large business actors. More fundamentally, scholars argue that one can identify the existence of a general interest of big business in the form of a "class-wide rationality" next to the individual interests of firms in the form of a "company rationality" (Himmelstein 1997). Broad overlapping business coalitions, especially among corporate actors, often exist on general questions regarding the regulatory environment and liberal trade and investment practices in the international arena, for instance: "The apparent business pluralism coalesces at key points around a fundamental narrow orthodoxy that views business and the market status quo as essentially benign and views government interference in existing market structures and arrangements for the purpose of achieving social goals as illegitimate" (Pertschuk 1984, 498).

In spite of these constraints on competition among business actors in the political and economic realm, however, the continued existence and relevance of this competition cannot be denied. The acknowledgement of this competition, in fact, is crucial for understanding constraints on positive contributions of individual business actors to global governance. Neither society nor the environment benefit if companies pursue the best environmental and social practices possible but are forced out of the market by competition in consequence. Thus, the existence of competition serves as a reminder of the importance of institutional frameworks that create a level playing field.

Finally, a potential additional constraint on the political power of

business arises from actors whom scholars perceive to be major beneficiaries of globalization as well. These actors are consumers and
consumer associations. Scholars suggest that consumers rather than
citizens and voters are the ones that can effectively form a *gegenmacht* (counterforce) and control business actors today (Beck 2002).
Clearly, consumer boycotts have from time to time brought even corporate giants to their knees. The advantage of consumers as a control
mechanism is that consumers, just like businesses, do not need to
organize as actors. A sufficient number of individual consumption
choices will effectively exert control.

In order to be effective as a general constraint on business conduct, however, consumers need to overcome major difficulties with
respect to the provision of information, not to mention adverse incentive structures. Consumer associations may help here and have indeed
successfully pushed issues of consumer protection and information
on the political agendas. However, most consumer associations will
also point out both the uphill battle they are fighting in the political
arenas and their resource scarcity relative to the amount of consumer
products on the market, the technical complexities of consumer protection, and the socioeconomic constraints existing for political consumerism (Fuchs and Lorek 2005).

In sum, a number of constraints on business power in global governance exist, including constraints imposed by the vulnerability of
business's legitimacy as a political actor, by competition among business interests, and by consumer pressure. Together these constraints
translate into uncertainty and risk for business actors in their efforts
to conduct their economic activities as well as in their attempts to
exercise political power.

Implications for Politics

The analysis has highlighted the importance of reintroducing a discussion of power in general and the power of business in particular in
the global governance debate and thereby laid the foundation for a
"politicization" of this debate (Guzzini 2005). It has suggested that
business indeed has gained political power (i.e., increased its capability to influence political outcomes) and pointed out the various
dimensions in which this growth in power can be noticed—even if
constraints and the potential divergence between activities and influence are taken into account. Thereby, the analysis has revealed poten-

tial concerns for a democratic balance in global governance. Clearly, the participation of business in politics in general and global governance in particular does have positive aspects. Still, from traditional notions of representative democracy and legitimacy, a *disproportionate* influence of business would be problematic. What are the implications of this development for politics, then? On one hand, this development implies that regulators have increasing responsibilities for providing a regulatory framework that allows for a balance of interests in the political arena. On the other hand, business actors likely will have to accept that with growing political power, their responsibilities toward society grow as well. Let us look at each of these actors' responsibilities in turn.

A clear implication of the analysis's findings is the increasing need for regulators to ensure a balance of interests in the political arena. At this point in time, the balance clearly is far from functioning. In this context, furthermore, the present analysis has demonstrated that a regulatory framework aimed at ensuring the balance of interests in the political arena requires a sufficiently broad approach. Different forms of regulation are needed for different forms of the political power of interest groups. As the analysis has shown, the regulation of the political activities of interest groups has to continue to involve the regulation of lobbying and campaign and party finance activities, of course. But it cannot stop there. The creation of an appropriate framework for PPPs and self-regulatory arrangements needs to be considered. Such a framework would help to reduce the potential costs associated with the voluntary nature and concerns about lax standards of respective arrangements while allowing the reaping of the benefits of decentralized governance, efficient mechanisms, and business support. As noted earlier, such a framework is also important to protect business actors with high aims in PPPs or self-regulatory arrangements and therefore is being demanded by business actors themselves in some cases in which they find themselves unable to provide it.

Likewise, the regulation of political activities by business has to take into account the important role discursive governance plays in today's politics. In consequence, it needs to consider a legal framework for corporate political speech. Similarly, sponsoring activities in schools, as they exist most prominently in the United States, need to be reassessed and a sufficient share of public funding for education, research, and the provision of information to the public needs to be assured. Finally and perhaps most important, an adequate regulatory framework would have to take into account the fundamental question of the interdependent relationship between private media conglomerates and business. In fact, corresponding to the broad intervention of discursive power in the political process, it is here that regulation needs to consider the widest range of potential needs and strategies.

This is also the area, however, where regulatory intervention is likely to be the most controversial. After all, the freedom of the press is considered an elementary precondition of democracy due to the assumption that diversity in views and sources helps to inform the public and to ensure the accountability of elected representatives. Any attempts to regulate the ability of business to exercise discursive power via the mass media thus would step on extremely sensitive ground. Similarly, the definition of what constitutes political speech already is a question of interpretation. In fact, the California Supreme Court had to consider the question whether Nike's claim to have improved its social record constituted politically protected speech in a recent case.

An additional issue that needs to be taken into account when deliberating questions of the control of business's political power is public access to information. After all, public scrutiny frequently is considered an effective control on business conduct, in particular in the case of global governance. Such scrutiny, however, is only possible if the respective civil society actors have easy access to the relevant information. At this point, public scrutiny tends to concentrate on a few highly visible corporate actors from developed countries in critical sectors and/or engaged in the production of consumer goods. Second-tier corporate actors or even some of the largest corporate actors operating less immediately in the public eye receive much less attention. At the same time, the websites of organizations such as Corporate Watch and Corporate Europe Observatory reach only a small number of consumers and citizens. In other words, if the control of business conduct through civil society is supposed to function, consumers and citizens at a minimum need to be provided with much more comprehensive and easily accessible information.[5] This last point draws attention to the fact that a functioning democratic system is not just the responsibility of regulators or business, of course, but also of civil society. Given the imbalances in resources, however, civil society does require support to be able to carry out its role. Improved information flows are also in the interest of those business actors who find it difficult to communicate their own responsible behavior in the midst of information campaigns on similar issues by less sincere competitors, of course.

Finally, to the extent that a strong imbalance in resources among interests constitutes a concern for democratic legitimacy, attention should also be paid to antitrust regulation. In the past, antitrust regulation has primarily been considered to limit economic power arising from monopoly positions. As competition among business actors also works as a constraint on their political power, it becomes clear that antitrust regulation is important in this regard as well. Antitrust regulation has existed for a considerable time, of course, but it is applied with different standards in different countries. More important, antitrust agencies were already outnumbered and incapable of thoroughly evaluating cases in the 1970s (Mueller 1975), and they continue to lack resources as well as opportunities and incentives for cooperation. Today, therefore, critical observers perceive antitrust regulation to be insufficient.

The major difficulty with regulating the political activities of business in global governance, however, is that such regulation is difficult to achieve at the global level. Agreement on appropriate measures is likely to be difficult to obtain, as is consensus on the need for such regulation in different areas and contexts. Such a lack of global regulation does not necessarily have to keep national governments from introducing and enforcing respective measures. Yet, substantial differences across countries and gaps in regulation would disadvantage domestic business actors as well as offer loopholes for relevant political activities by others and thereby may undermine well-intended efforts of individual countries. This would be the case especially if dominant countries or regions in the international system, such as the United States, the European Union, or other major OECD countries, were to choose to refrain from implementing the relevant regulations.

Instead of pondering options to reaffirm democracy in the traditional sense of electoral participation and representation, one may also consider more fundamentally changing the rules of the game. Thus, scholars have started to explore alternative concepts and sources of democratic legitimacy and practice (Wendler 2002). Fritz Scharpf (1998), for instance, has outlined a shift to output-based criteria for legitimacy, specifically the effectiveness and efficiency of solutions to existing problems. Even for the determination of output-based legitimacy, however, political decisions regarding the identification of problems and appropriate political responses as well as the evaluation of the output need to be made; in other words, issues of participation still matter. In consequence, the concepts of "deliberative democracy" and "participatory governance" are receiving increasing attention in the academic and popular debate (Gbikpi and Grote 2002). Specifically, scholars advance an approach to governance that relies on consensus-seeking deliberations and balances participation and effectiveness, or in other words, incorporates input- and output-based criteria, with governments performing an "end of pipe" control (Schneider 2002; Wolf 2002).[6] Even for such models, the politics of inclusion/exclusion and the balance of interests remain an issue, however. Questions regarding the provision of sufficient opportunity structures for (effective) participation will need to be addressed.

Next to regulators, business itself also faces pertinent implications from the developments in its power. The growth in business's political power is leading to an increase in public demands for business to take on societal responsibility. The World Summit on Sustainable Development in Johannesburg, South Africa, for instance, witnessed public actors calling on private actors to take on further responsibilities regarding the promotion of sustainable production and consumption patterns. Similar developments can be observed in the area of conflict prevention. In consequence, business increasingly may find itself facing expectations regarding its political role that it may not be able or willing to fulfill. In fact, some business representatives will point out that with respect to the environmental and social governance tasks they carry out today already, they are finding themselves in a role that they did not ask for.

Taking on societal responsibility is in business's economic and political self-interest partly due to such normative expectations on the part of the public. As pointed out in Chapter 5, some contributions to rule-setting activities by business actors are just that: acknowledgments of the need to take on responsibility in the face of a lack of government will or capacity to provide necessary regulatory frameworks—whether business actors engage in these activities out of moral conviction or "just" to reduce political and economic risk and create a level playing field. At the same time, business actors need to be very careful and walk the fine line of taking on sufficient responsibility while avoiding the impression of undue influence or incompetence. A seeming failure to fulfill governance tasks will damage business's legitimacy and therefore political power, whether these tasks were taken up voluntarily or forced onto business. Likewise, perceptions of an abuse of power would greatly damage business's legitimacy as a political actor, as discussed earlier.

The threat of a backlash resulting from perceptions of private governance failure and/or abuses of power affects the different dimensions of business's political power and the associated political activities to varying degrees. First and foremost, it affects the highly vulnerable discursive power of business. It is therefore not surprising that one can notice very careful behavior by business actors in the exercise of this power. While some individual business leaders do seem to have a knack for communicative disasters, political communication by corporate actors and business associations in general tends to be highly skilled and aware of dominant public sentiments today.

Threats of private governance failure and/or abuse of power are particularly relevant for rule-setting activities. In this context, it is important to note that the front-runners in ethical business conduct have incentives to severely reduce free-riding behavior by others. If "bad apples" feed into perceptions of the Global Compact as a "blue-washing" exercise or Responsible Care as a "greenwashing" one, those who have invested sincere efforts in these initiatives are likely to find their image tarnished and their investments undermined as well. The willingness and ability of the average consumer, citizen, and even regulator to differentiate between private governance initiatives and especially actors within an initiative is limited. Failures of some initiatives to institutionalize appropriate sanctioning mechanisms, whether they are due to lacking monitoring and enforcement capacities or the short-sightedness of the actors involved, may prove quite damaging from this perspective.

Finally, lobbying and campaign-finance activities tend to be somewhat removed from the public eye. Even here, however, we can notice signals of a careful evaluation of potential costs and benefits by business actors and the intent to avoid impressions of undue political influence. Shell, for instance, announces in its Business Principles its intent to refrain completely from campaign/party finance activities: "Shell companies do not make payments to political parties, organisations or their representatives or take any part in party politics."

Thus, the growth in business's political power delineated in this analysis has implications for regulators and their role in ensuring a balance of interests in the political arena. It also has an impact on business's political conduct and the expectations business actors face regarding their societal responsibilities. While not discussed as extensively, responsibility for a functioning democratic process also rests with civil society, of course, and its willingness to get involved. Likewise, the responsibilities of IGOs come into play regarding the question of a balance of interests at the supranational level and the difficulties existing with respect to the development of global rules for business's political conduct noted earlier. Clearly, an increase in business's political power has implications for all actors in global governance.

Implications for Research

In addition to implications for politics and policy, the findings of the present analysis have consequences for further research. On the basis of the differentiated picture of the role of business in global governance developed by the analysis, pivotal questions and approaches for further academically interesting and politically relevant research on this topic can be identified. First, there is clearly more need for inquiries into the discursive power of business. Such inquiries need to pay attention, for instance, to the place of business in society in general and the relationship among the media, business, and politics in particular. Moreover, they need to examine the interaction between larger legitimizing norms and ideas and business's ability to pursue concrete political strategies and proposals. In this context, the ability of businesses to provide consumption opportunities, employment, and careers needs to be addressed as well. After all, providing positive incentives such as material and immaterial opportunities is an important contribution to the discursive power of business. Finally, the many facets of the exercise of discursive power by business actors via the media are underexplored in political science. Drawing on insights by scholars and practitioners in marketing, public relations, and communication science will allow some valuable insights in this respect. Further analytical and empirical progress in this area is urgently needed, however.

Second, the interactions between business power and state power as well as the power of civil society deserve more attention. As the analysis has shown, it is increasingly difficult to differentiate among these actors, due to formal and especially informal collaborations. In particular, the border between public and private actors is becoming increasingly blurred. From such a perspective, the question arises whether some corporate actors are more advantaged than others in the political game due to their relationship to certain state actors. Specifically, do corporations headquartered in the United States occupy the pole position in global governance? Assuming that national governments still are more inclined to support the interests of their "domestic" corporations, and given the powerful position of the US government in the international system, American corporations may have relatively more influence on global governance arrangements than their counterparts (see also Strange 1988). At the same time, with high levels of anti-American sentiments in many parts of the world, they may also face more contestation at the local or regional level.

Third, it may be worthwhile to explore policy field–specific differences in the activities and power of business in global governance. Thus, it would be interesting to tease out variations in the general trends identified in this analysis, which may result from differences in the relevant institutional structures and regulatory contexts. Some scholars find, for example, that civil society is particularly present in the area of environmental policy (Lipschutz 1999; Wapner 1995). In consequence, the opportunities for business to influence policy and politics may be more restricted in this field than in others. Findings on this question are not unambiguous, however. Even in the environmental arena, numerous studies report a strong influence of corporate actors (Dauvergne 1999; Gonzalez 2001; Newell and Levy 2006). Edgar Grande and Louis Pauly (2005) have developed a broader model on the influence of transnational actors in general on political decisionmaking. They find that this influence is particularly high in low-level politics such as environmental policy and technical standardization, medium in welfare state politics, and low in high-level politics such as foreign and security politics. Critical observers suspecting a strong influence of the military industrial complex or oil interests on US foreign policy would disagree, though (Yergin 1991).

Fourth, the question of the power of business vis-à-vis the power of investors deserves further consideration. After all, top-level management more than ever has to take into account investor interests, in particular those of institutional investors, when planning a company's economic and political activities. Interestingly, attempts by business actors to obtain regulatory protection against hostile takeovers frequently failed to win the political struggle against opposing business interests in national and international arenas. Analyses of the relationship between investors and management do exist in the business management literature. Political scientists, however, may do well to invest more time and energy in research on the role of investor power vis-à-vis business power in global governance.

Finally, the further exploration of the "big picture" of global governance, its development and patterns, hot spots and gaps, and their causes and consequences is necessary. The present analysis has contributed to the understanding of the role of business in global governance as one significant piece of the puzzle. It has suggested that inquiries into the overall pattern and patchwork of global governance need to pay particular attention to business's interests and power, especially its rule-setting and discursive powers, in the definition of global problems as well as the definition, adoption, implementation, and enforcement of governance solutions. Similarly systematic and comprehensive assessments of some of the other actors will add other pieces to the puzzle. Moreover, even with respect to business, a range of questions deserves further inquiry, as just pointed out. In sum, global governance continues to be a highly relevant and promising topic for research and debate.

Outlook

Where will the trends in the power of business depicted here lead? This question cannot be answered with any degree of certainty at the present time. On one hand, the developments described suggest a substantial potential for business to further expand its political activities and exercise of power in global governance. On the other hand, however, a few specific developments, which have taken place just in the past four to five years, highlight that the contest over the legitimacy and power of business is bigger than ever.

Responding to a number of dramatic corporate scandals, the United States has introduced legislation implying a rather substantial overhaul of accounting industry law. The changes include the expansion of the definition of corporate fraud, the introduction of tougher sentencing for white-collar criminals and the requirement that CEOs and chief financial officers certify financial reports, and the imposition of restrictions on consulting services auditors can provide to their audit clients. These reforms do not undermine business influence on politics as such, of course, since they address accountability to investors rather than citizens. But they do highlight that the scandals did hurt the image of corporations in the United States.

Other trends also suggest a potential increase in the contestation of business interests. At the global level, the failure of the WTO's Doha Round, which was to include an agreement on investment, due to a renewed cohesion among developing countries and their opposition to continued subsidies in US and EU agricultural markets is an indicator of this development. This failure is not a completely new development in this context, of course, but can be interpreted as in line with the failure of WTO meetings in Seattle, Washington, and Cancun, Mexico, and antiglobalization protests at G7/G8 meetings. In Seattle, however, the protests derived mainly from NGOs and activists, while in Cancun and thereafter solid opposition also arose from governmental actors.

Likewise, recent and ongoing cut-backs in the provision of social benefits and welfare guarantees in many OECD countries will likely cause further contestation of business interests by threatening existing societal compromises. As Daniel Fusfeld (1989) argues, "as long as the economic system provides an acceptable degree of security, growing material wealth, and opportunity for further increase for the next generation, the average American does not ask who is running things or what goals are being pursued" (172). With a decline in these benefits, however, Americans as well as the citizens of other OECD countries may return to such questions of power and interest. The growing antiglobalization movement, which contains strong elements of an anticorporate movement, is an indicator of this dynamic.

At the same time, however, one can also find indicators for an increasing individual focus on financial security and career perspectives, income, and status due to growing societal and economic pressures and insecurity and a decreasing willingness to engage in collective political activities. This dynamic, then, would suggest a likely decline in effective contestation of the political influence of business actors in general and corporate actors in particular.

Meanwhile, many business actors are investing in governance mechanisms to improve the ethical record of the global economy. We can notice efforts by a substantial number of large and small business actors to improve environmental and social conduct. To what extent these developments will serve to soften concerns about business's conduct and political power will depend on the breadth and depth of the involvement of the business community, however. Moreover, a reduction in the contestation of business and its environmental and social conduct would require the systematic and comprehensive integration of relevant efforts into everyday business practice. Together, these factors will determine, then, how convincing business's investment in ethics, sustainable development, and governance is in the eyes of the general public as well as governments.

Finally, the return of security issues to the top of the agenda is a development the consequences of which have yet to be seen for the role of business. Security issues still tend to bring realist approaches to world politics back to the fore, as can be seen in the present US administration. This, in turn, could prompt a reshifting of power back toward the state (at least in the case of "strong states"). At the same time, the security arena is one where privatization trends are particularly noteworthy. Moreover, some business actors are, of course, well-connected in the security arena and benefit from a return of security concerns to the top of the agenda. Finally, fears of terrorism influence developments in an additional and very different way as well. Security concerns in the United States are leading to a reduction in information provision. Thus, the Homeland Security Department and Patriot II legislation, for instance, are calling for chemical plant data, on which NGOs depend for the monitoring of business's environmental conduct, to no longer be public.

Clearly, numerous questions remain to be answered, both from the perspective of science and from the perspective of politics. The topic of business's political power continues to be highly relevant for scholars and practitioners, and it will be fascinating to observe future developments. After all, business's political role and legitimacy are key concerns for governments, business, and civil society alike in the common pursuit of democracy in a global market economy.

Notes

1. Such a perspective may still arrive at a positive evaluation of the involvement of nonstate actors in global governance, of course.

2. Note that "political communication" has replaced "privatization," which had been used in the respective table in Chapter 3, as a heading for the activities. As was indicated in Chapter 3, the privatizing trend is an indirect reflection in the increase of the business sector's discursive power and was used there as a placeholder until a better heading indicating relevant activities by business could be found, thus providing a parallel to the other column headings in the table. Based on the results of Chapter 6, "political communication" now is used, as it captures the range of activities in the discursive power of business, including media campaigns, as well as the influence on ideas and norms via sponsoring and coalitions with NGOs, or corporate philanthropy. Political communication, in this context, would also include communication directed at "purely commercial" objectives such as advertising. As Chapter 6 pointed out, even such communication involves political aspects as it speaks to underlying norms and values of societal organization.

3. This also implies that general business lobbies are often paralyzed

due to internal divisions and disagreements among their members (Smith 2000), which in turn highlights that the ability and increasing inclination of corporate actors to pursue their political objectives individually or in small coalitions even in corporatist systems is a very important development from the perspective of analyses of business's political power.

4. In addition, the primary beneficiaries of globalization and an associated decline in state capacity in some developing countries may be informal markets and illegal activities.

5. Here, the development and implementation of sufficiently sophisticated ratings or labels could be considered, for example.

6. In environmental policy and politics, "end of pipe" controls have a negative connotation today due to views that it would be more efficient and effective to intervene at earlier stages of the production process. Such a connotation is not intended here, however.

Acronyms
and Abbreviations

BCRA	Bipartisan Campaign Reform Act
BDI	Federation of German Industries
BIPAC	Business Industry Political Action Committee
CEO	chief executive officer
CSR	corporate social responsibility
ECOSOC	United Nations Economic and Social Council
ERT	European Roundtable of Industrialists
EU	European Union
FSC	Forest Stewardship Council
GATS	General Agreement of Trade in Services
GATT	General Agreement on Tariffs and Trade
GDP	gross domestic product
GNP	gross national product
GRI	Global Reporting Initiative
ICC	International Chamber of Commerce
IGO	international governmental organization
ILO	International Labour Organization
IMF	International Monetary Fund
IPC	Intellectual Property Committee
IPE	international political economy
IR	international relations
ISO	International Standards Organization
MAI	Multilateral Agreement on Investment
MNC	multinational corporation
MNE	multinational enterprise
NGO	nongovernmental organization

OECD	Organization for Economic Cooperation and Development
OFII	Organization for International Investment
PAC	political action committee
PPP	public-private and private-private partnerships
TABD	transatlantic business dialogue
TBT	technical barriers to trade
TNC	transnational corporation
UN	United Nations
UNCED	United Nations Conference on Environment and Development
UNCTAD	United Nations Conference on Trade and Development
UNCTC	United Nations Center on Transnational Corporations
UNDP	United Nations Development Program
UNEP	United Nations Environmental Program
UNICE	Union of Industrial and Employers' Confederations of Europe
UNICEF	United Nations Children's Fund
USCIB	US Council for International Business
WEF	World Economic Forum
WHO	World Health Organization
WTO	World Trade Organization

Bibliography

Adams, Roger. 1998. *Linking Environmental and Financial Performance: A Survey of Best Practice Techniques*. Geneva: UNCTAD.

Adams, Walter, and James Brock. 1986. "Corporate Power and Economic Sabotage." *Journal of Economic Issues* 20(4): 919–940.

———. 1987. "Corporate Size and the Bailout Factor." *Journal of Economic Issues* 21(1): 61–85.

Ake, Claude. 1999. "Globalization, Multilateralism and the Shrinking Democratic Space." In Michael Schechter (ed.), *Future Multilateralism: The Political and Social Framework*. New York: Palgrave Macmillan.

Albert, Mathias, Lothar Brock, Stephan Hessler, Ulrich Menzel, and Jürgen Neyer. 1999. *Die neue Weltwirtschaft: Entstofflichung und Entgrenzung der Ökonomie*. Frankfurt a.M.: Suhrkamp.

Alemann, Ulrich von, and Rolf Heinze (eds.). 1979. *Verbände und Staat. Vom Pluralismus zum Korporatismus: Analysen, Positionen, Dokumente*. Opladen, Germany: Westdeutscher Verlag.

Alemann, Ulrich von, and Stefan Marschall. 2002. *Parteien in der Mediendemokratie*. Opladen, Germany: Westdeutscher Verlag.

Alemann, Ulrich von, and Bernhard Weßels (eds.). 1997. *Verbände in vergleichender Perspektive. Beiträge zu einem vernachlässigten Feld*. Berlin: edition sigma.

Almond, Gabriel. 1963. "A Comparative Study of Interest Groups and the Political Process." In Harry Eckstein and David Apter (eds.), *Comparative Politics*. New York: Free Press.

Altvater, Elmar, and Birgit Mahnkopf. 1996. *Grenzen der Globalisierung*. Münster: Westfälisches Dampfboot.

———. 2002. *Globalisierung der Unsicherheit*. Münster: Westfälisches Dampfboot.

Ambrosius, Gerold. 1994. "Privatisierung in historischer Perspektive." *Staatswissenschaft und Staatspraxis* 5: 415–438.

Amoore, Louise. 2000. "International Political Economy and the 'Contested Firm.'" *New Political Economy* 5(2): 183–204.

———. 2006. "Making the Modern Multinational." In Christopher May (ed.), *Global Corporate Power*. Boulder, CO: Lynne Rienner.

Andrews, David. 1994. "Capital Mobility and State Autonomy." *International Studies Quarterly* 38(2): 193–218.

Andrews, David, C. Randall Henning, and Louis Pauly (eds.). 2002. *Governing the World's Money*. Ithaca, NY: Cornell University Press.

Ansolabehere, Stephen, John de Figueiredo, and James Snyder. 2003. "Why Is There So Little Money in US Politics?" *Journal of Economic Perspectives* 17(1): 105–130.

Apeldoorn, Bastian van. 2002. "The European Round Table of Industrialists: Still a Unique Player?" In Justin Greenwood (ed.), *The Effectiveness of EU Business Associations*. Basingstoke, UK: Palgrave.

Apollonio, D. E. 2003. "The Decision to Lobby." Paper presented at the Annual Meeting of the Midwestern Political Science Association, Chicago, April 3–6.

Archibugi, Daniele, David Held, and Martin Kohler (eds.). 1998. *Re-Imagining Political Community: Studies in Cosmopolitan Democracy*. Cambridge, UK: Polity.

Arendt, Hannah. 1970. *On Violence*. London: Penguin.

Arentsen, Maarten, and Rolf Künneke (eds.). 2003. *National Reforms in European Gas*. Amsterdam: Elsevier.

Arnim, Hans Herbert von. 1984. "Verfassungsrechtliche Aspekte der Neuregelung der Parteienfinanzierung." *Aus Politik und Zeitgeschichte* 8: 9–25.

———. 2000. "Strukturprobleme des Parteienstaates." *ApuZ* 16: 30–38.

Arthurs, Harry. 2001. "The Re-constitution of the Public Domain." In Daniel Drache (ed.), *The Market or the Public Domain?* London: Routledge.

Arts, Bas. 2003. "Non-State Actors in Global Governance: Three Faces of Power." Reprint, Max-Planck-Projektgruppe, Recht der Gemeinschaftsgüter, 003/4. Bonn: Max-Planck-Gesellschaft.

Austen-Smith, David. 1995. "Campaign Contributions and Access." *American Political Science Review* 89(3): 566–581.

Bachrach, Peter, and Morten Baratz. 1962. "Two Faces of Power." *American Political Science Review* 56: 947–952.

———. 1970. *Power and Poverty: Theory and Practice*. New York: Oxford University Press.

Backhaus-Maul, Holger, and Thomas Olk. 1994. "Von Subsidiarität zu 'outcontracting': Zum Wandel der Beziehungen von Staat und Wohlfahrtsverbänden in der Sozialpolitik." In Wolfgang Streeck (ed.), *Staat und Verbände*. Opladen, Germany: Westdeutscher Verlag.

Bagdikian, Ben. 1997. *The Media Monopoly*. Boston: Beacon.

Balanyá, Belén, Ann Doherty, Olivier Hoedeman, Adam Ma'anit, and Erik Wesselius. 2000. *Europe Inc.: Regional and Global Restructuring and the Rise of Corporate Power*. London: Pluto.

Baldwin, David. 2002. "Power and International Relations." In Walter Carlsnaes, Thomas Risse, and Beth Simmons (eds.), *Handbook of International Relations*. London: Sage.

Baldwin, Robert, and Christopher Magee. 2000. *Congressional Trade Votes: From NAFTA Approval to Fast-Track Defeat*. Washington, DC: Institute for International Economics.

Bansal, Pratima, and Kendall Roth. 2000. "Why Companies Go Green: A Model of Ecological Responsiveness." *Academy of Management Journal* 434: 717–736.

Barber, Benjamin. 1995. *Jihad Versus McWorld*. New York: Random House.

Barnet, Richard, and Ronald Müller. 1974. *Global Reach: The Power of the Multinational Corporations*. New York: Simon and Schuster.

Bassiry, Reza. 1980. *Power vs. Profit: Multinational Corporation–Nation State Interaction*. New York: Arno.

Bauer, Raymond, Ithiel de Sola Pool, and Lewis Anthony Dexter. 1963. *American Business and Public Policy*. New York: Atherton.

Bauman, Zygmunt. 1998. *Globalization: The Human Consequences*. New York: Columbia University Press.

Baumgartner, Frank, and Beth Leech. 1998. *Basic Interests: The Importance of Groups in Politics and Political Science*. Princeton, NJ: Princeton University Press.

Baumgartner, Frank, Jeffrey Berry, Marie Hojnacki, David Kimball, and Beth Leech. 2001. "Issue Advocacy and Interest Group Influence." Paper presented at the meeting of the ECPR, Canterbury, September 6–10.

Beck, Ulrich. 1997. *Was ist Globalisierung?* Frankfurt a.M.: Suhrkamp.

———. 1999. *World Risk Society*. Cambridge, UK: Polity.

———. 2002. *Macht und Gegenmacht im globalen Zeitalter. Neue weltpolitische Ökonomie*. Frankfurt a.M.: Suhrkamp.

Becker, Gary. 1983. "A Theory of Competition Among Pressure Groups for Political Influence." *Quarterly Journal of Economics* 143(3): 371–400.

Beisheim, Marianne, Sabine Dreher, Gregor Walter, Bernhard Zangl, and Michael Zürn. 1999. *Im Zeitalter der Globalisierung? Thesen und Daten zur gesellschaftlichen und politischen Denationalisierung*. Baden-Baden: Nomos.

Bennedsen, Morten, and Sven Feldman. 2000. "Lobbying Legislatures." *Discussion Paper 2000/04*, Center for Industrial Economics, University of Copenhagen.

Bennis, Phyllis. 2001. "Mit der Wirtschaft aus der Finanzkrise?" In Tanja Brühl, Tobias Debiel, Brigitte Hamm, Hartwig Hummel, and Jens Martens (eds.), *Die Privatisierung der Weltpolitik*. Bonn: Dietz.

Bergsdorf, Wolfgang. 1980. *Die vierte Gewalt. Einführung in die politische Massenkommunikation*. Mainz: v. Hase and Köhler.

Bernauer, Thomas. 2000. *Staaten im Weltmarkt. Zur Handlungsfähigkeit von Staaten trotz wirtschaftlicher Globalisierung*. Opladen, Germany: Leske and Budrich.

Berry, Jeffrey. 1977. *Lobbying for the People: The Political Behavior of Interest Groups.* Princeton, NJ: Princeton University Press.
————. 1997. *The Interest Group Society.* New York: Longman.
Beyme, Klaus von. 1995. "Steuerung und Selbstregelung. Zur Entwicklung zweier Paradigmen." *Journal für Sozialforschung* 35: 197–217.
Beyme, Klaus von. 2000. *Parteien im Wandel. Von den Volksparteien zu den professionalisierten Wählerparteien.* Opladen, Germany: Westdeutscher Verlag.
Bhagwati, Jagdish. 1993. "The Case for Free Trade." *Scientific American* 269(5): 42–49.
Bieling, Hans-Jürgen, and Jochen Steinhilber. 2000. "Finanzmarktintegration und Corporate Governance in der Europäischen Union." *Zeitschrift für Internationale Beziehungen* 9(1): 39–74.
Biersteker, Thomas. 2000. "Globalization as a Mode of Thinking in Major Institutional Actors." In Ngaire Woods (ed.), *The Political Economy of Globalization.* New York: St. Martin's.
Björklund, Jan, and Sten Berglund. 2001. "From the *Canterbury Tales* to the Canterbury Conference. The Governance Perspective: What It Has Been, What It Is and What It Could Be." Paper presented at the meeting of the ECPR, Canterbury, September 6–10.
Boddewyn, Jean, and Thomas Brewer. 1994. "International-Business Political Behavior: New Theoretical Directions." *Academy of Management Review* 19(1): 119–143.
Bonefeld, Werner, and John Holloway (eds.). 1995. *Global Capital, National State, and the Politics of Money.* New York: St. Martin's.
Börzel, Tanja, and Thomas Risse. 2005. "Public-Private Partnerships." In Edgar Grande and Louis Pauly (eds.), *Complex Sovereignty.* New York: Columbia University Press.
Bowman, Scott. 1996. *The Modern Corporation and American Political Thought: Law, Power, and Ideology.* University Park: Pennsylvania State University Press.
Boylan, Richard. 2002. "Private Bills: A Theoretical and Empirical Study of Lobbying." *Public Choice* 111(1, 2): 19–47.
Boyer, Robert, and Daniel Drache (eds.). 1996. *States Against Markets: The Limits of Globalization.* London: Routledge.
Braithwaite, John, and Peter Drahos. 2000. *Global Business Regulation.* Cambridge, UK: Cambridge University Press.
Brand, Ulrich, Achim Brunnengräber, Lutz Schrader, Christian Stock, and Peter Wahl. 2000. *Global Governance. Alternative zur neoliberalen Globalisierung?* Münster: Westfälisches Dampfboot.
Braun, Rainer. 2001. "Konzerne als Beschützer der Menschenrechte?" In Tanja Brühl, Tobias Debiel, Brigitte Hamm, Hartwig Hummel, and Jens Martens (eds.), *Die Privatisierung der Weltpolitik.* Bonn: Dietz.
Brettschneider, Frank. 1997. "Massenmedien und politische Kommunikation." In Oscar Gabriel and Everhard Holtmann (eds.), *Handbuch Politisches System der Bundesrepublik Deutschland.* München: Oldenbourg.

Brink, Patrick ten (ed.). 2002. *Voluntary Environmental Agreements.* Sheffield, UK: Greenleaf.

Brinkmann, Johanna. 2004. "Corporate Citizenship und Public-Private Partnerships. Zum Potential der Kooperation zwischen Privatwirtschaft, Entwicklungszusammenarbeit und Zivilgesellschaft." WZGE-Studien 04-1. Wittenberg: Wittenberg Center for Global Ethics.

Broadhurst, Arlene. 2000. "Corporations and the Ethics of Social Responsibility." *Business Ethics* 9(2): 86–98.

Brock, Lothar. 1993. "Im Umbruch der Weltpolitik." *Leviathan* 21(2): 163–173.

———. 1998. "Die Grenzen der Demokratie." *Politisches Vierteljahresschrift* 39: 271–292.

Brosius, Hans-Bernd. 1997. *Modelle und Ansätze der Medienwirkungsforschung—Überblick über ein dynamisches Forschungsfeld.* Bonn: ZV Zeitungsverlags-Service.

Brown, Clyde, and Herbert Waltzer. 2002. "Buying National Ink: Advertorials by Organized Interests in *TIME* Magazine, 1985–2000." Paper presented at the Annual Meeting of the Southern Political Science Association, Savannah, GA, November 6–9.

Brühl, Tanja, Tobias Debiel, Brigitte Hamm, Hartwig Hummel, and Jens Martens (eds.). 2001. *Die Privatisierung der Weltpolitik.* Bonn: Dietz.

Brühl, Tanja, Heidi Feldt, Brigitte Hamm, Hartwig Hummel, and Jens Martens (eds.). 2004. *Unternehmen in der Weltpolitik. Politiknetzwerke, Unternehmensregeln und die Zukunft des Multilateralismus.* Bonn: Dietz.

Bruijn, Theo de, and Arnold Tukker (eds.). 2002. *Partnership and Leadership: Building Alliances for a Sustainable Future.* Dordrecht: Kluwer Academic.

Brunnengräber, Achim, Ansgar Klein, and Heike Walk (eds.). 2001. *NGOs als Legitimationsressource.* Opladen, Germany: Leske and Budrich.

Buchanan, James, Robert Tollison, and Gordon Tullock (eds.). 1980. *Toward a Theory of the Rent-Seeking Society.* College Station: Texas A&M Press.

Buchanan, James, and Gordon Tullock. 1962. *The Calculus of Consent.* Ann Arbor: University of Michigan Press.

Buckley, Peter, and Mark Casson. 1976. *The Future of the Multinational Enterprise.* London: Macmillan.

Bührer, Werner. 2000. "Auf dem Weg zum Korporatismus?" In Werner Bührer and Edgar Grande (eds.), *Unternehmerverbände und Staat in Deutschland.* Baden-Baden: Nomos.

Bührer, Werner, and Edgar Grande (eds). 2000. *Unternehmerverbände und Staat in Deutschland.* Baden-Baden: Nomos.

Burtless, Gary, Robert Lawrence, Robert Litan, and Robert Shapiro. 1998. *Globaphobia: Confronting Fears About Open Trade.* Washington, DC: Brookings Institution.

Busch, Andreas. 2003. *Staat und Globalisierung.* Opladen, Germany: VS Verlag.

Busch, Andreas, and Thomas Plümper (eds.). 1999. *Nationaler Staat und internationale Wirtschaft. Anmerkungen zum Thema Globalisierung.* Baden-Baden: Nomos.

Cadot, Olivier, and Douglas Webber. 2002. "Banana Splits: Policy Process, Particularistic Interests, Political Capture, and Money in Transatlantic Trade Politics." *Business and Politics* 4(1): 5–39.

Cairncross, Frances. 1997. *The Death of Distance: How the Communications Revolution Will Change Our Lives.* London: Orion Business.

Campbell, John, J. Rogers Hollingsworth, and Leon Lindberg (eds.). 1991. *The Governance of the American Economy.* Cambridge, UK: Cambridge University Press.

Caporaso, James, and Stephan Haggard. 1989. "Power in the International Political Economy." In Richard Stoll and Michael Ward (eds.), *Power in World Politics.* Boulder, CO: Lynne Rienner.

Carmines, Edward, and Robert Huckfeldt. 1996. "Political Behavior: An Overview." In Robert Goodin and Hans-Dieter Klingemann (eds.), *A New Handbook of Political Science.* New York: Oxford University Press.

Cashore, Benjamin. 2002. "Legitimacy and the Privatization of Environmental Governance." *Governance* 8(4): 503–529.

Caves, Richard. 1982. *The Multinational Enterprise and Economic Analysis.* Cambridge, UK: Cambridge University Press.

Cerny, Philip. 1990. *The Changing Architecture of Politics: Structure, Agency, and the Future of the State.* London: Sage.

———. 1997. "Paradoxes of the Competition State: The Dynamics of Political Globalization." *Government and Opposition* 32(2): 251–274.

———. 1998. "Globalisierung und die neue Logik kollektiven Handelns." In Ulrich Beck (ed.), *Politik der Globalisierung.* Frankfurt a.M.: Suhrkamp.

Charter, Martin, and Ursula Tischner. 2001. *Sustainable Solutions.* Sheffield, UK: Greenleaf.

Chatterjee, Pratap, and Matthias Finger. 1994. *The Earth Brokers.* London: Routledge.

Choate, Pat. 1990. *Agents of Influence: How Japan's Lobbyists in the United States Manipulate America's Political and Economic System.* New York: Knopf.

Cigler, Alan, and Burdett Loomis (eds.). 1995. *Interest Group Politics.* Washington, DC: Congressional Quarterly Press.

Clapp, Jennifer. 1998. "The Privatization of Global Environmental Governance: ISO 14000 and the Developing World." *Global Governance* 4: 295–316.

———. 2001. *Toxic Exports. The Transfer of Hazardous Wastes from Rich to Poor Countries.* Ithaca, NY: Cornell University Press.

Clark, Cal, and Steven Chan. 1995. "MNCs and Developmentalism: Domestic Structure as an Explanation for East Asian Dynamism." In Thomas Risse-Kappen (ed.), *Bringing Transnational Relations Back In.* Cambridge, UK: Cambridge University Press.

Clawson, Dan, Alan Neustadt, and Denise Scott. 1992. *Money Talks*. New York: Basic.

Clayton, Richard, and Jonas Pontusson. 1998. "Welfare-State Retrenchment Revisited: Entitlement Cuts, Public Sector Restructuring, and Inegalitarian Trends in Advance Capitalist Societies." *World Politics* 51: 67–98.

Clegg, Stewart. 1989. *Frameworks of Power*. London: Sage.

Clemens, Elisabeth. 1997. *The People's Lobby*. Chicago: University of Chicago Press.

Coase, Ronald. 1988. *The Firm, the Market, and the Law*. Chicago: University of Chicago Press.

Coen, David. 2005. "Environmental and Business Lobbying Alliances in Europe." In David Levy and Peter Newell (eds.), *The Business of Environmental Governance*. Cambridge, MA: MIT Press.

Cohen, Benjamin. 1998. *The Geography of Money*. Ithaca, NY: Cornell University Press.

Cohen, Bernhard. 1963. *The Press and Foreign Policy*. Princeton, NJ: Princeton University Press.

Cohen, Joshua, and Joel Rogers. 1994. "Solidarity, Democracy, Association." In Wolfgang Streeck (ed.), *Staat und Verbände*. Opladen, Germany: Westdeutscher Verlag.

Commission of the European Communities. 2001. *European Governance: A White Paper*. Brussels: Commission of the European Communities.

Commission on Global Governance. 1995. *Our Global Neighborhood*. Oxford: Oxford University Press.

Committee of Experts on Tobacco Industry Documents. 2000. *Tobacco Company Strategies to Undermine Tobacco Control Activities at the World Health Organization*. Geneva: WHO.

Common Cause. 2000. *The Half Billion Dollar Shakedown*. Washington, DC: Common Cause.

———. 2001. *A Reporter's Guide to Money in Politics: Campaign 2000*. Washington, DC: Common Cause.

———. 2002a. *Political Meltdown*. Washington, DC: Common Cause.

———. 2002b. *The 2002 Election: A Quick Guide*. Washington, DC: Common Cause.

———. 2003. "National Parties Raise Record $470.6 Million in Soft Money During the 2001–2002 Election Cycle Before New Law Takes Effect." http://www.commoncause.org/publications/jan03/010603_2.htm, last visited October 14, 2003.

Cooper, Christopher, and Anthony Nownes. 2003. "Money Well Spent? An Experimental Investigation of the Effects of Advertorials on Citizen Opinion." Working Paper, Department of Political Science, Western Carolina University.

Cox, John. 2006. *The Suborning of American Democracy: The Triumph of Corporate Power*. Frederick, MD: PublishAmerica.

Cox, Robert. 1987. *Production, Power, and World Order*. New York: Columbia University Press.

———— (ed.). 1996. *Business and the State in International Relations*. Boulder, CO: Westview.

Cutler, Claire. 1999. "Locating 'Authority' in the Global Political Economy." *International Studies Quarterly* 42: 59–81.

————. 2000. "Theorizing the 'No-Man's-Land' Between Politics and Economics." In Thomas Lawton, James Rosenau, and Amy Verdun (eds.), *Strange Power*. Aldershot, UK: Ashgate.

————. 2006. "Transnational Business Civilization, Corporations, and the Privatization of Global Governance." In Christopher May (ed.), *Global Corporate Power*. Boulder, CO: Lynne Rienner.

Cutler, Claire, Virginia Haufler, and Tony Porter (eds.). 1999. *Private Authority and International Affairs*. Albany: State University of New York Press.

Czada, Roland. 1994. "Konjunkturen des Korporatismus: Zur Geschichte eines Paradigmenwechsels in der Verbändeforschung." In Wolfgang Streeck (ed.), *Staat und Verbände*. Opladen, Germany: Westdeutscher Verlag.

Czempiel, Ernst-Otto. 1992. "Governance and Democratization." In James Rosenau and Ernst-Otto Czempiel (eds.), *Governance Without Government*. Cambridge, UK: Cambridge University Press.

Dahl, Robert. 1957. "The Concept of Power." *Behavioral Science* 2: 201–215.

————. 1961. *Who Governs?* New Haven, CT: Yale University Press.

————. 1994. *The New American (Dis)Order*. Berkeley, CA: Institute of Governmental Studies.

Dahrendorf, Ralf. 1970. "Zu einer Theorie des sozialen Konflikts." In Wolfgang Zapf (ed.), *Theorien des sozialen Wandels*. Köln: Kiepenheuer and Witsch.

Dalton, Russell, and Martin Wattenberg (eds.). 2000. *Parties Without Partisans: Political Change in Advanced Industrial Democracies*. Oxford: Oxford University Press.

Daly, Herman, and Robert Goodland. 1994. "An Ecological-Economic Assessment of Deregulation of International Commerce Under GATT." *Ecological Economics* 9: 73–92.

Damania, Richard. 2001. "When the Weak Win: The Role of Investment in Environmental Lobbying." *Journal of Environmental Economics and Management* 42(1): 1–22.

Danley, John. 1994. *The Role of the Modern Corporation in a Free Society*. London: University of Notre Dame Press.

Dauvergne, Peter. 1999. "Corporate Power in the Forests of the Solomon Islands." *Pacific Affairs* 71(4): 524–546.

Desai, Meghnad, and Paul Redfern. 1995. *Global Governance: Ethics and Economics of the World Order*. London: Pinter.

Detomasi, David. 2002. "International Institutions and the Case for Corporate Governance." *Global Governance* 8: 421–442.

Deutsch, Karl. 1970. *Politische Kybernetik*. Freiburg: Rombach.

Deutscher Bundestag (ed.). 2002. *Schlussbericht der Enquete-Kommission*

Globalisierung der Weltwirtschaft. Opladen, Germany: Leske and Budrich.

Diez, Thomas. 2005. "Constructing the Self and Changing Others: Reconsidering 'Normative Power Europe.'" *Millennium: Journal of International Studies* 33(3): 613–636.

DiMaggio, Paul, and Walter Powell (eds.). 1991. *The New Institutionalism in Organizational Analysis*. Chicago: University of Chicago Press.

Doremus, Paul, William Keller, Louis Pauly, and Simon Reich. 1998. *The Myth of the Global Corporation*. Princeton, NJ: Princeton University Press.

Drache, Daniel (ed). 2001. *The Market or the Public Domain?* London: Routledge.

Drucker, Peter. 1943. *The Future of Industrial Man—A Conservative Approach*. London: Heinemann.

Du Gay, Paul, and Michael Pryke (eds.). 2002. *Cultural Economy: Cultural Analysis and Commercial Life*. London: Sage.

Dugger, William. 1989. "Power: An Institutional Framework of Analysis." In Marc Tool and Warren Samuels (eds.), *The Economy As a System of Power*. New Brunswick, NJ: Transaction.

Dunning, John. 1988. *Explaining International Production*. London: Unwin Hyman.

——— (ed.). 1997. *Governments, Globalization, and International Business*. New York: Oxford University Press.

Eberlein, Burkard, and Edgar Grande. 2003. "Die Europäische Union als Regulierungsstaat: Transnationale Regulierungsnetzwerke und die Informalisierung des Regierens in Europa." In Markus Jachtenfuchs and Beate Kohler-Koch (eds.), *Europäische Integration*. Opladen, Germany: Leske and Budrich.

Eckersley, Robyn (ed.). 1995. *Markets, the State, and the Environment*. Houndmills, UK: Macmillan.

Eden, Lorraine, and Evan Potter (eds.). 1993. *Multinationals in the Global Political Economy*. New York: St. Martin's.

Eichengreen, Barry. 1996. *Globalizing Capital: A History of the International Monetary System*. Princeton, NJ: Princeton University Press.

Eising, Rainer. 2001. "Interessenvermittlung in der Europäischen Union." In Werner Reutter and Peter Rütters (eds.), *Verbände und Verbandssysteme in Westeuropa*. Opladen, Germany: Leske and Budrich.

Eising, Rainer, and Beate Kohler-Koch. 1994. "Inflation und Zerfaserung: Trends der Interessenvermittlung in der Europäischen Gemeinschaft." In Wolfgang Streeck (ed.), *Staat und Verbände*. Opladen, Germany: Westdeutscher Verlag.

Eppler, Erhard. 2002. *Vom Gewaltmonopol zum Gewaltmarkt*. Frankfurt a.M.: Suhrkamp.

Epstein, Edwin. 1969. *The Corporation in American Politics*. Englewood Cliffs, NJ: Prentice Hall.

———. 1984. "PACs and the Modern Political Process." In Betty Bock, Harvey Goldschmid, Ira Millstein, and F. M. Scherer (eds.), *The Impact of the Modern Corporation*. New York: Columbia University Press.

Esser, Josef. 1994. "Germany: Symbolic Privatizations in a Social Market Economy." In Vincent Wright (ed.), *Privatization in Western Europe*. London: Pinter.

Fach, Wolfgang, and Georg Simonis. 2000. "Die Welt des Autors." *Zeitschrift für Internationale Beziehungen* 7(2): 385–398.

Fagre, Nathan, and Louis Wells. 1982. "Bargaining Power of Multinationals and Host Governments." *Journal of International Business Studies* 13: 9–23.

Falk, Richard. 1999a. "Liberalism at the Global Level." In Errol Harris and James Yunker (eds.), *Toward Genuine Global Governance*. Westport, CT: Praeger.

———. 1999b. *Predatory Globalization: A Critique*. Cambridge, UK: Polity.

Falter, Jürgen, and Andrea Römmele. 2002. "Professionalisierung bundesdeutscher Wahlkämpfe, oder: wie amerikanisch kann es werden?" In Thomas Berg (ed.), *Aspekte des modernen Wahlkampfes—(Ein) Blick hinter die Kulissen*. Opladen, Germany: Leske and Budrich.

Farnsworth, Kevin. 2004. *Corporate Power and Social Policy in a Global Economy*. Bristol, UK: Policy.

Ferguson, Niall. 2001. *Politik ohne Macht. Das fatale Vertrauen in die Wirtschaft*. Stuttgart: Deutsche Verlags-Anstalt.

Ferguson, Yale, and Richard Mansbach. 1999. "Global Politics at the Turn of the Millennium: Changing Bases of 'Us' and 'Them.'" *International Studies Review* 1: 77–107.

Figueiredo, John de, and Emerson Tiller. 2001. "The Structure and Conduct of Corporate Lobbying: How Firms Lobby the Federal Communications Commission." *Journal of Economics and Management Strategy* 10(1): 91–122.

Finger, Matthias. 2002. "The Instrumentalization of the State by Transnational Corporations: The Case of Public Services." In Doris Fuchs and Friedrich Kratochwil (eds.), *Transformative Change and Global Order*. Münster: LIT Verlag.

Finger, Matthias, and Jeremy Allouche. 2002. *Water Privatisation: Transnational Corporations and the Re-regulation of the Water Industry*. London: Spon.

Finkelstein, Lawrence. 1995. "What Is Global Governance?" *Global Governance* 1(3): 367–372.

Finnemore, Martha, and Kathryn Sikkink. 1998. "International Norm Dynamics and Political Change." *International Organization* 52(4): 887–917.

Fischer, Klemens. 1997. *Lobbying und Kommunikation in der Europäischen Union*. Berlin: Berlin Verlag.

Fischer, Kurt, and Johan Schot (eds). 1993. *Environmental Strategies for Industry*. Washington, DC: Island.

Fleisher, Craig. 1993. "Assessing the Effectiveness of Corporate Public Affairs Efforts." In Barry Mitnick (ed.), *Corporate Political Agency.* Newbury Park, CA: Sage.

Florio, Massimo. 2002. "Economists, Privatization in Russia, and the Waning of the 'Washington Consensus.'" *Review of International Political Economy* 9(2): 374–415.

Fluck, Jürgen, and Thomas Schmitt. 1998. "Selbstverpflichtungen und Umweltvereinbarungen—rechtlich gangbarer Königsweg deutscher und europäischer Umweltpolitik?" *Verwaltungs-Archiv* 220–263.

Foucault, Michel. 1980. *Power/Knowledge: Selected Interviews and Other Writings, 1972–1977.* Brighton, UK: Harvester.

Fowler, Henry, and Francis Fowler. 1964. *The Concise Oxford Dictionary of Current English,* 5th ed. Oxford: Oxford University Press.

Frank, Andre Gunder. 1978. *Dependent Accumulation and Underdevelopment.* London: Macmillan.

Frieden, Jeffry, and David Lake. 1991. *International Political Economy: Perspectives on Global Power and Wealth.* New York: St. Martin's.

Friends of the Earth International. 1999. *Food and Food Security: The Implications of Current Trade Negotiations.* Seattle Series of Briefings, No. 4. http://www.foei.org/publications/gmo/ food.html, last visited October 14, 2003.

Fuchs, Doris. 2005. "Commanding Heights? The Strength and Fragility of Business Power in Global Politics." *Millennium* 33(3): 771–803.

———. 2006a. "Global Governance—An International Relations Perspective on Tropical Forests." In Sharon Spray and Michael Moran (eds.), *Understanding Environmental Challenges—A Multi-Disciplinary Approach: Tropical Deforestation.* New York: Rowman and Littlefield.

———. 2006b. "Transnational Corporations and Global Governance: The Effectiveness of Private Governance." In Stefan Schirm (ed.), *Globalization. State of the Art of Research and Perspectives.* London: Routledge.

Fuchs, Doris, and Daniel Mazmanian. 1998. "The Greening of Industry: Needs of the Field." *Business Strategy and the Environment* 7(4): 193–203.

Fuchs, Doris, and Sylvia Lorek. 2005. "Sustainable Consumption Governance: A History of Promises and Failures." *Journal on Consumer Policy* 28(3): 261–288.

Fusfeld, Daniel. 1989. "The Rise of the Corporate State in America." In Marc Tool and Warren Samuels (eds.), *The Economy As a System of Power.* New Brunswick, NJ: Transaction.

Gabriel, Oscar W., Oskar Niedermayer, and Richard Stöss (eds.). 2002. *Parteiendemokratie in Deutschland.* Opladen, Germany: Westdeutscher Verlag.

Galbraith, John Kenneth. 1958. *The Affluent Society.* Boston: Houghton Mifflin.

———. 1984. *The Anatomy of Power.* Boston: Houghton Mifflin.

Gallup International. 1999. *Gallup International Millennium Survey*. London: Gallup International Association.

Galtung, Johan. 1969. "Violence, Peace, and Peace Research." *Journal of Peace Research* 6: 167–191.

———. 1971. "A Structural Theory of Imperialism." *Journal of Peace Research* 2: 81–117.

Gamble, Cliff. 1994. *Timewalkers: The Prehistory of Global Colonization*. Cambridge, MA: Harvard University Press.

Ganghof, Steffen. 2005. "The Politics of (Income) Tax Structure." Paper presented at the Yale Conference on Distributive Politics, New Haven, CT, April 29–30.

Garcia-Johnson, Ronie. 2000. *Exporting Environmentalism: US Multinational Chemical Corporations in Brazil and Mexico*. Cambridge, MA: MIT Press.

Garrett, Geoffrey. 1998. "Global Markets and National Politics: Collision Course or Virtuous Circle?" *International Organization* 52(4): 787–824.

———. 2000. "Globalization and National Autonomy." In Ngaire Woods (ed.), *The Political Economy of Globalization*. New York: St. Martin's.

Garrod, Brian. 1998. "Are Economic Globalization and Sustainable Development Compatible? Business Strategy and the Role of the Multinational Enterprise." *International Journal for Sustainable Development* 1(1): 43–62.

Gbikpi, Bernard, and Jürgen Grote. 2002. "From Democratic Government to Participatory Governance." In Jürgen Grote and Bernard Gbikpi (eds.), *Participatory Governance: Political and Societal Implications*. Opladen, Germany: Leske and Budrich.

Geiger, Stephanie. 2003. "Governance und Reformen des Regierens in der EU." Paper presented at the Meeting of the Nachwuchsgruppe of the DGfP, Tutzing, Germany, November 21.

Gellhorn, Ernest. 1984. "Commentators' Remarks." In Betty Bock, Harvey Goldschmid, Ira Millstein, and F. M. Scherer (eds.), *The Impact of the Modern Corporation*. New York: Columbia University Press.

Genschel, Philipp. 1995. "Dynamische Verflechtung in der internationalen Standardisierung." In Renate Mayntz and Fritz Scharpf (eds.), *Gesellschaftliche Selbstregelung und politische Steuerung*. Frankfurt a.M.: Campus.

———. 2000. "Der Wohlfahrtsstaat im Steuerwettbewerb." *Zeitschrift für Internationale Beziehungen* 7(2): 267–296.

Getz, Kathleen. 1997. "Research in Corporate Political Action." *Business and Society* 36(1): 32–73.

Gibson, Robert (ed.). 1999. *Voluntary Initiatives*. Peterborough, UK: Broadview.

Gill, Stephen. 1995. "Globalisation, Market Civilisation, and Disciplinary Neoliberalism." *Millennium: Journal of International Studies* 24(3): 399–423.

————. 2002. *Power and Resistance in the New World Order.* New York: Palgrave Macmillan.

Gill, Stephen, and David Law. 1993. "Global Hegemony and the Structural Power of Capital." In Stephen Gill (ed.), *Gramsci, Historical Materialism, and International Relations.* Cambridge, UK: Cambridge University Press.

Gilpin, Robert. 1975. *US Power and the Multinational Corporation.* New York: Basic.

————. 2000. "The Retreat of the State?" In Thomas Lawton, James Rosenau, and Amy Verdun (eds.), *Strange Power.* Aldershot, UK: Ashgate.

Glossop, Ronald. 1999. "Global Governance Requires Global Government." In Errol Harris and James Yunker (eds.), *Toward Genuine Global Governance.* Westport, CT: Praeger.

Glotz, Peter. 1980. "Die Privatisierung der Öffentlichkeit. Gesellschaftliche Wirkungen der Telekommunikation." *Leviathan* 8(2): 233–244.

Goidel, Robert, Donald Gross, and Todd Shields. 1999. *Money Matters: Consequences of Campaign Finance Reform in US House Elections.* Lanham, MD: Rowman and Littlefield.

Goldman, Ian, and Ronen Palan. 2006. "Corporate Citizenship." In Christopher May (ed.), *Global Corporate Power.* Boulder, CO: Lynne Rienner.

Gonzalez, George. 2001. *Corporate Power and the Environment: The Political Economy of US Environmental Policy.* Lanham, MD: Rowman and Littlefield.

Gramsci, Antonio. 1971. *Selections from the Prison Notebooks.* New York: International.

————. 1995. *Further Selections from the Prison Notebooks.* Minneapolis: University of Minnesota Press.

Grande, Edgar. 2000. "Verbände und Verbändeforschung in Deutschland." In Werner Bührer and Edgar Grande (eds.), *Unternehmerverbände und Staat in Deutschland.* Baden-Baden: Nomos.

————. 2001a. "Die neue Unregierbarkeit: Globalisierung und die Grenzen des Regierens jenseits des Nationalstaats." *Working Paper No. 2/2001,* Technische Universität München, Lehrstuhl für Politische Wissenschaft.

————. 2001b. "Institutions and Interests: Interest Groups in the European System of Multi-Level Governance." *Working Paper No. 1/2001,* Technische Universität München, Lehrstuhl für Politische Wissenschaft.

————. 2003. "How the Architecture of the EU Political System Influences Business Associations." In Justin Greenwood (ed.), *The Challenge of Change in EU Business Associations.* Houndmills, UK: Palgrave Macmillan.

Grande, Edgar, and Burkard Eberlein. 1999. "Der Aufstieg des Regulierungsstaates im Infrastrukturbereich." *Working Paper No. 2/1999,* Technische Universität München, Lehrstuhl für Politische Wissenschaft.

Grande, Edgar, and Louis Pauly. 2005. "Conclusions: Trends Toward Transnational Governance?" In Edgar Grande and Louis Pauly (eds.), *Complex Sovereignty: Reconstituting Political Authority in the Twenty-first Century*. Toronto: University of Toronto Press.

Gray, John. 1998. *False Dawn: The Delusions of Global Capitalism*. London: Granta.

Grayson, Kyle. 2001. "Human Security in the Global Era." In Daniel Drache (ed.), *The Market or the Public Domain?* London: Routledge.

Greenwood, Justin. 1998. "Regulating Lobbying in the European Union." *Parliamentary Affairs* 51(4): 587–599.

———. 2002. *Inside the EU Business Associations*. Basingstoke, UK: Palgrave.

Greenwood, Justin, and Clive Thomas. 1998. "Introduction: Regulating Lobbying in the Western World." *Parliamentary Affairs* 51(4): 487–499.

Greider, William. 1997. *One World, Ready or Not: The Manic Logic of Global Capitalism*. London: Allen Lane.

Grenzke, Janet. 1989. "PACs in the Congressional Supermarket: The Currency Is Complex." *American Journal of Political Science* 33: 1–24.

Griffin, David. 1999. "Global Government: Objections Considered." In Errol Harris and James Yunker (eds.), *Toward Genuine Global Governance*. Westport, CT: Praeger.

Grossman, Gene, and Elhanan Helpman. 1994. "Protection for Sale." *American Economic Review* 84(4): 833–850.

———. 2001. *Special Interest Politics*. Cambridge, MA: MIT Press.

Grote, Jürgen, and Bernard Gbikpi (eds.). 2002. *Participatory Governance: Political and Societal Implications*. Opladen, Germany: Leske and Budrich.

Guzzini, Stefano. 2005. "The Concept of Power: A Constructivist Analysis." *Millennium: Journal of International Studies* 33(3): 495–522.

Haas, Peter. 1990. *Saving the Mediterranean*. New York: Columbia University Press.

Habermas, Jürgen. 1981. *Theorie des kommunikativen Handelns*, Vols. 1 and 2. Frankfurt a.M.: Suhrkamp.

Hajer, Maarten. 1997. *The Politics of Environmental Discourse: Ecological Modernization and the Policy Process*. Oxford: Clarendon.

———. 2003. "A Decade of Discourse Analysis of Environmental Politics: Achievements, Challenges, Perspectives." Paper presented at the 2003 Hamburg Conference "Does Discourse Matter?" Hamburg, Germany, July 11–13.

Hall, Peter, and David Soskice (eds.). 2001. *Varieties of Capitalism: The Institutional Foundations of Comparative Advantage*. Oxford: Oxford University Press.

Hall, Richard. 1990. "Buying Time: Moneyed Interests and the Mobilization of Bias in Congressional Committees." *American Political Science Review* 84: 797–820.

Hall, Richard, and Alan Deardorff. 2006. "Lobbying as Legislative Subsidy." *American Political Science Review* 100(1): 69–84.

Hansen, Wendy, and Neil Mitchell. 2001. "Globalization or National Capitalism: Large Firms, National Strategies, and Political Activities." *Business and Politics* 3(1): 5–19.

Harris, Errol. 1999. "Global Governance or World Government?" In Errol Harris and James Yunker (eds.), *Toward Genuine Global Governance.* Westport, CT: Praeger.

Harris, Errol, and James Yunker (eds.). 1999. *Toward Genuine Global Governance.* Westport, CT: Praeger.

Harrison, Kathryn. 1999. "Talking with the Donkey: Cooperative Approaches to Environmental Regulation." *Journal of Industrial Ecology* 2(3): 51–72.

Harrod, Jeff. 2006. "The Century of the Corporation." In Christopher May (ed.), *Global Corporate Power.* Boulder, CO: Lynne Rienner.

Hart, Stuart. 1997. "Beyond Greening: Strategies for a Sustainable World." *Harvard Business Review* 75: 66–76.

Hart, Stuart, and Gautam Ahuja. 1996. "Does It Pay to Be Green?" *Business Strategy and the Environment* 5: 30–37.

Hasenclever, Andreas, Peter Maier, and Volker Rittberger. 1997. *Theories of International Regimes.* Cambridge, UK: Cambridge University Press.

Haufler, Virginia. 1993. "Crossing the Boundary Between Public and Private." In Volker Rittberger (ed.), *Regime Theory and International Relations.* Oxford: Clarendon.

———. 2001. *A Public Role for the Private Sector.* Washington, DC: Carnegie Endowment for International Peace.

———. 2006. "Global Governance and the Private Sector." In Christopher May (ed.), *Global Corporate Power.* Boulder, CO: Lynne Rienner.

Hayward, Clarissa Rile. 2000. *De-Facing Power.* Cambridge, UK: Cambridge University Press.

Heclo, Hugh. 1978. "Issue Networks and the Executive Establishment." In Anthony King (ed.), *The New American Political System.* Washington, DC: American Enterprise Institute.

Heinelt, Hubert. 2002a. "Civic Perspectives on a Democratic Transformation of the EU." In Jürgen Grote and Bernard Gbikpi (eds.), *Participatory Governance: Political and Societal Implications.* Opladen, Germany: Leske and Budrich.

Heinelt, Hubert. 2002b. "Preface." In Jürgen Grote and Bernard Gbikpi (eds.), *Participatory Governance: Political and Societal Implications.* Opladen, Germany: Leske and Budrich.

Heinz, John, Edward Laumann, Robert Nelson, and Robert Salisbury. 1993. *The Hollow Core: Private Interests in National Policymaking.* Cambridge, MA: Harvard University Press.

Heinze, Rolf, and Josef Schmid. 1994. "Mesokorporatistische Strategien im Vergleich: Industrieller Strukturwandel und die Kontingenz politischer Steuerung in drei Bundesländern." In Wolfgang Streeck (ed.), *Staat und Verbände.* Opladen, Germany: Westdeutscher Verlag.

Held, David. 1995. *Democracy and the Global Order: From the Modern State to Cosmopolitan Governance.* Cambridge, MA: Polity.

Held, David, Anthony McGrew, David Goldblatt, and Jonathan Perraton. 1999. *Global Transformations: Politics, Economics, and Culture*. Cambridge, UK: Polity.

Helleiner, Gerald. 2001. "Markets, Politics, and Globalization: Can the Global Economy Be Civilized?" *Global Governance* 7(3): 243–263.

Hennis, Wilhelm, Peter Graf Kielmansegg, and Ulrich Matz (eds.). 1977. *Regierbarkeit. Studien zu ihrer Problematisierung*. Bd. 1. Stuttgart: Klett-Cotta.

———. 1979. *Regierbarkeit. Studien zu ihrer Problematisierung*. Bd. 2. Stuttgart: Klett-Cotta.

Héritier, Adrienne (ed.). 2002. *Common Goods: Reinventing European and International Governance*. Lanham, MD: Rowman and Littlefield.

Herrnson, Paul, Ronald Shaiko, and Clyde Wilcox. 1998. *The Interest Group Connection: Electioneering, Lobbying, and Policymaking in Washington*. Chatham, MD: Chatham House.

Hewson, Martin, and Timothy Sinclair (eds.). 1999. *Approaches to Global Governance Theory*. Albany: State University of New York Press.

Higgott, Richard, Geoffrey Underhill, and Andreas Bieler (eds.). 2000. *Non-State Actors and Authority in the Global System*. London: Routledge.

Hildebrandt, Eckart. 1995. "Ökologisch erweiterte Arbeitspolitik als Gegenstand der Umweltsoziologie." In Wilfried Müller (ed.), *Der ökologische Umbau der Industrie*. Münster: LIT Verlag.

Hillebrand, Ernst. 2001. "Schlüsselstellung im globalisierten Kapitalismus." In Tanja Brühl, Tobias Debiel, Brigitte Hamm, Hartwig Hummel, and Jens Martens (eds.), *Die Privatisierung der Weltpolitik*. Bonn: Dietz.

Hillman, Amy, and Michael Hitt. 1999. "Corporate Political Strategy Formulation." *Academy of Management Review* 24(4): 825–842.

Himmelstein, Jerome. 1997. *Looking Good and Doing Good. Corporate Philanthropy and Corporate Power*. Bloomington: Indiana University Press.

Hirsch, Joachim. 1998. *Vom Sicherheitsstaat zum nationalen Wettbewerbsstaat*. Berlin: ID-Verlag.

Hirscher, Gerhard, and Roland Sturm (eds.). 2001. *Die Strategie "des Dritten Weges."* München: Olzog.

Hirsch-Kreinsen, Hartmut. 1998. "Shareholder Value: Unternehmensstrategien und neue Strukturen des Kapitalmarkts." In Hartmut Hirsch-Kreinsen and Harald Wolf (eds.), *Arbeit, Gesellschaft, Kritik*. Berlin: edition sigma.

Hirsch-Kreinsen, Hartmut, and Harald Wolf (eds.). 1998. *Arbeit, Gesellschaft, Kritik*. Berlin: edition sigma.

Hirst, Paul. 1997. *From Statism to Pluralism: Democracy, Civil Society, and Global Politics*. Bristol, UK: UCL-Press.

Hirst, Paul, and Grahame Thompson. 1996. *Globalization in Question: The International Economy and the Possibilities of Governance*. Oxford: Polity.

Hodess, Robin. 2001. "The Contested Competence of NGOs and Business in Public Life." In Daniel Drache (ed.), *The Market or the Public Domain?* London: Routledge.

Hoffman, Andrew. 1999. "Institutional Evolution and Change: Environmentalism and the US Chemical Industry." *Academy of Management Journal* 42(4): 351–371.

Hoffmann-Riem, Wolfgang. 2000. "Politiker in den Fesseln der Mediengesellschaft." *Politische Vierteljahresschrift* 41(1): 107–127.

Hojnacki, Marie, and David Kimball. 1998. "Organizational Interests and the Decision of Whom to Lobby in Congress." *American Political Science Review* 92(4): 775–790.

Holliday, Charles, Stephan Schmidheiny, and Philip Watts. 2002. *Walking the Talk. The Business Case for Sustainable Development.* Sheffield, UK: Greenleaf.

Hollingsworth, J. Rogers, and Robert Boyer (eds.). 1997. *Contemporary Capitalism: The Embeddedness of Institutions.* Cambridge, UK: Cambridge University Press.

Holzinger, Katharina, Christoph Knill, and Dirk Lehmkuhl. 2003. *Politische Steuerung im Wandel: Der Einfluß von Ideen und Problemstrukturen.* Opladen, Germany: Leske and Budrich.

Holzscheiter, Anna. 2003. *"Power of Discourse* and *Power in Discourse*— Investigating the Symbolic Capital of Non-State Actors." Paper presented at the 2003 Hamburg Conference "Does Discourse Matter?" Hamburg, Germany, July 11–13.

———. 2005. "Discourse as Capability: Non-State Actors' Capital in Global Governance." *Millennium* 33(3): 723–746.

Hornung, Robert. 1999. "The VCR Doesn't Work." In Robert Gibson (ed.), *Voluntary Initiatives.* Peterborough, Ontario: Broadview.

Huffschmid, Jörg. 1999. *Politische Ökonomie der Finanzmärkte.* Hamburg: VSA-Verlag.

Hula, Kevin. 2000. *Lobbying Together: Interest Group Coalitions in Legislative Politics.* Washington, DC: Georgetown University Press.

Hummel, Hartwig. 2001. "Die Privatisierung der Weltpolitik." In Tanja Brühl, Tobias Debiel, Brigitte Hamm, Hartwig Hummel, and Jens Martens (eds.), *Die Privatisierung der Weltpolitik.* Bonn: Dietz.

Hurd, Ian. 1999. "Legitimacy and Authority in International Politics." *International Organization* 53(2): 379–408.

Huws, Ursula. 2006. "The Restructuring of Global Value Chains and the Creation of a Cybertariat." In Christopher May (ed.), *Global Corporate Power.* Boulder, CO: Lynne Rienner.

Hymer, Stephen. 1976. *The International Operations of National Firms: A Study of Direct Foreign Investment.* Cambridge, MA: MIT Press.

Isely, Philip. 1999. "A Critique of 'Our Global Neighborhood.'" In Errol Harris and James Yunker (eds.), *Toward Genuine Global Governance.* Westport, CT: Praeger.

Iyengar, Shanto, and Adam Simon. 1993. "News Coverage of the Gulf Crisis and Public Opinion: A Study of Agenda-Setting, Priming, and Framing." *Communication Research* 20(3): 365–383.

Jacobsen, Gary. 1980. *Money in Congressional Elections*. New Haven, CT: Yale University Press.

Jacoby, Neil. 1974. "Myths of the Corporate Economy." In John Weston (ed.), *Large Corporations in a Changing Society*. New York: New York University Press.

Jessop, Bob. 1997. "Die Zukunft des Nationalstaates—Erosion oder Reorganisation? Grundsätzliche Überlegungen zu Westeuropa." In Steffen Becker, Thomas Sablowski, and Wilhelm Schumm (eds.), *Jenseits der Nationalökonomie? Weltwirtschaft und Nationalstaat zwischen Globalisierung und Regionalisierung*. Hamburg: Argument-Verlag.

Johansen, Robert. 1999. "Enforcement Without Military Combat: Toward an International Civilian Police." In Raimo Väyrynen (ed.), *Globalization and Global Governance*. Lanham, MD: Rowman and Littlefield.

Jordan, Grant, and Andrew McLaughlin. 1993. "The Rationality of Lobbying in Europe." In Sonia Mazey and Jeremy Richardson (eds.), *Lobbying in the European Community*. Oxford: Oxford University Press.

Kaiser, Karl. 1998. "Globalisierung als Problem der Demokratie." *Internationale Politik* 4: 3–11.

Kaiser, Wolfram. 2000. "Europäisch und pragmatisch: Der Bundesverband der Deutschen Industrie, Europa, und die Welt, 1949–1973." In Werner Bührer and Edgar Grande (eds.), *Unternehmerverbände und Staat in Deutschland*. Baden-Baden: Nomos.

Karliner, Joshua. 1994. "The Environmental Industry." *Ecologist* 24(2): 60–61.

———. 1997. *The Corporate Planet: Ecology and Politics in the Age of Globalization*. San Francisco: Sierra Club.

Katzenstein, Peter, and Yukata Tsujinaka. 1995. "'Bullying,' 'Buying,' and 'Binding': US-Japanese Transnational Relations and Domestic Structures." In Thomas Risse-Kappen (ed.), *Bringing Transnational Relations Back In*. Cambridge, UK: Cambridge University Press.

Kaul, Inge. 2001. "Public Goods." In Daniel Drache (ed.), *The Market or the Public Domain?* London: Routledge.

Keat, Russel. 2000. *Cultural Goods and the Limits of the Market: Beyond Commercial Modelling*. New York: St. Martin's.

Keck, Margaret, and Kathryn Sikkink. 1998. *Activist Beyond Borders: Advocacy Networks in International Politics*. Ithaca, NY: Cornell University Press.

Kell, George, and John Ruggie. 2001. "Global Markets and Social Legitimacy: The Case of the 'Global Compact.'" In Daniel Drache (ed), *The Market or the Public Domain?* London: Routledge.

Keohane, Robert, and Joseph Nye. 1977. *Power and Interdependence*. Boston: Longman.

Kepplinger, Hans Mathias. 1998. *Die Demontage der Politik in der Informationsgesellschaft*. Freiburg: Alber.

————. 1999. "Die Mediatisierung der Politik." In Jürgen Wilke (ed.), *Massenmedien und Zeitgeschichte*. Konstanz: Uvk Medien.

Kerwer, Dieter. 2002. "Standardizing as Governance." In Adrienne Héritier (ed.), *Common Goods: Reinventing European and International Governance*. Lanham, MD: Rowman and Littlefield.

Kindleberger, Charles, and David Audretsch (eds.). 1983. *The Multinational Corporation in the 1980s*. Cambridge, MA: MIT Press.

King, Andrew, and Michael Lenox. 2000. "Industry Self-Regulation Without Sanctions." *Academy of Management Journal* 43(4): 698–716.

Kingdon, John. 1984. *Agendas, Alternatives, and Public Policies*. New York: Harper Collins.

Klein, Naomi. 2000. *No Logo: Taking Aim at the Brand Bullies*. Toronto: Knopf.

Knill, Christoph. 2001. "Private Governance Across Multiple Arenas: European Interest Associations as Interface Actors." *Journal of European Public Policy* 8(2): 227–246.

Knill, Christoph, and Dirk Lehmkuhl. 2002. "Private Actors and the State." *Governance* 5(1): 41–63.

Kobrin, Stephen. 1997. "The Architecture of Globalization." In John Dunning (ed.), *Governments, Globalization, and International Business*. New York: Oxford University Press.

Kohler-Koch, Beate. 1996. "Die Gestaltungsmacht organisierter Interessen." In Markus Jachtenfuchs and Beate Kohler-Koch (eds.), *Europäische Integration*. Opladen, Germany: Leske and Budrich.

————. 2000. "Unternehmensverbände im Spannungsfeld von Europäisierung und Globalisierung." In Werner Bührer and Edgar Grande (eds.), *Unternehmerverbände und Staat in Deutschland*. Baden-Baden: Nomos.

Kohler-Koch, Beate, and Rainer Eising (eds.). 1999. *The Transformation of Governance in the European Union*. London: Routledge.

Kolk, Ans, and Rob van Tulder. 2002. "The Effectiveness of Self-Regulation: Corporate Codes of Conduct and Child Labour." *European Management Journal* 20(3): 260–271.

————. 2004. "Ethics in International Business: Multinational Approaches to Child Labor." *Journal of World Business* 39(1): 49–60.

Koller, Peter. 1991. "Facetten der Macht." *Analyse und Kritik* 13: 107–133.

Kollman, Kelly. 2003. "Marketing Good Behavior: The Role of Transnational Business Networks in Promoting Standards of Corporate Responsibility." Paper presented at the ISA/IEESA conference, Budapest, Hungary, June 26–28.

Kollman, Ken. 1998. *Outside Lobbying: Public Opinion and Interest Group Strategies*. Princeton, NJ: Princeton University Press.

König, Klaus, and Angelika Benz (eds.). 1997. *Privatisierung und staatliche Regulierung*. Baden-Baden: Nomos.

Kooiman, Jan. 2002. "Governance: A Socio-Political Perspective." In Jürgen

Grote and Bernard Gbikpi (eds.), *Participatory Governance: Political and Societal Implications*. Opladen, Germany: Leske and Budrich.

Korten, David. 1995. *When Corporations Rule the World*. West Hartford: Kumarian Press.

Krasner, Stephen. 1999. *Sovereignty*. Princeton, NJ: Princeton University Press.

Kratochwil, Friedrich. 1995. "Was wissen wir über den Wandel der Beziehungen zwischen Staat, Markt und Gesellschaft?" *Welttrends* 7: 114–132.

———. 1997. "International Organization: Globalization and the Disappearance of Publics." In Jin-Young Chung (ed.), *Global Governance*. Seoul: Sejong.

———. 2002. "Globalization: What It Is and What It Is Not." In Doris Fuchs and Friedrich Kratochwil (eds.), *Transformative Change and Global Order*. Münster: LIT Verlag.

Kratochwil, Friedrich, and John Ruggie. 1986. "The State of the Art on the Art of the State." *International Organization* 40: 753–776.

Kropp, Sabine. 2000. "Parteienfinanzierung im 'Parteienstaat.'" *Gegenwartskunde* 49(4): 435–446.

Kroszner, Randall, and Thomas Stratmann. 2000. "Congressional Committees as a Reputation-building Mechanism." *Business and Politics* 2(1): 35–52.

Krumbein, Wolfgang. 1998. "Wider die Veränderungsdramatik. " In Regine Stötzel (ed.), *Ungleichheit als Projekt*. Marburg: BdWi-Verlag.

Krut, Riva, and Harris Gleckman. 1998. *ISO 14001: A Missed Opportunity for Sustainable Global Industrial Development*. London: Earthscan.

Kurbjuweit, Dirk. 2003. *Unser effizientes Leben. Die Diktatur der Ökonomie und ihre Folgen*. Reinbek: Rowohlt.

Kuttner, Robert. 1997. *Everything for Sale*. New York: Alfred Knopf.

Lagerlof, Johan. 1997. "Lobbying, Information, and Private and Social Welfare." *European Journal of Political Economy* 13(3): 615–637.

Landfried, Christine. 2001. "Politik in einer entgrenzten Welt." In Christine Landfried (ed.), *Politik in einer entgrenzten Welt*. Köln: Verlag Wissenschaft und Politik.

Lange, Stefan, and Dietmar Braun. 2000. *Politische Steuerung zwischen System und Akteur*. Opladen, Germany: Leske and Budrich.

Langhorne, Richard. 2001. *The Coming of Globalization: Its Evolution and Contemporary Consequences*. Houndsmills, UK: Palgrave.

Lasswell, Harold, and Abraham Kaplan. 1950. *Power and Society: A Framework for Political Inquiry*. New Haven, CT: Yale University Press.

Latham, Robert. 1999. "Politics in a Floating World." In Martin Hewson and Timothy Sinclair (eds.), *Approaches to Global Governance Theory*. Albany: State University of New York Press.

Lawton, Thomas, and Kevin Michaels. 2000. "The Evolving Global Production Structure." In Thomas Lawton, James Rosenau, and Amy Verdun (eds.), *Strange Power*. Aldershot, UK: Ashgate.

Lawton, Thomas, James Rosenau, and Amy Verdun (eds.). 2000. *Strange Power*. Aldershot, UK: Ashgate.

Leander, Anna. 2001. "Global Ungovernance: Mercenaries, States, and the Control over Violence." Working Paper, Copenhagen Peace Research Institute.

———. 2005. "The Power to Construct International Security: On the Significance of Private Military Companies." *Millennium: Journal of International Studies* 33(3): 803–826.

Lederer, Markus. 1998. "Probleme der Organisation von internationalen Märkten am Beispiel des 'Multilateralen Abkommens über Investitionen.'" Magisterarbeit, Ludwig-Maximilians-Universität München.

———. 2002. "Changing Frameworks: 'Exchange' and 'Regulation' instead of 'Markets' and 'States.'" In Doris Fuchs and Friedrich Kratochwil (eds.), *Transformative Change and Global Order*. Münster: LIT Verlag.

———. 2003. *Exchange and Regulation in European Capital Markets*. Münster: LIT Verlag.

Ledgerwood, Grant, and Arlene Idol Broadhurst. 2000. *Environment, Ethics, and the Corporation*. New York: St. Martin's.

Lehmbruch, Gerhard. 1977. "Liberal Corporatism and Party Government." *Comparative Political Studies* 10: 91–126.

Lehmbruch, Gerhard, and Philippe Schmitter (eds.). 1982. *Patterns of Corporatist Policy-Making*. London: Sage.

Lenway, Stefanie, and Kathleen Rehbein. 1991. "Leaders, Followers, and Free Riders: An Empirical Test of Variation in Corporate Political Involvement." *Academy of Management Journal* 34(4): 893–905.

Levy, David. 1995. "The Environmental Practices and Performance of Transnational Corporations." *Transnational Corporations* 4(1): 44–68.

Levy, David, and Daniel Egan. 2000. "Corporate Political Action in the Global Polity." In Richard Higgott, Geoffrey Underhill, and Andreas Bieler (eds.), *Non-State Actors and Authority in the Global System*. London: Routledge.

Levy, David, and Peter Newell. 2000. "Oceans Apart? Business Responses to Global Environmental Issues in Europe and the United States." *Environment* 42(9): 8–20.

———. 2002. "Business Strategy and International Environmental Governance: A Neo-Gramscian Synthesis." *Global Environmental Politics* 2(4): 84–101.

——— (eds.). 2005. *The Business of Environmental Governance*. Cambridge, MA: MIT Press.

Liemt, Gijsbert van. 1998. *Codes of Conduct and International Subcontracting: A 'Private' Road Toward Ensuring Minimum Labour Standards in Export Industries*. Geneva: ILO.

Lindblom, Charles. 1977. *Politics and Markets*. New York: Basic.

Linder, Steve. 2003. "The Transformation of Global Warming from Policy Problem to Cultural Sign." Paper presented at the 2003 Hamburg Conference "Does Discourse Matter?" Hamburg, Germany, July 11–13.

Lipschutz, Ronnie. 1999. "From Local Knowledge and Practice to Global Environmental Governance." In Martin Hewson and Timothy Sinclair (eds.), *Approaches to Global Governance Theory*. Albany: State University of New York Press.

Loader, Brian (ed.). 1998. *Cyberspace Divide: Equality, Agency, and Policy in the Information Society*. London: Routledge.

Lock, Peter. 2001. "Sicherheit *a la carte?*" In Tanja Brühl, Tobias Debiel, Brigitte Hamm, Hartwig Hummel, and Jens Martens (eds.), *Die Privatisierung der Weltpolitik*. Bonn: Dietz.

Lord, Michael. 2000. "Constituency-based Lobbying as Corporate Political Strategy: Testing an Agency Theory Perspective." *Business and Politics* 2(3): 289–308.

Lorentzen, Jochen. 2000. "Foreign Capital, Host-Country-Firm Mandates, and the Terms of Globalisation." In Richard Higgott, Geoffrey Underhill, and Andreas Bieler (eds.), *Non-State Actors and Authority in the Global System*. London: Routledge.

Lowi, Theodore. 1964. "American Business, Public Policy, Case Studies, and Political Theory." *World Politics* 16(4): 677–693.

———. 1979. *The End of Liberalism*. New York: Norton.

Luhmann, Niklas. 1975. *Macht*. Stuttgart: Enke.

Lukes, Steven. 1974. *Power, a Radical View*. London: Macmillan.

———. 2004. *Power, a Radical View*. 2nd ed. London: Palgrave Macmillan.

Luttwak, Edward. 1999. *Turbo-Kapitalismus. Gewinner und Verlierer der Globalisierung*. Hamburg: Europa Verlag.

Lütz, Susanne. 1995. "Politische Steuerung und die Selbstregelung korporativer Akteure." In Renate Mayntz and Fritz Scharpf (eds.). *Gesellschaftliche Selbstregelung und politische Steuerung*. Frankfurt a.M.: Campus.

———. 2003. "Governance in der politischen Ökonomie—zum Stand der Debatte." *Politische Vierteljahresschrift* 44(2): 231–243.

Mahon, John. 1989. "Corporate Political Strategy." *Business in the Contemporary World* 2(1): 50–62.

Mair, Peter, Wolfgang Müller, and Fritz Plasser (eds.). 1999. *Party Responses to the Erosion of Voter Loyalties in Western Europe*. London: Sage.

Majone, Giandomenico (ed.). 1996. *Regulating Europe*. London: Routledge.

Majone, Giandomenico. 1997. "From the Positive to the Regulatory State: Causes and Consequences of Changes in the Mode of Governance." *Journal of Public Policy* 17(2): 139–167.

Mann, Michael. 1986. *The Sources of Social Power*, vol. 1. Cambridge, UK: Cambridge University Press.

———. 1993. *The Sources of Social Power*, vol. 2. Cambridge, UK: Cambridge University Press.

Manners, Ian. 2002. "Normative Power Europe: A Contradiction in Terms?" *Journal of Common Market Studies* 40(2): 235–258.

Manzetti, Luigi. 1999. *Privatization South American Style*. New York: Oxford University Press.

Marazzi, Christian. 1995. "Money in the World Crisis: The New Basis of Capitalist Power." In Werner Bonefeld and John Holloway (eds.), *Global Capital, National State, and the Politics of Money*. New York: St. Martin's.

March, James, and Johan Olsen. 1984. "The New Institutionalism: Organizational Factors in Political Life." *American Political Science Review* 78(3): 734–749.

Marsh, David, and Colin Hay (eds.). 2000. *Demystifying Globalization*. London: Macmillan.

Martin, Glen. 1999. "A Planetary Paradigm for Global Government." In Errol Harris and James Yunker (eds.), *Toward Genuine Global Governance*. Westport, CT: Praeger.

Mast, Claudia (ed.). 1996. *Markt-Macht-Medien: Publizistik im Spannungsfeld zwischen gesellschaftlicher Verantwortung und ökonomischen Zielen*. Konstanz: Uvk.

Mathews, Jessica. 1997. "Power Shift." *Foreign Affairs* 76(1): 50–66.

Matthews, Duncan, and John Pickering. 2000. "Business Strategy and Evolving Rules in the Single European Market." In Richard Higgott, Geoffrey Underhill, and Andreas Bieler (eds.), *Non-State Actors and Authority in the Global System*. London: Routledge.

May, Christopher (ed.). 2006a. *Global Corporate Power*. Boulder, CO: Lynne Rienner.

———. 2006b. "Global Corporate Power and the UN Global Compact." In Christopher May (ed.), *Global Corporate Power*. Boulder, CO: Lynne Rienner.

Mayntz, Renate. 2002. "Common Goods and Governance." In Adrienne Héritier (ed.), *Common Goods*. Lanham, MD: Rowman and Littlefield.

Mayntz, Renate, and Fritz Scharpf (eds.). 1995. *Gesellschaftliche Selbstregelung und politische Steuerung*. Frankfurt a.M.: Campus.

Mayntz, Renate, and Volker Schneider. 1995. "Die Entwicklung technischer Infrastruktursysteme zwischen Steuerung und Selbstorganisation." In Renate Mayntz and Fritz Scharpf (eds.), *Gesellschaftliche Selbstregelung und politische Steuerung*. Frankfurt a.M.: Campus.

Mazey, Sonja, and Jeremy Richardson. 1997. "Policy Framing: Interest Groups and the Lead Up to the 1996 Inter-Governmental Conference." *West European Politics* 20(3): 111–133.

McCombs, Maxwell, and D. L. Shaw. 1972. "The Agenda-Setting Function of the Mass Media." *Public Opinion Quarterly* 36: 176–187.

McDowell, Stephen D. 2006. "Commercial Control of Global Electronic Networks." In Christopher May (ed.), *Global Corporate Power*. Boulder, CO: Lynne Rienner.

McGinnis, Michael. 1999. "Rent-Seeking, Redistribution, and Reform in the Governance of Global Markets." In Aseem Prakash and Jeffrey Hart (eds.), *Globalization and Governance*. London: Routledge.

Menzel, Ulrich. 1998. *Globalisierung und Fragmentierung*. Frankfurt a.M.: Edition Suhrkamp.

Messner, Dirk. 2002. "The Concept of the 'World Economic Triangle.'" *IDS Working Paper 173*. Institute of Development Studies, Brighton, UK.

Messner, Dirk, and Franz Nuscheler. 1996a. "Global Governance. Challenges to German Politics on the Threshold of the Twenty-first Century." *Policy Paper 2*. Bonn: SEF, Development and Peace Foundation.

————. 1996b. "Global Governance, Organisationselemente und Säulen einer Weltordnungspolitik." In Dirk Messner and Franz Nuscheler (eds.), *Weltkonferenzen und Weltberichte*. Bonn: Dietz.

————. 2003. "Das Konzept Global Governance. Stand und Perspektiven." *INEF Report 67*. Duisburg: Institut für Entwicklung und Frieden.

Midttun, Atle (ed.). 1997. *European Electricity Systems in Transition: A Comparative Analysis of Policy and Regulation in Western Europe*. Amsterdam: Elsevier.

Milbrath, Lester. 1963. *The Washington Lobbyists*. Chicago: Rand McNally.

Miliband, Ralph. 1969. *The State in Capitalist Society*. London: Weidenfeld and Nicolson.

Miller, Arthur Selwyn. 1972. "Legal Foundations of the Corporate State." *Journal of Economic Issues* 6(1): 59–79.

Mills, C. Wright. 1956. *The Power Elite*. New York: Oxford University Press.

Milner, Helen. 1991. "The Assumption of Anarchy in International Relations Theory: A Critique." *Review of International Studies* 17: 67–85.

Milyo, Jeffrey, David Primo, and Timothy Groseclose. 2000. "Corporate PAC Campaign Contributions in Perspective." *Business and Politics* 2(1): 75–88.

Mintzer, Irving, and J. Amber Leonard (eds.). 1994. *Negotiating Climate Change: The Inside Story of the Rio Convention*. Cambridge, UK: Cambridge University Press.

Mirbach, Martin von. 1999. "Demanding Good Wood." In Robert Gibson (ed.), *Voluntary Initiatives*. Peterborough, Ontario: Broadview.

Mittelman, James, and Robert Johnston. 1999. "The Globalization of Organized Crime, the Courtesan State, and the Corruption of Civil Society." *Global Governance* 5(1): 103–127.

Mitnick, Barry (ed.). 1993. *Corporate Political Agency: The Construction of Competition in Public Affairs*. Newbury Park, CA: Sage.

Moffet, John, and Francois Bregha. 1999. "Non-Regulatory Environmental Measures." In Robert Gibson (ed.), *Voluntary Initiatives*. Peterborough, Ontario: Broadview.

Mol, Arthur. 2001. *Globalization and Environmental Reform*. Cambridge, MA: MIT Press.

Moore, Stephen, Sidney Wolfe, Deborah Lindes, and Clifford Douglas. 1994. "Epidemiology of Failed Tobacco Control Legislation." *Journal of the American Medical Association* 272: 1171–1175.

Morgenthau, Hans. 1948. *Politics Among Nations: The Struggle for Power and Peace*. New York: Knopf.

Mucciaroni, Gary. 1995. *Reversals of Fortune: Public Policy and Private Interests*. Washington, DC: Brookings Institution.

Muchlinski, Peter. 1997. "'Global Bukowina' Examined." In Gunther Teubner (ed.), *Global Law Without a State*. Aldershot: Dartmouth.

Mueller, Dennis. 1986. *The Modern Corporation*. Lincoln: University of Nebraska Press.

Mueller, Willard. 1975. "Antitrust in a Planned Economy." *Journal of Economic Issues* 9(2): 159–179.

Muldoon, Paul, and Ramani Nadarajah. 1999. "A Sober Second Look." In Robert Gibson (ed.), *Voluntary Initiatives*. Peterborough, Ontario: Broadview.

Müller, Harald. 1993. *Die Chance der Kooperation: Regime in den Internationalen Beziehungen*. Darmstadt: Wiss. Buchgesellschaft.

———. 1994. "Internationale Beziehungen als kommunikatives Handeln." *Zeitschrift für Internationale Beziehungen* 1(1): 15–44.

Müller, Philipp. 2002. "Imag[in]ing Globalization: Therapy for Policy Makers." In Doris Fuchs and Friedrich Kratochwil (eds.), *Transformative Change and Global Order*. Münster: LIT Verlag.

Müller, Wilfried (ed.). 1995. *Der ökologische Umbau der Industrie*. Münster: LIT Verlag.

Mürle, Holger. 1998. "Global Governance. Literaturbericht und Forschungsfragen." *INEF-Report 32*, Duisburg: Institute for Development and Peace.

Murphy, Craig. 1994. *International Organization and Industrial Change: Global Governance Since 1850*. New York: Oxford University Press.

Mytelka, Lynn. 2000. "Knowledge and Structural Power in the International Political Economy." In Thomas Lawton, James Rosenau, and Amy Verdun (eds.), *Strange Power*. Aldershot, UK: Ashgate.

Nadvi, Khalid, and Frank Wältring. 2002. "Making Sense of Global Standards." *INEF Report 58*, Institute for Development and Peace, University of Duisburg.

Nash, Jennifer, and John Ehrenfeld. 1997. "Codes of Environmental Management Practice." *Annual Review of Energy and Environment* 22(1): 487–535.

Naßmacher, Karl-Heinz. 2002. "Die Kosten der Parteitätigkeit in westlichen Demokratien." *Österreichische Zeitschrift für Politikwissenschaft* 2002(1): 7–20.

——— (ed.). 2001. *Foundations for Democracy: Approaches to Comparative Political Finance*. Baden-Baden: Nomos.

Nelson, Jane. 1998. *Building Competitiveness and Communities: How World Class Companies Are Creating Shareholder Value and Societal Value*. London: Prince of Wales Business Leaders Forum.

Nennenkamp, Peter. 1999. "Grenzenloser Handel und Kapitalverkehr? Was wirtschaftspolitisch zu tun und zu lassen ist." *Internationale Politik* 54(1): 3–10.

Neuman, Mark, Asaf Bitton, and Stanton Glantz. 2002. "Tobacco Industry

Strategies for Influencing European Community Tobacco Advertising Legislation." *Lancet* 359: 1323–1330.

Newell, Peter, and David Levy. 2006. "The Political Economy of the Firm in Global Environmental Governance." In Christopher May (ed.), *Global Corporate Power*. Boulder, CO: Lynne Rienner.

Newell, Peter, and Matthew Paterson. 1998. "A Climate for Business." *Review of International Political Economy* 5(4): 679–703.

Neyer, Jürgen. 2002. "Politische Herrschaft in nicht-hierarchischen Mehrebenensystemen." *Zeitschrift für Internationale Beziehungen* 9(1): 9–38.

Noelle-Neumann, Elisabeth. 1973. "Return to the Concept of Powerful Media." *Studies of Broadcasting* 9: 67–112.

———. 1996. *Öffentliche Meinung: Die Entdeckung der Schweigespirale*. Frankfurt a.M.: Ullstein.

Noland, Marcus. 1999. *The New Protectionists: The Privatisation of US Trade Policy*. London: Institute of Economic Affairs.

Nölke, Andreas. 2000. "Regieren in transnationalen Politiknetzwerken?" *Zeitschrift für Internationale Beziehungen* 7(2): 331–358.

———. 2005. "Governance by Coordination Service Firms: The Private Infrastructure of Financial Capitalism." Paper presented at the Annual Meeting of the International Studies Association, Honolulu, March 1–5.

Nollert, Michael. 1997. "Verbändelobbying in der Europäischen Union—Europäische Dachverbände im Vergleich." In Ulrich von Alemann and Bernhard Wessels (eds.), *Verbände in vergleichender Perspektive*. Berlin: edition sigma.

Nye, Joseph. 1991. *Bound to Lead: The Changing Nature of American Power*. New York: Basic.

———. 2002. *The Paradox of American Power*. Oxford: Oxford University Press.

Oberreuter, Heinrich (ed.). 1996. *Parteiensystem am Wendepunkt? Wahlen in der Fernsehdemokratie*. Landsberg: Olzog.

O'Brien, Robert, Anne Goetz, Jan Aart Scholte, and Marc Williams. 2000. *Contesting Global Governance*. Cambridge, UK: Cambridge University Press.

OECD. 1998. *Harmful Tax Competition. An Emerging Global Issue*. Paris: Organization for Economic Cooperation and Development.

Offe, Claus, and Helmut Wiesenthal. 1980. "Two Logics of Collective Action: Theoretical Notes on Social Class and Organizational Form." *Political Power and Social Theory* 1: 67–115.

Ohmae, Kenichi. 1990. *The Borderless World: Power and Strategy in the Global Market Place*. London: HarperCollins.

———. 1996. *The End of the Nation State: The Rise of Regional Economies*. New York: Free Press.

Olson, Mancur. 1965. *The Logic of Collective Action: Public Goods and the Theory of Groups*. Cambridge, MA: Harvard University Press.

———. 1982. *The Rise and Decline of Nations*. New Haven, CT: Yale University Press.

Omestad, Thomas. 1989. "Selling Off America." *Foreign Policy* 76: 119–140.

Ong, Elisa, and Stanton Glantz. 2000. "Tobacco Industry Efforts Subverting International Agency for Research on Cancer's Second-hand Smoke Study." *Lancet* 355: 1253–1259.

Ostrom, Elinor. 1990. *Governing the Commons: The Evolution of Institutions for Collective Action.* Cambridge, UK: Cambridge University Press.

Ottoway, Marina. 2001. "Corporatism Goes Global: International Organizations, Nongovernmental Organization Networks, and Transnational Business." *Global Governance* 7: 265–292.

Ougaard, Morten. 2006. "Instituting the Power to Do Good?" In Christopher May (ed.), *Global Corporate Power.* Boulder, CO: Lynne Rienner.

Palan, Ronen. 1992. "The Second Structuralist Theories of International Relations: A Research Note." *International Studies Notes* 17(3): 22–29.

———. 1999. "Global Governance and Social Closure *or* Who Is to Be Governed in the Era of Global Governance?" In Martin Hewson and Timothy Sinclair (eds.), *Approaches to Global Governance Theory.* Albany: State University of New York Press.

Pappi, Franz Urban, and Christian Henning. 1998. "Policy Networks: More Than a Metaphor?" *Journal of Theoretical Politics* 10(4): 553–575.

Parsons, Talcott. 1967. *Sociological Theory and Modern Society.* New York: Free Press.

Parto, Saeed. 1999. "Aiming Low." In Robert Gibson (ed.), *Voluntary Initiatives.* Peterborough, Ontario: Broadview.

Patel, Indraprasad. 1995. "Global Economic Governance: Some Thoughts on Our Current Discontents." In Meghnad Desai and Paul Redfern, *Global Governance: Ethics and Economics of the World Order.* London: Pinter.

Paul, James. 2001. "Der Weg zum *Global Compact.*" In Tanja Brühl, Tobias Debiel, Brigitte Hamm, Hartwig Hummel, and Jens Martens (eds.), *Die Privatisierung der Weltpolitik.* Bonn: Dietz.

Pauly, Louis. 1995. "Capital Mobility, State Autonomy, and Political Legitimacy." *Journal of International Affairs* 48: 369–388.

———. 1997. *Who Elected the Bankers? Surveillance and Control in the World Economy.* Ithaca, NY: Cornell University Press.

———. 2003. "Global Markets, National Authority, and the Problem of Legitimation." In Rodney Bruce Hall and Thomas Biersteker (eds.), *The Emergence of Private Authority in Global Governance.* Cambridge, UK: Cambridge University Press.

Pauly, Louis, and Simon Reich. 1997. "National Structures and Multinational Corporate Behavior." *International Organization* 5(1): 1–30.

Pegg, Scott. 2006. "World Leaders and Bottom Feeders: Divergent Strategies Toward Social Responsibility and Resource Extraction." In Christopher May (ed.), *Global Corporate Power.* Boulder, CO: Lynne Rienner.

Peltzman, Sam. 1976. "Toward a More General Theory of Regulation." *Journal of Law and Economics* 19(2): 211–240.

Pertschuk, Michael. 1984. "Commentators' Remarks." In Betty Bock, Harvey Goldschmid, Ira Millstein, and F. M. Scherer (eds.), *The Impact of the Modern Corporation*. New York: Columbia University Press.

Pierre, Jon (ed.). 2000. *Debating Governance: Authority, Steering, and Democracy*. Oxford: Oxford University Press.

Pijl, Kees van der. 2001. "Private Weltpolitik." In Tanja Brühl, Tobias Debiel, Brigitte Hamm, Hartwig Hummel, and Jens Martens (eds.), *Die Privatisierung der Weltpolitik*. Bonn: Dietz.

Pitofsky, Robert. 1984. "Commentators' Remarks." In Betty Bock, Harvey Goldschmid, Ira Millstein, and F. M. Scherer (eds.), *The Impact of the Modern Corporation*. New York: Columbia University Press.

Plehwe, Dieter, and Berhard Walpen. 1998. "Eine 'Art von internationaler fünfter Kolonne des Liberalismus.'" In Regine Stötzel (ed.), *Ungleichheit als Projekt*. Marburg: BdWi-Verlag.

Polk, Andreas. 2002. "The Economics of Lobbying and Special Interest Groups." Dissertation, Universität Zürich.

Porter, Michael, and Claas van der Linde. 1995. "Green and Competitive: Ending the Stalemate." *Harvard Business Review* 73: 120–134.

Porter, Tony. 2005. "The Private Production of Public Goods: Private and Public Norms in Global Governance." In Edgar Grande and Louis Pauly (eds.), *Complex Sovereignty*. Toronto: University of Toronto Press.

Posner, Richard. 1974. "Power in America: The Role of the Large Corporation." In John Weston (ed.), *Large Corporations in a Changing Society*. New York: New York University Press.

Poulantzas, Nicos. 1978. *Political Power and Social Classes*. London: Verso.

Prakash, Aseem. 2000. *Greening the Firm*. Cambridge, UK: Cambridge University Press.

———. 2002. "Beyond Seattle: Globalization, the Nonmarket Environment, and Corporate Strategy." *Review of International Political Economy* 9(3): 513–537.

Prakash, Aseem, and Jeffrey Hart (eds.). 1999. *Globalization and Governance*. London: Routledge.

Princen, Thomas, and Matthias Finger. 1994. *Environmental NGOs in World Politics: Linking the Local and the Global*. London: Routledge.

Purcell, Mark. 2002. "The State, Regulation, and Global Restructuring." *Review of International Political Economy* 9(2): 298–332.

Pury, David (ed.). 1998. "Wer regiert die Weltwirtschaft?" *Internationale Politik* 53(11): 25–30.

Reese-Schäfer, Walter. 1999. "Supranationale oder transnationale Identität. Zwei Modelle kultureller Integration in Europa." In Reinhold Viehoff and Rien Segers (eds.), *Identität—Kultur—Europa*. Frankfurt a.M.: Suhrkamp.

———. 2001. "Internationale Gerechtigkeit als Gegenstand von Theorie und Praxis universalistischer Moralität. Ein Kommentar zu Thomas Pogge." In Karl Graf Ballestrem (ed.), *Internationale Gerechtigkeit*, Opladen, Germany: Leske and Budrich.

Reinicke, Wolfgang. 1998. *Global Public Policy. Governing Without Governments?* Washington, DC: Brookings Institution.

Reljiç, Dušan. 2001. "Der Vormarsch der Megamedien und die Kommerzialisierung der Weltöffentlichkeit." In Tanja Brühl, Tobias Debiel, Brigitte Hamm, Hartwig Hummel, and Jens Martens (eds.), *Die Privatisierung der Weltpolitik*. Bonn: Dietz.

Reutter, Werner. 2001. "Korporatismus, Pluralismus, und Demokratie." In Werner Reutter and Peter Rütters (eds.), *Verbände und Verbandssysteme in Westeuropa*. Opladen, Germany: Leske and Budrich.

Reutter, Werner, and Peter Rütters (eds.). 2001. *Verbände und Verbandssysteme in Westeuropa*. Opladen, Germany: Leske and Budrich.

Rhodes, Martin. 1991. "The Social Dimension of the Single European Market: National versus Transnational Regulation." *European Journal of Political Research* 19: 245–280.

Rhodes, R.A.W., and David Marsh. 1992. "New Directions in the Study of Policy Networks." *European Journal of Political Research* 21: 181–205.

Rifkin, Jeremy. 1995. *The End of Work: The Decline of the Global Labor Force and the Dawn of the Post-Market Era*. New York: Putnam.

Riker, William. 1986. *The Art of Political Manipulation*. New Haven: Yale University Press.

———. 1996. *The Strategy of Political Rhetoric*. New Haven, CT: Yale University Press.

Risse, Thomas. 2000. "Let's Argue!: Communicative Action in World Politics." *International Organization* 54(1): 1–39.

Robé, Jean-Philippe. 1997. "Multinational Enterprises: The Constitution of a Pluralistic Legal Order." In Gunther Teubner (ed.), *Global Law Without a State*. Aldershot, UK: Dartmouth.

Roberts, Alasdair. 2001. "The Informational Commons at Risk." In Daniel Drache (ed), *The Market or the Public Domain?* London: Routledge.

Rodrik, Dani. 1999. *The New Global Economy and Developing Countries: Making Openness Work*. Washington, DC: Overseas Development Council.

Roloff, Ralf. 2001. *Europa, Amerika, und Asien zwischen Globalisierung und Regionalisierung*. Paderborn: Schöningh.

Römmele, Andrea. 2002. *Direkte Kommunikation zwischen Parteien und Wählern*. Wiesbaden: Westdeutscher Verlag.

Ronit, Karsten. 2000. "The Good, the Bad, or the Ugly?" In Karsten Ronit and Volker Schneider (eds.), *Private Organisations in Global Politics*. London: Routledge.

Ronit, Karsten, and Volker Schneider. 1997. "Organisierte Interessen in nationalen und supranationalen Politökologien—Ein Vergleich der G7-Länder mit der Europäischen Union." In Ulrich von Alemann and Bernhard Wessels (eds.), *Verbände in vergleichender Perspektive*. Berlin: edition sigma.

————. 1999. "Global Governance Through Private Organizations." *Governance* 12(3): 243–266.

———— (eds.). 2000. *Private Organizations in Global Politics.* London: Routledge.

Rosenau, James. 1992. "Governance, Order, and Change in World Politics." In Rosenau, James, and Ernst-Otto Czempiel (eds.). *Governance Without Government: Order and Change in World Politics.* Cambridge, UK: Cambridge University Press.

————. 1995. "Governance in the Twenty-First Century" *Global Governance* 1(1): 13–43.

————. 1999. "Toward an Ontology for Global Governance." In Martin Hewson and Timothy Sinclair (eds.), *Approaches to Global Governance Theory.* Albany: State University of New York Press.

————. 2000. "Change, Complexity, and Governance in a Globalizing Space." In Jon Pierre (ed.), *Debating Governance.* Oxford: Oxford University Press.

Rosenau, James, and Ernst-Otto Czempiel (eds.). 1992. *Governance Without Government: Order and Change in World Politics.* Cambridge, UK: Cambridge University Press.

Rowlands, Ian. 2000. "Beauty and the Beast?" *Environment and Planning C: Government and Policy* 18(3): 339–354.

Ruggie, John. 1993. "Territoriality and Beyond: Problematizing Modernity in International Relations." *International Organization* 47(1): 139–174.

————. 2001. "global_governance.net: The Global Compact as Learning Network." *Global Governance* 7: 371–378.

Rugman, Alan. 1996. *The Theory of Multinational Enterprise.* Cheltenham, UK: Edward Elgar.

Rutherford, Paul. 2003. "Whatever Happened to the Environment? Environmentalism and Business Discourse." Paper presented at the 2003 Hamburg Conference "Does Discourse Matter?" Hamburg, Germany, July 11–13.

Sabatier, Paul, and Henk Jenkins-Smith (eds.). 1993. *Policy Change and Learning: An Advocacy Coalition Approach.* Boulder, CO: Westview.

Salisbury, Robert. 1969. "An Exchange Theory of Interest Groups." *Midwest Journal of Political Science* 13: 1–32.

Sandholtz, Wayne, and John Zysman. 1989. "Recasting the European Bargain." *World Politics* 42: 95–128.

Sarcinelli, Ulrich (ed.). 1998. *Politikvermittlung und Demokratie in der Mediengesellschaft.* Bonn: Bundeszentrale für politische Bildung.

Sassen, Saskia. 1996. *Losing Control: Sovereignty in an Age of Globalization.* New York: Columbia University Press.

Scharpf, Fritz. 1991. "Die Handlungsfähigkeit des Staates am Ende des zwanzigsten Jahrhunderts." *Politische Vierteljahresschrift* 32(4): 621–634.

————. 1998. "Demokratie in der transnationalen Politik." In Ulrich Beck (ed.), *Politik der Globalisierung.* Frankfurt a.M.: Suhrkamp.

———. 1999. *Regieren in Europa. Effektiv und demokratisch?* Frankfurt a.M.: Campus.

Schattschneider, Elmer. 1960. *The Semi-Sovereign People: A Realist's View of Democracy in America.* New York: Holt, Rinehart, and Winston.

Schatz, Heribert, Patrick Rössler, and Jörg-Uwe Nieland. 2002. *Politische Akteure in der Mediendemokratie. Politiker in den Fesseln der Medien.* Wiesbaden: Westdeutscher Verlag.

Schechter, Michael. 1999. *The Revival of Civil Society. Global and Comparative Perspectives.* New York: Palgrave Macmillan.

Scherrer, Christoph. 1999. *Globalisierung wider Willen?* Berlin: edition sigma.

Scherrer, Christoph, and Thomas Greven. 2000. *Global Rules.* Münster: Westfälisches Dampfboot.

Schimmelfennig, Frank. 1997. "Rhetorisches Handeln in den Internationalen Beziehungen." *Zeitschrift für Internationale Beziehungen* 1(1): 219–253.

———. 1998. "Macht und Herrschaft in Theorien der Internationalen Beziehungen." In Peter Imbusch (ed.), *Macht und Herrschaft. Sozialwissenschaftliche Konzeptionen und Theorien.* Opladen, Germany: Leske and Budrich.

Schirm, Stefan. 2001. "Wie Globalisierung nationale Regierungen stärkt. Zur politischen Ökonomie staatlicher Antworten auf Globalisierung." In Christine Landfried (ed.), *Politik in einer entgrenzten Welt.* Köln: Verlag Wissenschaft und Politik

———. 2002. *Globalization and the New Regionalism. Global Markets, Domestic Politics, and Regional Cooperation.* Cambridge, UK: Polity.

——— (ed.). 2004. *New Rules for Global Markets. Public and Private Governance in the World Economy.* New York: Palgrave Macmillan.

Schlozman, Kay Lehman, and John Tierney. 1983. "More of the Same: Washington Pressure Group Activity in a Decade of Change." *Journal of Politics* 45: 351–377.

Schmidheiny, Stephan. 1992. *Changing Course.* Cambridge, MA: MIT Press.

Schmidt, Brian C. 2005. "Competing Realist Conceptions of Power." *Millennium: Journal of International Studies* 33(3): 523–550.

Schmidt, Rudi. 1998. "Zur politischen Semantik von 'Globalisierung.'" In Hartmut Hirsch-Kreinsen and Harald Wolf (eds.), *Arbeit, Gesellschaft, Kritik.* Berlin: edition sigma.

Schmitt-Beck, Rüdiger. 2000. *Politische Kommunikation und Wählerverhalten. Ein internationaler Vergleich.* Opladen, Germany: Westdeutscher Verlag.

Schmitt-Beck, Rüdiger, and Barbara Pfetsch. 1994. "Amerikanisierung von Wahlkämpfen? Kommunikationsstrategien und Massenmedien im politischen Mobilisierungsproze." In Michael Jäckel and Peter Winterhorff-Spurk (eds.), *Politik und Medien. Analysen zur Entwicklung der politischen Kommunkation.* Berlin: Vistas.

Schmitter, Philippe. 1974. "Still the Century of Corporatism?" *Review of Politics* 36: 85–131.

———. 2002. "Participation in Governance Arrangements: Is There Any Reason to Expect It Will Achieve 'Sustainable and Innovative Policies in a Multilevel Context'?" In Jürgen Grote and Bernard Gbikpi (eds.), *Participatory Governance: Political and Societal Implications.* Opladen, Germany: Leske and Budrich.

Schmitter, Philippe, and Gerhard Lehmbruch (eds.). 1979. *Trends Towards Corporatist Intermediation.* Beverly Hills, CA: Sage.

Schmitter, Philippe, and Wolfgang Streeck. 1999. "The Organization of Business Interests: Studying the Associative Action of Business in Advanced Industrial Societies." Discussion paper, Max-Planck-Institut für Gesellschaftsforschung. Köln: MPIFG.

Schneider, Volker. 2002. "Private Actors in Political Governance: Regulating the Information and Communication Sectors." In Jürgen Grote and Bernard Gbikpi (eds.), *Participatory Governance: Political and Societal Implications.* Opladen, Germany: Leske and Budrich.

Scholte, Jan Aart. 2000a. *Globalization: A Critical Introduction.* Basingstoke, UK: Palgrave.

———. 2000b. "Global Civil Society." In Ngaire Woods (ed.), *The Political Economy of Globalization.* New York: St. Martin's.

Schuler, Douglas. 1996. "Corporate Political Strategy and Foreign Competition: The Case of the Steel Industry." *Academy of Management Journal* 39(3): 720–737.

———. 1999. "Corporate Political Action: Rethinking the Economic and Organizational Influence." *Business and Politics* 1(1): 83–97.

Schumann, Michael. 1998. "Frißt die Shareholder Value-Ökonomie die Modernisierung der Arbeit?" In Hartmut Hirsch-Kreinsen and Harald Wolf (eds.), *Arbeit, Gesellschaft, Kritik.* Berlin: edition sigma.

Schwartz, David. 1985. "Idealism and Realism: An Institutionalist View of Corporate Power in Regulated Utilities." *Journal of Economic Issues* 19(2): 311–331.

Schwarz, Michael. 1995. "Strategien und Handlungskonstellationen im betrieblichen Umweltschutz." In Wilfried Müller (ed.), *Der ökologische Umbau der Industrie.* Münster: LIT Verlag.

Scott, John. 1985. "Theoretical Framework and Research Design." In Frans Stokman, Rolf Ziegler, and John Scott (eds.), *Networks of Corporate Power.* Cambridge, UK: Cambridge University Press.

Sebaldt, Martin. 1997. *Organisierter Pluralismus: Kräftefeld, Selbstverständnis, und politische Arbeit deutscher Interessengruppen.* Opladen, Germany: Westdeutscher Verlag.

Seeleib-Kaiser, Martin. 1999. "Globalisierung und Wohlfahrtssysteme: Divergenz, Konvergenz oder divergente Konvergenz." *Zeitschrift für Sozialreform* 45(1): 3–23.

Sell, Susan. 2000. "Structures, Agents, and Institutions: Private Corporate Power and the Globalisation of Intellectual Property Rights." In Richard

Higgott, Geoffrey Underhill, and Andreas Bieler (eds.), *Non-State Actors and Authority in the Global System*. London: Routledge.

Shaffer, Brian. 1992. "Regulation, Competition, and Strategy: The Case of Automobile Fuel Economy Standards 1974–1991." In James Post (ed.), *Research in Corporate Social Performance and Policy*. Greenwich, CT: JAI Press.

Shaffer, Gregory. 2001. "The Blurring of the Intergovernmental: Public-Private Partnerships Behind US and EC Trade Claims." In Mark Pollack and Gregory Shaffer (eds.), *Transatlantic Governance in the Global Economy*. Lanham, MD: Rowman and Littlefield.

Shaiko, Ronald. 1998. "Lobbying in Washington: A Contemporary Perspective." In Paul Herrnson, Ronald Shaiko, and Clyde Wilcox (eds.), *The Interest Group Connection*. Chatham, MD: Chatham House.

Shapiro, Michael, and Hayward Alker (eds.). 1996. *Challenging Boundaries: Global Flows, Territorial Identities*. Minneapolis: University of Minnesota Press.

Sharma, Sanjay, and Harrie Vredenburg. 1998. "Proactive Corporate Environmental Strategy and the Development of Competitively Valuable Organizational Capabilities." *Strategic Management Journal* 19(8): 729–753.

Shepsle, Kenneth. 1979. "Institutional Arrangements and Equilibrium in Multidimensional Voting Models." *American Journal of Political Science* 23(1): 27–59.

Shonfield, Andrew. 1965. *Modern Capitalism: The Changing Balance of Public and Private Power*. London: Oxford University Press.

Sinclair, Timothy. 1999a. "Bond-Rating Agencies and Coordination in the Global Political Economy." In Claire Cutler, Virginia Haufler, and Tony Porter (eds.), *Private Authority and International Affairs*. New York: State University of New York Press.

———. 1999b. "Synchronic Global Governance and the International Political Economy of the Commonplace." In Martin Hewson and Timothy Sinclair (eds.), *Approaches to Global Governance Theory*. Albany: State University of New York Press.

Singer, Max, and Aaron Wildavsky. 1993. *The Real World Order: Zones of Peace, Zones of Turmoil*. Chatham, NJ: Chatham House.

Sklair, Leslie. 1998. "As Political Actors." *New Political Economy* 3(2): 284–287.

Sloof, Randolph. 2000. "Interest Group Lobbying and the Delegation of Policy Authority." *Economics and Politics* 12(3): 247–274.

Sloof, Randolph, and Frans van Winden. 2000. "Show Them Your Teeth First!" *Public Choice* 104: 81–120.

Smart, Bruce. 1992. *Beyond Compliance: A New Industry View of the Environment*. Washington, DC: World Resources Institute.

Smith, Mark. 2000. *American Business and Political Power: Public Opinion, Elections, and Democracy*. Chicago: University of Chicago Press.

Smouts, Marie-Claude. 1999. "Multilateralism from Below: A Prerequisite for Global Governance." In Michael Schechter (ed.), *Future Multilateralism: The Political and Social Framework*. New York: Palgrave Macmillan.

Smythe, Elizabeth. 2000. "Non-State Actors and the Negotiation of the Multilateral Agreement on Investment at the OECD." In Richard Higgott, Geoffrey Underhill, and Andreas Bieler (eds.), *Non-State Actors and Authority in the Global System*. London: Routledge.

Solomon, Michael. 2003. *Conquering Consumerspace*. New York: Amacom.

Sparrow, Malcom. 2000. *The Regulatory Craft: Controling Risks, Solving Problems, Managing Compliance*. Washington, DC: Brookings Institution.

Späth, Konrad. 2003. "Inside Global Governance. New Borders of a Concept." Working Paper, Critical Perspectives on Global Governance, http://www.cpogg.org.

Steffek, Jens. 2003. "The Legitimation of International Governance: A Discourse Approach." *European Journal of International Relations* 9(2): 249–275.

Steger, Ulrich. 2000. "Environmental Management Systems." *European Management Journal* 18(1): 23–32.

Stewart, Keith. 2001. "Avoiding the Tragedy of the Commons: Greening Governance Through the Market or the Public Domain." In Daniel Drache (ed.), *The Market or the Public Domain?* London: Routledge.

Stigler, George. 1971. "The Theory of Economic Regulation." *The Bell Journal of Economics and Management Science* 2(1): 3–21.

Stiglitz, Joseph. 2002. *Globalization and Its Discontents*. New York: Norton.

Stokman, Frans, Rolf Ziegler, and John Scott (eds.). 1985. *Networks of Corporate Power: A Comparative Analysis of Ten Countries*. Cambridge, UK: Cambridge University Press.

Stoll, Richard, and Michael Ward (eds.). 1989. *Power in World Politics*. Boulder, CO: Lynne Rienner.

Stopford, John, and Susan Strange. 1991. *Rival States, Rival Firms*. Cambridge, UK: Cambridge University Press.

Stötzel, Regine (ed.). 1998. *Ungleichheit als Projekt*. Marburg: BdWi-Verlag.

Strange, Susan. 1988. *States and Markets*. London: Blackwell.

———. 1993. "Big Business and the State." In Lorraine Eden and Evan Potter (eds.), *Multinationals in the Global Political Economy*. New York: St. Martin's.

———. 1996. *The Retreat of the State: The Diffusion of Power and Wealth in the World Economy*. Cambridge, UK: Cambridge University Press.

———. 1998. *Mad Money. When Markets Outgrow Governments*. Ann Arbor: University of Michigan Press.

Streeck, Wolfgang (ed.). 1994. *Staat und Verbände*. Opladen, Germany: Westdeutscher Verlag.

Streeck, Wolfgang, and Martin Höppner. 2003. *Alle Macht dem Markt? Fallstudien zur Abwicklung der Deutschland AG*. Frankfurt a.m.: Campus.

Streeck, Wolfgang, and Philippe Schmitter. 1985a. "Gemeinschaft, Markt und Staat—und die Verbände? Der mögliche Beitrag von Interessenregierungen zur sozialen Ordnung." *Journal für Sozialforschung* 25(2): 133–159.

——— (eds.). 1985b. *Private Interest Government: Beyond the Market and State*. London: Sage.

Streeck, Wolfgang, and Philippe Schmitter. 1991. "From National Corporatism to Transnational Pluralism: Organized Interests in the Single European Market." *Politics and Society* 19(2): 133–161.

Sturm, Roland, Gabriele Dautermann, and Jürgen Dieringer. 2000. *Regulierung und Deregulierung im wirtschaftlichen Transformationsprozess*. Opladen, Germany: Leske and Budrich.

Susskind, Lawrence. 1992. "New Corporate Roles in Global Environmental Treaty-Making." *Columbia Journal of World Business* 27: 62–73.

Suter, Keith. 2005. *Curbing Corporate Power: How Can We Control Transnational Corporations?* London: Zed.

Sutter, Daniel. 2002. "Constitutional Prohibitions in a Rent Seeking Model." *Public Choice* 111(1-2): 105–125.

Swank, Duane. 2002. *Global Capital, Political Institutions, and Policy Change in Developed Welfare States*. Cambridge, UK: Cambridge University Press.

Tenbrücken, Marc. 2001. *Corporate Lobbying in the European Union*. Frankfurt a.M.: Peter Lang.

Teubner, Gunther (ed.). 1997. *Global Law Without a State*. Aldershot, UK: Dartmouth.

Thomas, Caroline. 2000. *Global Governance, Development, and Human Security*. London: Pluto.

Thomas, Clive. 1998. "Interest Group Regulation Across the United States: Rationale, Development, and Consequences." *Parliamentary Affairs* 51(4): 500–515.

Thompson, Peter, and Laura Strohm. 1996. "Trade and Environmental Quality: A Review of the Evidence." *Journal of Development Economics* 5(4): 363–388.

Tool, Marc, and Warren Samuels (eds.). 1989. *State, Society, and Corporate Power*. New Brunswick, NJ: Transaction.

Tooze, Roger. 2000. "Ideology, Knowledge, and Power in International Relations and International Political Economy." In Thomas Lawton, James Rosenau, and Amy Verdun (eds.), *Strange Power*. Aldershot, UK: Ashgate.

Traxler, Franz, and Philippe Schmitter. 1994. "Perspektiven europäischer Integration, verbandlicher Interessenvermittlung und Politikformulierung. " In Volker Eichener and Helmut Voelzkow (eds.), *Europäische Integration und verbandliche Regulierung*. Marburg: Metropolis.

Tripathi, Micky. 2000. "PAC Contributions and Defense Contracting." *Business and Politics* 2(1): 53–73.

Truman, David. 1951. *The Governmental Process*. New York: Knopf.

Tullock, Gordon. 1972. "The Purchase of Politicians." *Western Economic Journal* 10: 354–355.

UNCTAD. 2000. *World Investment Report 2000*. New York: United Nations.

———. 2002. *World Investment Report 2002*. New York: United Nations.

Underhill, Geoffrey. 1995. "Keeping Governments out of Politics: Transnational Securities Markets, Regulatory Cooperation, and Political Legitimacy." *Review of International Studies* 21: 251–278.

———. 2001. "The Public Good Versus Private Interests and the Global Financial and Monetary System." In Daniel Drache (ed.), *The Market or the Public Domain?* London: Routledge.

UNDP. 2002. *Human Development Report 2002*. New York: United Nations.

Useem, Michael. 1984. *The Inner Circle*. New York: Oxford University Press.

Utting, Peter. 2004. "Neue Ansätze zur Regulierung Transnationaler Konzerne. Potential und Grenzen von Multistakeholder-Initiativen." In Tanja Brühl, Heidi Feldt, Brigitte Hamm, Hartwig Hummel, and Jens Martens (eds.), *Unternehmen in der Weltpolitik. Politiknetzwerke*. Bonn: Dietz.

Vaillancourt Rosenau, Pauline. 2000. *Public-Private Partnerships*. Cambridge, MA: MIT Press.

VanNijnatten, Debora. 1999. "The Day the NGOs Walked Out." In Robert Gibson (ed.), *Voluntary Initiatives*. Peterborough, Ontario: Broadview.

Väyrynen, Raimo (ed.). 1999. *Globalization and Global Governance*. Lanham, MD: Rowman and Littlefield.

Verba, Sidney, and Gary Orren. 1985. *Equality in America*. Cambridge, MA: Harvard University Press.

Verdun, Amy. 2000. "Money Power: Shaping the Global Financial System." In Thomas Lawton, James Rosenau, and Amy Verdun (eds.), *Strange Power*. Aldershot, UK: Ashgate.

Vernon, Raymond. 1971. *Sovereignty at Bay: The Multinational Spread of US Enterprises*. New York: Basic.

———. 1993. "Sovereignty at Bay: Twenty Years After." In Lorraine Eden and Evan Potter (eds.), *Multinationals in the Global Political Economy*. New York: St. Martin's.

Vogel, Stephen. 1996. *Freer Markets, More Rules: Regulatory Reforms in Advancing Industrial Countries*. Ithaca, NY: Cornell University Press.

Vorländer, Hans. 1997. *Hegemonialer Liberalismus. Politisches Denken und Politische Kultur in den USA 1776–1920*. Frankfurt a.M.: Campus.

Wagschal, Uwe. 1999. "Blockieren Vetospieler Steuerreformen?" *Politische Vierteljahresschrift* 40: 628–640.

———. 2003. "Die Politische Ökonomie der Besteuerung." In Herbert Obinger, Uwe Wagschal, and Bernhard Kittel (eds.), *Politische Ökonomie*. Opladen, Germany: Leske and Budrich.

Wallerstein, Immanuel. 1979. *The Capitalist World Economy*. Cambridge, UK: Cambridge University Press.

Walter, Andrew. 1998. "Do They Really Rule the World?" *New Political Economy* 3(2): 288–292.

———. 2000. "Globalisation and Policy Convergence: The Case of Direct Investment Rules." In Richard Higgott, Geoffrey Underhill, and Andreas Bieler (eds.), *Non-State Actors and Authority in the Global System*. London: Routledge.

———. 2001. "NGOs, Business, and International Investment." *Global Governance* 7: 51–73.

Waltz, Kenneth. 1979. *Theory of International Politics*. Reading, MA: Addison-Wesley.

Wapner, Paul. 1995. "Politics Beyond the State: Environmental Activism and World Civic Politics." *World Politics* 47: 311–340.

Waters, Malcolm. 1995. *Globalization*. London: Routledge.

Webb, Kernaghan (ed.). 2004. *Voluntary Codes: Private Governance, the Public Interest, and Innovation*. Ottawa: Carleton University Press.

Webb, Michael C. 2006. "Shaping Corporate Taxation." In Christopher May (ed.), *Global Corporate Power*. Boulder, CO: Lynne Rienner.

Weber, Max. 1978. *Economy and Society,* vol. 1. Edited by Guenther Roth and Claus Wittich. Los Angeles: University of California Press.

———. 1980. *Wirtschaft und Gesellschaft*. Tübingen, Germany: Mohr.

Weiser, John, and Simon Zadek. 2000. *Conversations with Disbelievers: Persuading Companies to Address Social Challenges*. New York: Ford Foundation.

Weiss, Linda. 1998. *The Myth of the Powerless State: Governing the Economy in a Global Era*. Cambridge, UK: Polity.

——— (ed.). 2003. *States in the Global Economy: Bringing Domestic Institutions Back In*. Cambridge, UK: Cambridge University Press.

Wells, Louis, and Alvin Wint. 1993. "Marketing Strategies to Attract Foreign Investment." In Lorraine Eden and Evan Potter (eds.). *Multinationals in the Global Political Economy*. New York: St. Martin's.

Wendler, Frank. 2002. "Neue Legitimationsquellen für Europa?" *Zeitschrift für Internationale Beziehungen* 9(2): 253–274.

Wendt, Henry. 1993. *Global Embrace: Corporate Challenges in a Transnational World*. New York: Harper Business.

West, Darrell. 2000. *Checkbook Democracy: How Money Corrupts Political Campaigns*. Boston: Northeastern University Press.

West, Darrell, and Burdett Loomis. 1999. *The Sound of Money: How Political Interests Get What They Want*. New York: Norton.

Wichterich, Christa. 1998. *Die globalisierte Frau. Berichte aus der Zukunft der Ungleichheit*. Reinbek, Germany: Rowohlt.

Wilkin, Peter. 1997. "New Myths for the South: Globalization and the Conflict Between Private Power and Freedom." In Caroline Thomas and Peter Wilkin (eds.), *Globalization and the South*. London: Macmillan.

Williamson, Oliver. 1975. *Markets and Hierarchies*. New York: Free Press.

Willke, Helmut. 1992. *Ironie des Staates*. Frankfurt a.M.: Suhrkamp.

Wilson, Graham. 1990. *Interest Groups*. Oxford: Blackwell.

Windolf, Paul, and Michael Nollert. 2001. "Institutionen, Interessen, Netzwerke. Unternehmensverflechtung im internationalen Vergleich." *Politische Vierteljahresschrift* 42(1): 51–78.

Wolf, Klaus Dieter. 2002. "Contextualizing Normative Standards for Legitimate Governance Beyond the State." In Jürgen Grote and Bernard Gbikpi (eds.), *Participatory Governance. Political and Societal Implications*. Opladen, Germany: Leske and Budrich.

Woods, Ngaire (ed.). 2000. *The Political Economy of Globalization*. New York: St. Martin's.

Wright, John. 1990. "Contributions, Lobbying, and Committee Voting in the US House of Representatives." *American Political Science Review* 84: 417–438.

Wriston, Walter. 1986. *Risk and Other Four Letter Words*. New York: Harper Row.

Wriston, Walter (ed.). 1992. *The Twilight of Sovereignty: How the Information Revolution Is Transforming Our World*. New York: Scribner.

Wylynko, Bradley. 1999. "Beyond Command and Control." In Robert Gibson (ed.), *Voluntary Initiatives*. Peterborough, Ontario: Broadview.

Yergin, Daniel. 1991. *The Prize: The Epic Quest for Oil, Money, and Power*. New York: Touchstone.

Yergin, Daniel, and Joseph Stanislaw. 1998. *The Commanding Heights*. New York: Simon and Schuster.

Yosie, Terry, and Tim Herbst. 1998. *The Journey Toward Corporate Environmental Excellence*. Washington, DC: Enterprise for the Environment.

Young, Brigitte. 1998. "Globalisierung und Genderregime." In Regine Stötzel (ed.), *Ungleichheit als Projekt*. Marburg: BdWi-Verlag.

Young, Oran (ed.). 1997. *Global Governance: Drawing Insights from the Environmental Experience*. Cambridge, MA: MIT Press.

Yunker, James. 1999. "A Pragmatic Route to Genuine Global Governance." In Errol Harris and James Yunker (eds.), *Toward Genuine Global Governance*. Westport, CT: Praeger.

Zacher, Marc. 1999. "Uniting Nations: Global Regimes and the United Nations System." In Raimo Väyrynen (ed.), *Globalization and Global Governance*. Lanham, MD: Rowman and Littlefield.

Zürn, Michael. 1998. *Regieren jenseits des Nationalstaates. Globalisierung und Denationalisierung als Chance*. Frankfurt a.M.: Suhrkamp.

Index

About the Book

Has the political power of big business, particularly transnational corporations (TNCs), increased in our globalizing world? What, if anything, constrains TNCs? Analyzing the role of business in the global arena, this systematic and theoretically grounded book addresses these questions.

Fuchs considers the implications of expanded lobbying efforts by businesses and business associations, the impact of capital mobility, and developments in self-regulation and public-private partnerships. She also highlights the role of business in framing policy issues and influencing public debate. Clearly identifying the sources of the marked increase in the political power of TNCs, she also provides evidence of the limitations and vulnerabilities that rein them in.

Doris Fuchs is professor of international relations and European integration at the University of Stuttgart. She is author of *An Institutional Basis for Environmental Stewardship*.